D0712245

DISCARD

Leadership
for
Higher Education

Leadership
for
Higher Education

The Campus View

EDITED BY
ROGER W. HEYNS

AMERICAN COUNCIL ON EDUCATION · · · · · *Washington, D.C.*

© 1977 by the American Council on Education
One Dupont Circle, Washington, D.C. 20036

Library of Congress Cataloging in Publication Data

American Council on Education.
  Leadership for higher education.

  Papers presented at the 59th annual meeting
of the American Council on Education, held in
New Orleans, October 6–8, 1976.
    1. Universities and Colleges—United States—
Administration—Congresses. I. Heyns, Roger
William, 1918– II. Title.
LB2341.A576 1977   378.73   77-10781
ISBN 0-8268-1341-0

9 8 7 6 5 4 3 2 1

Printed in the United States of America

WHITWORTH   LIBRARY
SPOKANE, WASH. 99251

Contributors

Mary F. Berry
Chancellor, University of Colorado

David W. Breneman
Senior Fellow, The Brookings Institution

Randolph W. Bromery
Chancellor, University of Massachusetts at Amherst

Lattie F. Coor
President, University of Vermont

Norman C. Crawford, Jr.
President, Salisbury State College

William E. Davis
President, University of New Mexico

Edward D. Eddy
President, Chatham College

Joe E. Elmore
Provost, and Dean of Academic Affairs, Earlham College

Laurine E. Fitzgerald
Dean of the Graduate School, University of Wisconsin—Oshkosh

Thomas W. Fryer, Jr.
Chancellor, Peralta Community College District

Patricia Albjerg Graham
Dean of the Radcliffe Institute and Professor of Education, Harvard University

Theodore M. Hesburgh, C.S.C.
President, University of Notre Dame

Stephen Horn
President, California State University, Long Beach

Harold Howe II
Vice President for Education and Research, The Ford Foundation

Frederick S. Humphries
President, Tennessee State University

Phillip E. Jones
Assistant Vice President and Director of Affirmative Action, University of Iowa

Beverly E. Ledbetter
Legal Counsel, University of Oklahoma

Charles R. Longsworth
President, Hampshire College

Myron J. Lunine
Dean, The Western College of Miami University

Cecil Mackey
President, Texas Tech University

Colette Mahoney, R.S.H.M.
President, Marymount Manhattan College

Maurice B. Mitchell
Chancellor, University of Denver

Alfred L. Moye
Vice Chancellor for Student Affairs, University of Pittsburgh

Frederick D. Patterson
Chairman, Board of Directors, Robert R. Moton Memorial Institute, Inc.

Terry Sanford
President, Duke University

Jesse N. Stone, Jr.
President, Southern University

George B. Vaughan
President, Mountain Empire Community College

Edmond L. Volpe
President, The College of Staten Island of the City University of New York

Donald E. Walker
President, Southeastern Massachusetts University

Steven Wenzel
General Counsel, University of South Florida

E. T. York, Jr.
Chancellor, State University System of Florida

Contents

Preface

BY DEFINITION, it is a prime concern and a principal responsibility of leaders of higher education to identify, understand, and find solutions to the problems facing our nation's colleges. We have learned in the past that one valuable contribution the American Council on Education can make to this process is to facilitate the exchange of ideas among educators, some of whom have arrived at workable solutions to pressing problems.

The American Council on Education, at its fifty-ninth Annual Meeting, held in New Orleans, October 6–8, 1976, provided a forum for this exchange. The meeting was designed to enable campus leaders to share their ways of dealing with major crises as well as day-to-day problems. The emphasis was on actuality rather than abstraction; on the pragmatic rather than the theoretical; on the practical experience of leaders who have administrative responsibilities rather than on the disinterested wisdom of experts.

The American Council publishes this volume of papers from the meeting in the hope that the discussions included in it will facilitate the process of resolving issues. The meeting owes much of its success to John F. Hughes and Donna C. Phillips, who directed and coordinated the plans and programs. The Council is indebted to the contributors to this volume and to the staff members who helped prepare for and carry out this Annual Meeting of the American Council on Education.

ROGER W. HEYNS

The Presidency:
A Personalist Manifesto

THEODORE M. HESBURGH, c.s.c.

I HAVE BEEN ASKED to say something today about presidential leadership in the field of higher education. In view of the fact that this is my twenty-fifth year as president of Notre Dame, I assume that I am expected to be somewhat personal, philosophical, frank, even blunt about the possibilities and challenges of being president.

First, let me abandon modesty by saying that the presidency of a college or university can be a great vocation: exciting, demanding, surprising, at times very satisfying, and occasionally great fun. Of course, it is also very hard work, tiring to the point of exhaustion, repetitive, very often exasperating, but never really hopeless or dull if you have the right attitude about it.

I suppose one can say the same thing of the presidency of any human organization. All presidents, because they are at the top of whatever organizational triangle they are asked to lead, have broad and diverse constituencies, all clamoring for attention. The president often pleases one of his constituencies at the price of alienating another. To paraphrase Lincoln, you can please some constituencies all the time and all the constituencies some of the time, but you cannot please all your constituencies all the time. I believe that a failure to recognize this basic fact and a futile attempt to please everyone all the time are the basic causes of most presidential failures. Clark Kerr in his 1963 Godkin Lectures at Harvard best described the difficulty facing the president:

> The university president in the United States is expected to be a friend of the students, a colleague of the faculty, a good fellow with the alumni, a sound administrator with the trustees, a good speaker with the public, an astute bargainer with the foundations and the federal agencies, a politician with the state legislature, a friend of industry, labor, and agriculture, a persuasive diplomat with donors, a champion of education generally, a supporter of the professions (particularly law and medicine),

a spokesman to the press, a scholar in his own right, a public servant at the state and national levels, a devotee of opera and football equally, a decent human being, a good husband and father, an active member of a church. Above all, he must enjoy traveling in airplanes, eating his meals in public, and attending public ceremonies. No one can be all of these things. Some succeed at being none.

He should be firm, yet gentle; sensitive to others, insensitive to himself; look to the past and the future, yet be firmly planted in the present; both visionary and sound; affable, yet reflective; know the value of a dollar and realize that ideas cannot be bought; inspiring in his visions, yet cautious in what he does; a man of principle, yet able to make a deal; a man with broad perspective who will follow the details conscientiously; a good American, but ready to criticize the status quo fearlessly; a seeker of truth where the truth may not hurt too much; a source of public policy pronouncements when they do not reflect on his own institution. He should sound like a mouse at home and look like a lion abroad. He is one of the marginal men in a democratic society— of whom there are many others—on the margin of many groups, many ideas, many endeavors, many characteristics. He is a marginal man, but at the very center of the total process.[1]

Administrative principles

When my predecessor, Father John Cavanaugh, introduced me to the presidency, he gave me some very brief and very good advice that I will share with you today. May I say that I have tried to follow this advice and following it has in large measure accounted for whatever sanity and equilibrium I still maintain after all these years.

First, Father John said, the heart of administration is making decisions. When you make a decision, however large or small, do not ask, "What is the easy thing to do?" or "What will cost the least money?" or "What will make me the most loved or popular by those affected by the decision?" Just ask what is the *right* decision, all things considered. Once you have made that judgment—and you'll make it better once you have been burned a few times—then just do it, decide it, no matter how difficult it is, no matter how costly, no matter how unpopular. In the long run, whatever the immediate uproar or inconveniences, people, your people, will respect you for following your conscience, for doing what you thought right, even though they do not agree with you. No other position is in the least way defensible, even in the short run. As Winston Churchill once said so well: "The only guide to a man is his conscience. The only shield to his memory is the rectitude and sincerity of his actions. It is very

1. *The Uses of the University* (Cambridge, Mass.: Harvard University Press, 1963), pp. 29–30.

imprudent to walk through life without this shield, because we are so often mocked by the failure of our hopes; but with this shield [of conscience] whatever our destiny may be, we always march in the ranks of honor."[2] Martin Luther said the same thing more briefly, "Here I stand."

Every decision is not, of course, a great moral crisis. But I have found few decisions that did not have a moral dimension that could only be ignored with considerable risk, not just for oneself, but particularly for justice, whose final spokesmen all presidents are. When the president abdicates this fundamental responsibility, people are hurt.

One sees easily that what this attitude often calls for in the president is personal courage, often lonely courage, because everyone else below has passed the buck. If a person does not have the courage to stand alone, quite often, sometimes daily during times of crisis, then the presidency can be an agony. Without courage, it is always a failure. Of that I am sure.

The president's situation is unique. Politicians try to please everybody; presidents must please their conscience, ultimately God. Budget officers understandably try to find the most economical solution. It is not always the right one. Cowards, of course, seek the easy, undemanding path. Pasternak said in *Doctor Zhivago* that "gregariousness is the refuge of the mediocre." The uncertain always walk in a crowd. The leader most often finds himself marching single file at the head of a thin column. If you are to be a good president, you will often enough find yourself in that situation, which brings me to the second Cavanaugh principle for the presidency: Don't expect a lot of praise or plaudits for what you do. If you need continual compliments to sustain you, you are in for a great surprise and letdown, because you are not going to get many thanks, even for the best things you do, the best decisions you make. Face it. People, as a group, are fickle, often insensitive, and the academic community is made up of people. As the Congressman running for re-election was asked by a farmer he had helped greatly in the past: "What have you done for me lately, and what will you do for me tomorrow?"

In the last analysis, this second principle reverts to the first: You make a decision simply because it is right in your judgment, not because someone will be grateful to you for making it. I grant you this is a difficult truism to accept because we are all human beings who enjoy an occasional pat on the back. I must assure you it is more realistic to expect numerous kicks in another part of your anatomy when you make a mistake. Criticism will be a far greater part of your presidential life than plaudits and gratitude. As John Cavanaugh said, you will sleep better if you recognize that from the beginning and don't court disappointment and personal hurt by expecting what you will not get.

2. Tribute to Neville Chamberlain in the House of Commons, November 12, 1940.

One of the best early decisions I made elicited one letter of thanks from several hundred faculty members who were greatly benefited by the decision. I thought it might get better as the years passed, but, believe me, it does not. Better to expect very little because that is what you will get in the way of praise or thanks. Once you accept this fact, then you can get on with doing what you do because it is the right thing to do. Besides, you get paid more than all the others, and they may think that is thanks enough. Whether it is or not, it will have to do, so accept what is, and don't be hurt.

The third bit of advice was very apropos because I was young and feisty at the time, also supremely confident as the young, thank God, always are. Cavanaugh principle number three was:

> Don't think you can do very much all by yourself. There are too many of them and only one of you. Leadership may appear to be a man on a white horse leading the multitude, but you'll do a lot better if you get off the horse and entice the best of the multitude to join you up front.

Of course, every leader has to have a personal vision of where he or she wants to lead, but just having it won't do it. Effective leadership means getting the best people you can find to share the vision and to help in achieving it. Whether you are talking about being President of the United States or president of Willow Grove College, the principle is equally valid. You cannot do it alone, all by yourself. You may be very intelligent, exceptionally talented, good looking, charismatic, whatever. You still need help, the very best help you can find. The third principle says: Find them quickly, and invite them aboard.

I remember, after hearing this, picking the five best people available and making them all vice presidents. They were all older than I was. Some were more intelligent. They all possessed talents that I lacked. They often disagreed with me, and often they were right, so I changed my mind. It was not always easy working with them, but it would have been impossible without them. They saved my life more times than I like to remember. My present associates are still saving my life today.

Cavanaugh added a few subthoughts to this third principle that one cannot be a good president all by himself or herself, making all the decisions unilaterally or intuitively, initiating everything all by yourself, always thinking and acting alone. Only God does that, and I believe even He is a trinity of persons. Cavanaugh's three subthoughts were varied, but very valid in my later experience:

• Don't think that you are the indispensable man or woman. "The day you leave, someone else will be doing your job," he said, "and quite probably doing it better." That rankled my pride, but I accepted it. I still do. Humility is not just a nice virtue; it is the truth. The cemeteries of the world are full of indispensable men and women, but somehow the world goes on. So does the world of colleges and universities.

• Be sure that all those who help you achieve your vision receive a large share of the credit. It should not always be, "The president announces." Let a few others announce, too, especially, let them announce what they do successfully, and let them get what credit goes with it. Don't be afraid to be off center stage once in a while. And although you may not get many thanks, make a point of seeing that all those who work closely with you get thanked, at least by you. If there is any long-range credit for what is well done in your institution, you will eventually get your share, maybe at their expense, so make sure that they get a good word of gratitude from you, right now.

• Never pass off on your associates all the dirty work of administration. Never let them pass their less tasty tasks to you either. As a general rule, you will and should take the blame in public for the large mistakes that would not have happened if you had been better informed, more involved, even more decisive. On the other hand, don't baby your associates when they tend to hide behind you—or get you to do what they find unpleasant. Tell them that you will handle your own unpleasant duties and that they will handle theirs. I once had a doorman who couldn't bring himself to tell people not to park in front of the University Inn where there was a large "No Parking" sign. After I chided him, his way out was to say to all comers, "Father Hesburgh doesn't want you to park here." After I heard of this, I said to him, "I'll make a deal with you. I won't interfere with the parking, if you don't use me to do it right."

The fourth principle was not spoken so much as lived by my predecessor. When an author in Renaissance Italy, around the time of Machiavelli, wanted to write about the science of governance, he asked the best governor he knew, the Duke of Mantua, what was the most important quality of the person who governs well. The Duke quickly answered in two words: *Essere umano,* to be human.

That may seem to be an oversimplification at first glance. After thinking about it, in the light of much experience, I would say that it strikes at the heart of what a good president should be, simply human. Those presidents who are generally unsuccessful often fail from lack of humanity. They lose the loyalty of those with whom they live and work. All our dealings are with people, all kinds of people: people who are intelligent and not so intelligent; people who are good or bad, but generally a mixture of both; people who have hopes, dreams, feelings, frustrations; people who are happy or unhappy; people who are satisfied or dissatisfied; people who generally want something that we can or cannot give. All of them deserve something from us that we can give, no matter what the outcome of our decisions—namely, to be treated as human beings, to be understood, even when that is difficult, to be accorded basic human consideration and compassion, even when they abuse our human dignity. In a word, people deserve to be treated with humane sensitivity, even when all our inclinations push us toward brusque rejection, not only of their proposals, but of them as persons. The president has to suffer fools, if not gladly, at least patiently.

Animals govern by growling or biting; human dictators rule by sheer force, terror, or quick punishment, even death. That is not what is or should be expected in a community of learners and teachers who have long been characterized by rationality, civility, urbanity, friendship, but, especially, humanity toward one another, even when they are intellectually or morally in disagreement.

There is a humane way of saying no, of denying an impassioned request, of telling someone that he or she has failed and will be terminated. There is a humane way of upholding a deeply held conviction, even when it is under brutal attack. One can be forceful and humane at the same time. But it is not easy.

It may be that the most difficult problem for a president is to be humane while doing many unpleasant, but necessary things that seem to others to be inhumane. *Essere umano,* to be human, a great quality in anyone having power over others. Power will not corrupt such a person.

Pleasing each constituency

I would now like to declare myself on some very specific opportunities and challenges that face every college or university president. The easiest way to do so is to discuss in some detail the relationships between the president and his central constituencies: the trustees, the faculty, the students. You have all heard the facetious comment that a successful president gives each group what it wants, the alumni, championship teams; the faculty, parking; and the students, sex. I find this cynical as well as bad policy.

The trustees are in a juridical sense the most important constituency, for they have, in our American structure for higher education, the very important task of setting basic policies for the administration of what is essentially a public trust. The trustees do not administer the institution, but their most important task is to see that it is well administered. Having selected and appointed the president, the least they should expect of him is honesty and clarity of purpose, even when the trustees may not agree. Disagreement there often may be between a president and his trustees, but never deceit.

There are times when a president will have to try to change trustees' minds regarding basic policy. At least he should leave no doubt about where he stands. Trustees need to be informed clearly and forcefully, on a continuing basis, regarding the institution's most basic needs. The president must resist when trustees interfere in the administration, attempting to govern rather than ensure good government. I have found that this stance is both appreciated and supported by trustees. A spirit of confidence on the part of a president begets confidence on the part of trustees.

Trustees should share bad as well as good news, problems as well as successes. Sometimes a president should simply admit that he or she has made a mistake. Most of the trustees I know do not expect perfection of a president, just competent effort and honest accounting of stewardship. In occasional times of great crisis, trustees must be reminded by a president that they are the court of last resort, that they must take a corporate stand, that no one is going to follow the sound of an uncertain trumpet.

There may even come a time when the president must say to the trustees, because only he or she can, "Here I stand." It may be the end of the relationship, but rarely is. Even trustees, or maybe especially trustees, respect integrity.

All in all, this has not been in my experience a difficult relationship, even though the president is always in the middle between the trustees and the rest of the institution. He must interpret both sides to each other, preserving the confidence of each side. I should admit that I have always been blessed with intelligent and competent trustees, well versed in the problems of higher education. Had it been otherwise, I might be telling a different story, although I believe my principles of operation would be the same.

The faculty is, from an educational point of view, the most important constituency of the president. Educationally, the faculty makes the institution what it is, good or bad or in between. The faculty is also the president's most difficult constituency. He is its leader, but the trustees appoint him. Every day of every year, year in and year out, the president must prove himself to the faculty. Especially in a large institution, there is no such thing as a completely cordial and trusting relationship. The president is, in some sense, the symbolic adversary, since he is ultimately the bearer of whatever bad news comes to the faculty these days.

On the positive side, and more important, he must proclaim to faculty members, in season and out, his vision of their institution, what it is and what it might yet be. Only they can make his dream come true, and only if they are convinced will they cooperate in the venture. In a word, he must create trust—no easy task, given the climate.

There is no leadership here by edict. All faculty members consider themselves his equal, if not his better, intellectually. Persuasion is the best mode of leadership where the faculty is involved. They must be part and parcel of the total educational process.

There are no easy answers here. Most presidents have been members of a teaching and research faculty and thus are fully conscious of the hopes and aspirations, as well as the very special nature of that body called faculty, made up of people who think otherwise.

And yet, they too must be led by the president. He must find a theme of unity in their diversity. He must inspire them, challenge them, question them, reason with them, occasionally say "no" to them, but, above all, he must persuade them to give their best talents and their most creative efforts to the realization of his educational vision.

This assumes, of course, that the president does have a clear vision for the institution, a vision that is educationally sound and integral, given the available resources. You cannot turn Pugwash into Princeton overnight. Whatever else he is clear and enthusiastic about, the president must most of all elaborate his specific vision, rethink it as times change, perfect it as he learns from experience or develops new resources. He may be the best administrator in the world, but without a clear and bright and, yes, beautiful vision, he is leading nowhere. Without a vision, the people perish. Each president will have his own style; but beyond all style must be substance. If a president cannot intelligently discuss education with his faculty, nothing else he discusses will matter. He will simply lose the faculty, and he will be unable to lead them anywhere, certainly not to the promised land.

The normal faculty criticisms of a president are many and varied, often contradictory. If he is always home, he is a nobody; if he is often away, he is neglecting his homework. If he spends little time with faculty members, he is aloof; if he spends much time with them, he is interfering in their proper business. If he balances the budget, he is stingy; if he cannot balance the budget, he is irresponsible and incompetent. If he is big on fringe and retirement benefits, the younger faculty can't meet their expenses; if he stresses faculty raises, the older faculty are impoverished on retirement. If he spends much time on fund raising, he is a huckster; if he doesn't, the financial situation gets worse. In a word, it is Scylla and Charybdis every day. We might as well admit that willy-nilly, the president will always be between the rock and the hard place.

Having admitted this, let us also admit that there is no better association in the world than a good academic relationship where civility rules disagreement and where comradeship is very real in an endeavor as fundamentally exalted as higher education. Despite all the normal and natural tensions between a good faculty and a good administration, this is in itself a healthy tension productive of an unusually good symbiotic effect—better governance by mutual understanding of the tasks proper to each.

I could understate the situation by saying that administrators should mainly administer and professors should mainly teach. When either intrudes unnecessarily on the other's task, both tasks are unduly complicated and rendered impossible. There are many other schemes of governance discussed widely and promoted actively today. In fact, sandbagging the administration by a constant threat of collective bargaining has become a popular indoor sport in colleges and universities. Despite this, I have yet to hear of any form of governance as good as what we generally have, especially when intelligently and competently administered, with the faculty deeply involved in the formation of educational policy and the administration sensitively and forcefully administering this policy, even prodding occasionally for a change of policy. Both functions are indispensable, the forming and the effecting of educational policy mutually agreed upon. There are, of course, many other tasks that the faculty and administration must do separately. Here, mutual understanding and cooperation are the order of the good day in academe.

Concern for students

Having already specified two constituencies as most important, do not be surprised if I declare that the students, as the main reason for which our institutions exist, are also, in that sense, a most important constituency of the president. Their needs and desires do not always coincide with those of the trustees and faculty, but they too must be heard. Let us admit that it took a recent student revolution for us to involve them more integrally in the total life of our institutions. Personally, I believe that the students have generally reacted well to this new responsibility as new members of most of our academic councils and committees.

The greatest gift a president can give his students is the example of his life. One could say the same of faculty members, but the president is in a highly visible position. He must be a kind of superprofessor to all the students. Young adults are, whether they admit it or not, looking for public models of the kind of person they would like to become. While the president cannot be a super "in loco parentis person," he cannot avoid transmitting to students the fact that he does or does not care deeply about the kinds of persons they are becoming, the interests and attitudes they presently portray, the concerns that bite deeply into their youthful hopes.

Despite anything he says, the president will declare much more by how he lives, the concerns he exemplifies, the causes he supports, the public service he renders. There are great moral issues facing young and old alike today. In an educational setting, one would hope that values would be all important and that the young would perceive clearly where we elders stand on issues such as human rights, world poverty and hunger, good government, preserving the fragile ecosphere, strengthening marriage and family life.

The president should also be deeply concerned that his students are being educated for tomorrow, not for yesterday; that they do emerge from the whole process knowing how to think, write, speak, and organize themselves effectively; that they have a sense of values and judge their world by reason and justice with love and not by blind emotional instinct; finally, that they have situated themselves and are at peace with themselves as they are and are becoming, as men and women, as Protestants, Catholics, or Jews, as members of a Western world that is part of a much poorer, less human, underdeveloped, and increasingly interdependent world. One would hope that beyond competence in doing something to earn a living, students would emerge from our institutions with some compassion for and commitment to the improvement of the larger, less favored world around them. If we, as presidents, do not show these concerns in our own lives and works, then I doubt that our students will take any of our words very seriously.

Each president will have to find some realistic and personal way of maintaining a continuing conversation with his students, not only for their benefit, but mainly for his own. Students will keep a president alive and honest, for they have an extraordinary radar for detecting double talk and the irrelevant. One must always level with them.

Again, I believe that under the pressure of the student revolution, there were too many concessions made to the bohemian type of students. It is time and overtime to revert to a student way of life that is more wholesome and less unstructured. I know of no way of building character without adhering to a definite set of moral standards and values that make for the good life. We have cast aside too many of these standards and values, like honesty, sobriety, fidelity, justice, and magnanimity. I believe many students, quite different from those of the late 1960s, would welcome a change, a reestablishment of student standards. Change will not come without presidential leadership.

I could, but will not, speak at length of other constituencies of the president: the alumni who are the best evidence of our productive and continuing efforts, the public who largely gave birth to our institutions and generously support them when we win their appreciation of our work. Both are important. I could also speak of the government, local, state, and federal, that today has such impact, maybe too much, on our institutions. However, I have said enough in these personal reflections on the presidency.

I will only say that I am concerned that so many recently appointed presidents are fleeing a task that could be very fulfilling and greatly productive if approached with vision, hope, and reasonable confidence. I have seen the presidency in its best and worst days. I did not enjoy the troubled times, but the good years before and since have more than compensated for that agony. I only regret that we lost so many good and stalwart presidents who were caught in a vortex for which there were no set rules of procedure, only improvisations, many of which simply did not work. Higher education must still produce a whole new generation of presidents who are their equals. It was a sad commentary that when *Change* magazine identified by popular poll last year the forty-four leaders of higher education, so very few of them were presidents of colleges and universities, only one of the top four.[3]

I would like to close on a very personal note which I trust you will indulge me. Over the years, I have stood at the graveside of many of my university colleagues and have contemplated the quiet nobility of their lives, so totally and unselfishly given to the higher education of young men and women. Some day, some of my lifelong associates will stand at my graveside. At that time, I would feel greatly honored if they will say, "Well, we worked together for a long time. We didn't always agree, but that never bothered our friendship or our forward march. At least, he was fair and tried to make the place better. Now he can rest in peace."

I'm not anxious for that day to come soon, but when it does, I would settle for those final sentiments. Who among us would ask for more? The respect of our colleagues is quite enough, assuming God's blessing, too. We won't get the one without the other.

Cooperative Leadership

TERRY SANFORD

LEADERSHIP is difficult to define. Obviously, those in higher education need to show some leadership, and producing leaders is certainly one of the chief missions of higher education.

Leaders can surface in unexpected places, and they often assume the role as a matter of chance. The story of how the great Southern cavalry

3. "Who's Who in Higher Education," *Change*, February 1975, pp. 24–31.

leader, Jeb Stuart, won his spurs illustrates the point. At the First Battle of Manassas (Bull Run), Stuart was leading his troops across a field when he spotted some infantry in red pants advancing toward him. An Alabama regiment that wore red pants as part of its uniform was supposed to be in the vicinity; Stuart assumed they were lost, so he rode up to tell them to change direction, that the Yankees were the other way. At the last minute he realized the men were not Confederates but were New York Zouaves, who also wore red pants. Hopelessly outnumbered and with no chance to escape, he did the only thing he could—he ordered a charge. The Zouaves were so startled at this suicidal plunge that they broke and ran. From that day on, Jeb Stuart was a leader and a hero.

We need leadership in higher education to combat the growing apprehension that we do not know where we are going. Someone once commented that no community is more prone to anxiety than an academic community. Lewis Mayhew reinforces this idea almost offhandedly; in commenting on a section of the report, he suggests that "a commission with the prestige of the Carnegie Commission could cause panic if it adopted a decidedly pessimistic view."[1] The only remedy I know for the anxiety that threatens panic is leadership.

Our need for leadership stems from the lack of a shared sense of direction. This loss of sense of direction has been aggravated, if not in part caused, by dwindling enrollments, declining endowments, and the fiscal strains facing all colleges and universities. A study on the financial state of higher education found nearly one half of all institutions of higher learning in "unhealthy" or "relatively unhealthy" financial situations; two thirds of private institutions were in those categories. Of these last, "many may be able to recover"[2]—meaning, more pointedly, that some will not and many may not.

Perhaps we have perceived money as the problem for so long that we are neglecting the more important questions. Stanford University psychologists performed a series of experiments in which groups of kittens were raised in environments composed only of horizontal or vertical lines. Later, when the environments were changed, the kittens raised in the horizontal environment could not perceive the vertical environment and vice versa.

I do not agree that money is the big problem of higher education. We can take care of the shortages of money. In an environment in which money—getting and spending and teaching others to find and spend it—

1. *The Carnegie Commission on Higher Education* (San Francisco: Jossey-Bass, 1973), p. 129.

2. Andrew H. Lupton, John Augenblick, and Joseph Heyison, "The Financial State of Higher Education," *Change*, September 1976, pp. 21–35.

is no factor, we can find out what we have in higher education. In other words, what should we worry about if we do not have to worry about money? Because we are preoccupied, do we act by institutional rote—the same old courses, same old departments, same divisions of knowledge? Does our concern for money hinder us from considering what sort of experience a student has in four years of college?

The student's perspective

Take a look at the seniors who have invested four years of their lives in faith that the college would give them something of immeasurable value. Have we done what we said we would do? They have received something, surely. They know more. They might even be close to being educated—for their age. They are probably happy enough with their experiences. Still, have we done with those irreplaceable years what we said we would do? Have we made the most of the sparkling intellect of youth? We promised a liberal education. Have we kept our promise?

When I put this question to my campus, I get some mundane answers. I give myself some lame excuses. The only reassurance is that we have done as well as any other university, that the senior could not have done better anywhere else. Beyond that . . . I do not want students at my university to feel cheated. I want them to be overwhelmed all their lives by the realization that Duke University made the difference in their lives. It made them people, it made them concerned. It made them compassionate. It made them thoughtful. It persuaded them to develop inquiring, doubting, challenging minds. It gave them an unquenchable thirst for learning throughout life.

The same question can be asked of any postsecondary institution. Institutions are not supposed to be the same. Joseph Schwab brought the industrial educator's challenge to the level of that of the Dartmouth history professor when he said, "Let such programs beware only that . . . they do not dispense also the habits of unquestioning conformity."[3] I ask questions from where I am; others can ask the same questions from where they are.

Have your students learned to seek answers, to doubt authorities? Will they dare their own individual creative impulses? Will they have a sense of duty to whatever, but especially a sense of duty to excellence? Do they have a sense of moral values, or at least do they know how to arrive at their own? Morality does not result from a course in moral values; it is the result of the total effect of faculty, institution, associations, experi-

3. Schwab, "Freedom and the Scope of Liberal Education," *The President as Educational Leader* (Washington: Association of American Colleges, 1976), p. 87.

ences as well as studies, and the institution's operations as well as its pronouncements.

Has the brilliant premedical student read any English literature? Has he or she looked at matters catalogued and compartmentalized under topics such as political science or sociology or economics? Is the sampling of strange subjects forbidden by the grade system and the graduate school requirements? Is this system what we proclaim to be liberal education? Are we letting the higher education process remain dull, helping it become merely a path to graduate or professional school or an entry to corporate business or a badge of social acceptability?

Our leadership efforts have been at best timid. We have allowed departments to evolve into feudal kingdoms, each jealously guarding its territory and subjects, both human and academic. As a rule, faculty members will not question faculty members—the brilliant, bold, inquiring mind of the laboratory or the library will seldom venture beyond the old framework of organized instruction. The path for a professor's academic success is as narrow as the student's path, and the arrangement in the end benefits neither as much as it might.

Consider the deterrents to being an excellent teacher with deep feelings for students. Dedicated faculty members realize that the better they teach, the more they must teach; the hard work of being exciting teachers draws more and more students into their classes, and they work even harder—all without much material reward on the tenure and promotion track. Dedicated teachers become good departmental counselors, genuinely concerned with students and their progress, so students flock to them—again without much material reward on the tenure and promotion track. In dealing with students, one hardly dares to be great.

Departmentalization

Forty years ago Robert Maynard Hutchins exposed his students to the major thinkers and creative figures of the past, linking current concerns with those of our predecessors. We need to interrelate past events and experiences as present events and activities are interrelated. The interrelation of ideas has not blossomed in many places partly because of one constant element of the academic scene—the specialization and parochialism of the departmental structure.

Leadership demands that we measure the usefulness of the departmental system against its disadvantages. The quest for national rankings, based on departmental peer opinion of graduate faculty, distorts the general university purpose. A distinguished specialist is of immense value to those who would raise their rating a notch, but a distinguished and brilliant generalist who is also capable of working in another discipline, and perhaps inclined to teach undergraduates, is of no such use in filling a departmental vacancy.

As the major organizing principle of higher education, the academic department has had a profound influence on our educational offerings and visions. It has helped produce significant research breakthroughs and major scholarly works. These efforts have improved the capacity for teaching, but they have not encouraged teaching in many of our major universities and colleges.

The specialization that contributes to research attainments makes coordination and cooperation across undergraduate disciplinary lines very difficult. Research and specialization at the graduate level are university hallmarks, but it is clear to me that the influence of departmental divisions hampers the general educational experience for undergraduates.

Should we abolish departments and organize along some other lines? I am sure that reorganization is not a good solution. We need specialization at the graduate level, but if we retain departments, we must abandon the habit of thinking that undergraduate courses are designed primarily to train and identify graduate students for the departments.

Students come from high schools drilled in disciplines similar in name to college departments. They pass on to graduate school, concentrating in one of those departments. In between, there is time for broad and broadening education, but generally the departmental tradition limits the breadth. We should not abolish departments; we should shake them up.

I want to see a college organized on the proposition that students come first and departments come somewhere behind our desire to provide an exciting environment for creative faculty members. The burden of leadership for such a change falls not on the college president but on the faculty members. The president can arrange budget items for such devices as joint appointments, but cooperation between disciplines must arise from faculty leadership. The role of the president in this matter is to ask questions, questions with answers too obvious to be ignored. This is a fair division of leadership.

The president's relationship with the faculty is only one of his duties, though it does mean that the faculty may be called on for the leadership to revive and improve undergraduate education. A president must also be plugged in to students, parents, alumni, the public, trustees, and those various groups that furnish institutional support to keep them all working toward the institutional goals.

I think there are too many departments in every college. Some should be combined, and some should be abolished. Some important areas of higher education should not be confined in departments, because departments can be justified to the extent that they organize disciplines. We need to devise a different, less rigorous structure. Areas of studies that are not separate disciplines should not be locked up in departments, but should be free to roam across the entire academic landscape. I suggest that policy sciences, urban problems, black studies, ecological and environmental concerns, and international affairs are not disciplines but are examples of bodies of knowledge that are too peripatetic to be incarcerated in one department.

Education departments, or even schools, should be freer than they have been, for the training of teachers is too broad to be called a discipline. Surely other areas should also escape departmental status. Some might be structured as institutes, but the way they are structured is less important than their purpose.

It is not enough to have these orbiting subjects circling and uniting the social sciences, the humanities, the biological sciences, the arts, the physical sciences. There need to be more joint efforts and joint appointments in math and philosophy, religion and economics, or almost any other apparently outrageous combination.

In addition, various other interdepartmental studies or majors might be encouraged, such as Canadian or comparative area studies, or maybe drama and journalism or comparative literature or medieval studies.

We need disciplines in recognizable departments for graduate specialization. We need to let them fly as loosely as possible for undergraduates. Faculty must be determined not to be bound by old constraints. The president's role as leader, beyond asking the questions, is to provide budgetary, tenure, promotion, and salary procedures that reward and do not penalize for such new directions.

Needed financial support

I began this examination of leadership by putting aside the concern for money just to see more clearly leadership's true goals, but leaders cannot ignore the need for financial support. I am convinced we can handle the money problems as stoop labor to be done late in the afternoon, after the freshness of the morning has been spent on improving education. Money must have a high priority in the allocation of leadership abilities, but not the highest priority. I have no fear that higher education will survive the present fiscal fears.

Public colleges will be supported by continued increases in state appropriations because the political pressures assure it and because it is a proper public policy. Low tuition at public institutions, with the cost differential covered by tax dollars, has served our society well and must remain the basic pattern. Private and public college leadership should join in support of that proposition.

Private colleges are suffering a financial strain. Most of those without any private financial resources are doomed to closing. But the resources of most are considerable. They have valuable physical plants and endowments that, although inadequate now, are generally sufficient to maintain independence.

Corporations are gradually beginning to be aware of their role in preserving the private sector of education, as a part of preserving all private enterprise, and the future of corporate contributions is promising. People are more concerned that the diversity of education be maintained, and the record of alumni groups points to greater support. The need for financial aid for students is beginning to be met by the federal government and may yet be designed to accord the student full choice in selection of a college.

The only fatal handicap faced by private colleges is the widening differential between public and private colleges. Too many public college administrators smugly suggest better management, which is usually the reverse of the fact. The differential is occurring because inflation is absorbed by the taxpayers in the public colleges and by the students in the private colleges. To increase public tuition would be detrimental to higher education. The answer is for states to provide, as many states are doing, an equalization grant for students who choose to go to private colleges. This equalization is fair to the student, saves money for the taxpayer, and will preserve the invaluable diversity of a dual system of higher education. The amount of the equalization grant must be enough to give the student a real choice; I have suggested that it should be 50 percent of the subsidy provided on behalf of the student in a public college. Private colleges must be forced to compete for students. If they are not forced to do so, many otherwise strong private colleges will close, and the dual system will be finished.

I find it appalling that the principal proponents of starving the private colleges off the land should be many leaders of public colleges. Those who promote such petty skirmishes are going to lose, because American society will insist that its dual system be preserved. It is up to us and our leadership efforts to make it well worth preserving.

The President's Role

HAROLD HOWE II

I SHALL ARGUE THREE POINTS: The task of leading a college or university is a more difficult job today than it was fifteen or twenty years ago; there is a special danger in these times of confusing leadership with management and conciliation; there is no reason for despair about higher education's leadership.

It is not news that leading a college or university is more difficult and demanding today than it was in the 1950s or early 1960s. Warren Bennis, the president of the University of Cincinnati, addressed the questions "where have all the leaders gone" and "why leaders can't lead" and in the process has given us all a lucid, thoughtful treatise on the frustrations of higher education leadership these days. Gail Parker, in an article in *Atlantic,* has exposed the villains of trustee waffling and faculty irresponsibility at a time of institutional crisis.[1] Despite these and other efforts, there may be a point in playing the record again. Perhaps a trustee or a tenured professor or an alumnus enamored of Adam Smith's economic precepts will hear it this time. Or maybe a state legislator or even a student hotly pursuing some cause will absorb a grain of understanding about the clash of interests and pressures that batter the college president's office. Perhaps all these parties will advance on the college president at a somewhat slower speed and even with a willingness to back up in the interest of others.

The overarching cause of the new complexity in steering an American college or university on a purposeful journey is the fog that has settled over American society itself. Americans have fewer shared purposes, more contending groups, and a less clear understanding of where we are heading than we did a few short years ago. As Stephen Bailey noted in a recent essay, "a confluence of technological and cultural forces . . . is turning America into a joyless, aimless, cynical, fragmented, and endlessly contentious society."[2] While Bailey's essay balances pessimistic views by pointing some ways out of the trap we have built for ourselves, I submit that all our institutions are afflicted by the aimlessness and contentiousness that characterize our national mood. To give a college or university a sense of purpose and direction in such a time demands resources of mind and spirit that challenge the most able men and women

1. "While Alma Mater Burns, Professors Fiddle, Trustees Temporize, Foundations Fumble," *Atlantic,* September 1976, p. 44.

2. *The Purposes of Education* (Bloomington, Ind.: Phi Delta Kappa, 1976), p. xii.

in the college presidency and that tempt many to fall back on a combination of management and treaty-making among warring constituencies as a substitute for leadership.

Problems facing the president

Just as the mood of the larger society complicates the exercise of effective leadership, so does the atmosphere of the smaller world of the college or university itself. Consider the following listing, which is an incomplete catalog of the difficulties confronting the president of a college or university:

1. In a time of the so-called steady state of higher education (a polite phrase to describe a combination of declining enrollments, diminishing public approbation, rapidly increasing costs, and unbalanced budgets), a president must referee highly intensified intramural warfare among departments and other divisions of the college or university, each of which identifies the continuation of its own welfare with the health and excellence of the institution.

2. The powerful new partner of both public and private higher education, the federal government, has not learned to be the relatively silent partner that it promised. Consequently, institutional resources, including scarce presidential time and energy, are increasingly devoted to sorting out issues that arise as the long arm of government follows its dollars more closely than many heads of institutions think it should.

3. The media are more alert to the small furors of academic life than they once were. Probably this constitutes a healthy openness, but it drains a president. Robert Menke, a trustee of Indiana University, has said that his institution contains fewer "clowns and good-time Charlies" than twenty-five years before, when he attended. "The difference is that today there are reporters living on the campus ... who provide factual material for the writers of lurid headlines for prurient adults who wish to have their opinions confirmed regarding degenerate youth on the big, unreconstructed, altruistic, American campus."

The college president must take these diversions seriously because they affect the confidence of alumni, the legislature, and the public. As the mores of the younger generation have departed dramatically from those of their fathers and mothers in recent years, the institutions that shelter the young are caught in the middle.

4. The demand for participation by students in the affairs of institutions has declined somewhat since the confrontations of the late 1960s. Although it has left a healthy residue of younger trustees, more open administration, and other benefits, it has also resulted in a situation that

makes many small decisions more complex than is warranted and frequently ties up important institutional issues in endless committee processes, all of which require wary tending by a responsible president.

5. The alumni of colleges and universities have always been a source of strength to institutions as well as a source of headaches. So they remain today, but a strong argument can be made that their migraine-producing capacity has increased as they have adopted more of the contentiousness and confrontational style that has characterized much of national life in recent years. A winning football team will no longer keep the neanderthals happy. They want in addition an economics department that accepts their views, and they argue such a cause in the name of academic freedom, a posture that would be amusing if it were not such a threat to academic freedom itself. Whether they are influential citizens imposing their views on a public institution or private persons threatening withdrawal of support from a private college, the president must spend more of his time dealing with them.

6. It may be no accident that boards of trustees frequently appoint lawyers to the college presidency these days. Warren Bennis says he has so many suits against him at the University of Cincinnati that his mother calls him "the defendant" rather than the president. Colleges and universities, as well as other institutions, suffer from our current tendency to resolve all conflicts by taking them to court, and this phenomenon takes its toll on the president as well. Attorneys who have a new place in the institutional hierarchy as decisionmakers ask the new question, "Who is going to sue us?" along with the old question, "Is it right and sensible?"

All these phenomena are frequently unappreciated by those who occasionally glimpse the college president in his traditional ceremonial role. They see the comfortable house that the college provides him along with someone to mow the lawn, and they think, what a cushy job! But the time demands alone of the college presidency are frequently self-defeating. Monopolized by the minutiae of participatory decisionmaking and inundated by committee reports, correspondence, and requests for speeches he has little time to prepare, today's college or university president suffers the same temptations as a high-level federal bureaucrat. The most insidious of those temptations is to spend twelve-hour days at the office meeting too many people for short appointments, talking on the telephone, and fussing with papers. Such days are followed by evenings and weekends at public functions or catching up on more paper. When does the president of an educational institution in the midst of such a routine think about education? The answer, at least for some presidents, is not very often.

Defining missions and goals

There is a growing danger of confusing leadership with some combination of management and skill at conciliation among opposing constituencies in an institution. Management and conciliating skills are important, but the sum of the highest possible development of each does not add up to leadership.

The leader's task is to hold before all persons connected with the institution some vision of what its mission is and how the institution can perform it more effectively. Because institutions exist in moral, political, social, and economic circumstances that are constantly changing, the burden of addressing an institution's purposes and performance never ends.

In arguing that the president has the primary role in defining missions and goals and assessing progress and problems, I am not suggesting that he should perform this function in a god-like fashion, handing down dicta from on high. He must constantly exchange ideas with students, faculty members, trustees, alumni, and others to enrich his own thinking. But after consultations, he must say what he thinks, not as a ukase for all to follow but as a thoughtful and significant contribution to a continuing conversation that shapes the future of his institution. His thinking can be the source of energizing people rather than controlling them. Although I agree with those who point out that it is difficult for a president to perform in this fashion, I disagree with those who contend that he should not try and that he can accomplish more through good management and conciliation.

There are, of course, great differences among colleges and universities. Some are small, well-integrated, natural communities; others are large, loose aggregations of special interest, many of which do not care a hoot for the others. Regardless of such differences, I doubt that a college or university has any reason to exist unless there is something to be said about its educational purpose. That is the most important part of the president's job and at the same time the part that is easiest to neglect.

In the last ten years, the theory and practice of managing higher education institutions have changed significantly. These developments constitute important contributions to the capacity of institutions to meet their fiscal problems and to operate efficiently. Systems for financial control and for planning, offices of institutional research, and the application to educational institutions of techniques developed in the realms of business and government have all become powerful new tools in college and university administration. But they are only tools. The ultimate purposes to which they are to be turned will continue to be defined by human judg-

WHITWORTH COLLEGE LIBRARY
SPOKANE, WASH. 99251

ment, and the president's principal job is to lead the process of arriving at that judgment.

The tragedy of today's presidency is that circumstances conspire to deny colleges and universities the most important contributions their presidents can make. Among those circumstances is the beguiling appeal of becoming so immersed in all the new systems of control and planning that independent thinking about educational issues is left by the wayside.

My advice to college presidents—offered in all seriousness—is to avoid as much as possible the process of systematic institutional management and to try to deal only with the results of the process. I am reminded of John Kenneth Galbraith's comments.

> Yesterday morning I held my first meeting with my Country Team, who act as a cabinet. I broke the news that meetings would be held irregularly. Meetings are a great trap. Soon you find yourself trying to get agreement and then the people who disagree come to think they have a right to be persuaded. Thus they acquire power; thus meetings become a source of opposition and trouble. However, they are indispensable when you don't want to do anything.[3]

In suggesting that presidents save some time to think about where their institutions are heading and to speak and write about their deliberations, I am probably running counter to some of the new wisdom about organizations provided by social scientists, who, like me, have never tried to lead a university or a college. Michael Cohen of the University of Michigan and James March of Stanford have studied the American college president for the Carnegie Commission on Higher Education, and they suggest that attempts to set long-term goals and to make changes that will move an institution toward them are not very useful. Furthermore, they have interviewed the presidents of forty-two institutions, and studied them and their institutions by using such scientific methods as having presidential secretaries log phone calls and by using elaborate systems to decide whether presidents should be categorized as "authoritative" or "mediative." There is no category in their research to determine whether any are *meditative*. They conclude that the American college or university today is characterized by "organized anarchy," a phrase that for me has a contradictory flavor. They observe:

> the American college or university . . . does not know what it is doing. Its goals are either vague or in dispute. Its technology is familiar but not understood. Its major participants wander in and out of the organization. These factors do not make the university a bad organization or

3. *Ambassador's Journal* (New York: Houghton Mifflin, 1969).

a disorganized one; but they do make it a problem to describe, organize and lead.[4]

I cannot compete with this sort of research, nor do I intend to try, although I do agree that colleges are difficult to lead. So are most other large, heterogeneous organizations. Also, I might quibble with the validity of research based on a log of a person's phone calls. I wrote two paragraphs of this paper while listening on the telephone to a gentleman trying to convince me that the Ford Foundation should support a zoo in Israel.

Actually, I have no quarrel with the thesis of these higher education scholars that there are various styles of leadership and that the less conspicuous, politically skillful, pragmatic, mediative style works better in today's atmosphere than the autocratic approach. A few college presidents still use the General Custer or Alamo mode of leadership; but it does not help their institutions much, even though they will be long remembered.

I am even willing to go along with the idea of Cohen and March that goals are clarified and identified to a considerable degree by day-to-day decisions worked out among the various constituencies of an institution rather than by the special rationality and wisdom of the president and the trustees. Clearly presidents have lost power to the faculty and other groups. Indeed, one of the most elusive chairs in the academic world is the seat of authority. No one knows who has it; many presume to it; and when anyone finally believes he is firmly in it, some unexpected party grabs it away. I suppose that this condition is a description of anarchy.

But all these qualifications about changes in the style of leadership and the difficulties of making a president an effective force for purposeful change in an institution do not vitiate the point that management and leadership are different activities. A president can end every day with a clean desk, answer all his phone calls the same day he receives them, meet all his appointments on time, keep more people happy than unhappy, end every year with a balanced budget, be admired by both trustees and alumni, and still not provide that extra something that is larger and more important than good management.

Indeed, I am prepared to defend the proposition that a president can be an indifferent manager and a successful leader if he has the right people to run around behind him and pick up the pieces resulting from his mismanagement. Wit, charm, a firm defense of academic freedom, and an interest in educational and scholarly values combined with a deep

4. Cohen and March, *Leadership and Ambiguity: The American College* (New York: McGraw-Hill, 1976), p. 3.

appreciation of the several sources of knowledge are still needed—even if they percolate through the institution less easily than they once did.

Hope for the future of leadership

I have always been suspicious of the glib statement "When the going gets tough, the tough get going," but maybe it is worth recalling in the present circumstance of colleges and universities. Actually, I believe that there are clear signs of this kind of response from today's leadership of higher education.

Although I have not researched the subject of leadership in higher education, I have seen many college presidents on a regular basis during the past five years. For instance, I have conferred for more than one hour with each of seventy-eight college presidents. These distinguished men and women did not come to see me to seek a transfusion of knowledge about higher education; they were seeking a transfusion of something much more tangible. Neither do I claim that these visitors to the Ford Foundation represent a valid national sample of higher education institutions. But this exposure does make me more optimistic about the leadership of higher education in our country today than any of the serious students of that subject appear to be. These presidents have difficult problems of institutional finance on their minds at a time when their costs are rising more rapidly than their incomes. But they are deeply concerned about many other matters that are close to the bone of education and scholarship as well as central to the issues confronted by American society. A few of these concerns at random are:

- how to introduce into programs of science and technology a new concern for the human values that are inevitably affected by technological development;
- how to rethink the concept of general education in a time of increasing specialization of learning and of growing demand for a vocational emphasis in college;
- how to expose students to the implications of today's thinking on ecological and environmental issues;
- how to meet the special needs and problems of minorities;
- how to teach college students to write;
- how to recognize new modes of learning without doing violence to educational standards;
- how to fashion for college-educated persons an adequate awareness of the world outside the United States and to escape what appears to be a growing insularity in both the academy and the country;
- how to design programs that will improve teaching in colleges;

- how to coordinate the experience of college and the world of work.

These educational questions are real and pressing. Unless the president of an institution is asking them, the questions may not be taken seriously. It is the president's job to ask such questions; it is reassuring to know that some are.

Whenever the president of an institution asks a serious question about its educational priorities and future plans, he automatically rocks someone's boat. So presidents with ideas constitute a threat to the status quo—particularly in these times when any new activity in a college requires that some other activity be dropped to provide the needed funds. Actually, it is not a bad definition of a president's job of leadership to say that his function is to be a threat to the status quo. He needs a nice sense of balance to avoid disruption. Someone once observed that it is all right if the alumni are sullen as long as they are not in revolt. Nevitt Sanford suggests that the important thing about a college president is not whether he is hated but why.[5]

Robert Hutchins, who had firm views about everything connected with education as well as about most things that are not, took a dim view of the possibility that a college president might have some useful thoughts:

> The president or rector and the deans are the bosses or foremen of the labor force and are responsible ... for the inspection and certification of the product, the maintenance of good public relations, and securing adequate financing. They are not chosen because of their commitment to the intellectual life or their ability to lead it. If they had the commitment and ability, they would not be in a position to lead it, because they have no time.... No man committed to the life of the mind can easily reconcile himself to being an administrator for his whole time or for very long.[6]

Such a statement helps Hutchins and the rest of us let off steam. I hope that college presidents will continue to express their frustrations in vivid language. They will surely continue to have them in growing measure. But Hutchins's career as president of the University of Chicago speaks loudly to the contrary. He was full of interesting thoughts about every aspect of the institution, and he enriched it and all of American education enormously. The charge is made that there are no such men around today, and I must agree that they are harder to find. John Gardner spoke some years ago of the antileadership vaccine that was subverting the

5. "On Filling a Role and on Being a Man: Leadership for Improved Conditions for Learning and Research," in *In Search of Leaders*, ed. G. Kerry Smith (Washington: American Association for Higher Education and National Education Association, 1967), p. 13.

6. *The Learning Society* (New York: Praeger, 1968), p. 118.

young; those college students are now old enough to be college presidents. Perhaps some of the inoculations were effective. All the more reason for those who hold major institutional responsibilities today to ask themselves the searching question "Am I so busy doing the possible that I fail to grasp for the difficult or impossible?"

The poet's generalization about human affairs was valid in the nineteenth century and will still be in the twenty-first—"Ah, but a man's reach should exceed his grasp, Or what's a heaven for?"[7] Most of us will live our lives somewhere between reaching for the stars and shouldering our everyday burdens; college presidents should stretch toward the long reach rather than the small beer.

7. Robert Browning, *Andrea del Sarto*, lines 98–99.

Faculty Governance

MARY F. BERRY

FOR A GUIDE to interpreting faculty governance, one need only look at the salient points in the history of the American university. The people of this country adapted the inherited British and continental models of the university to serve the more egalitarian, practical needs of a colonial and later a frontier society. They evolved the American concept of the liberal education. A natural consequence of the development of our distinctive traditions was that college and university faculties should hold a decisive voice in the formation and administration of policies governing the institutions. Not only were these institutions smaller than they are today, but also many were private in their origins—especially the church-related institutions—and therefore free from significant public control by legislatures.

The coming of the land grant era (1862) marked the beginning of the federal government's substantial interest in the development of university life and policy, while the states went ahead to create great state university systems. As universities grew and prospered throughout the late nineteenth and the twentieth centuries, so did state and federal participation in their financial support. Traditional faculty dominance in all aspects of decisionmaking yielded on two fronts. First, the institutions became sufficiently large to require professional, full-time administrators to manage the finances, the physical plant, and the student life on the campuses. Second, as more and more institutions came to depend on some form of public support for their growth and survival, public and quasi-public bodies began to assert a greater share of control over decisions.

The general results of this evolution were that faculties increasingly viewed themselves as exempt from the business of running the universities. They concentrated instead on establishing their prerogatives as the elite corps within the institutions of higher learning, retaining important veto powers when meeting occasionally in assembly and protecting traditional freedoms of expression in the classroom and in the scholarly journals.

Events on our campuses since the late 1960s provide a striking contrast to this background. The very recent history of faculty governance shows a convergence of some themes of contemporary social and political revolution with the themes of university life. Caught by surprise by pervasive changes in American society, the institutions of higher learning at first bent and then cracked in some places under the strain. Among the many responses to this stress was a widespread demand for renewed and significant participation by faculty members in decisionmaking affecting university life and for a more dominant role in the establishment of university policies. Translated into action, this response to unprecedented stress appeared as a proliferation of ad hoc committees, the emergence of numerous study commissions composed of faculty members inquiring into student life and related issues, and considerable vocal disagreement and dissension among various faculty members and among particular disciplines.

I believe very strongly in the efficacy and value of faculty participation in the governance of our institutions. I find it, therefore, even more necessary to take a critical posture with respect to some forms of participation that render faculty governance, as a whole, less effective.

Defining faculty governance

The issues of faculty governance turn on how we decide to characterize or define that governance. We members of the academic community may define faculty governance in three essential ways: (1) as a process in which the faculty has timely and effective input into the work of administering institutions of higher learning; (2) as a process in which key members of the administration are faculty members selected from the ranks of scholars and teachers; (3) as a process in which faculty participation is marked by the responsibility of those who advance policy to remain in the institution to face the implications and effects of those policies. If we can concur in these definitions, we define faculty governance and faculty leadership as the most essential resource within our institutions for the preservation of quality in university life. This situation, we hope, exists on every campus. But if faculty governance is characterized by perennial committees and study panels that meet ad hoc to review and call into question on a hit-or-miss basis administrative policies and decisions, then we must set some limits on this kind of participation.

During my first years as a faculty member in the late 1960s, my concern and interest in faculty governance were minimal. I knew little and cared less. I knew certainly that disciplines were grouped into faculties which exercised control over the various curricula and content of the students' educational programs. But in all candor, I had no interest in the total budget of the institution, or in who was responsible for the physical surroundings, or in whether the person who was the chief administrator and academic officer was called a president or a chancellor. Like most faculty members, I cared about my discipline, my own students, my own research, my own colleagues. Administrators and administration were not worth the expenditure of my time and energy.

The very recent history of events seems to indicate that a transformation has taken place, creating an intense desire among faculty members for participation in governance of the university. Whatever transformation has occurred, I do not believe that it has altered the basic, chosen roles of faculty members. Faculties have a long tradition of a closely related set of roles, only one of which includes leadership in the governance of the institution, and some of which require different behavior altogether. The faculty member is a teacher, mentor, confidante to students, researcher, writer, sometimes a visionary or a die-hard skeptic. He or she is also a record-keeper, an evaluator, a learner, a consultant, and a great deal more.

Limited interest and participation

It is therefore misleading, if not completely inaccurate, to assert that the popular inclination among faculty members is toward assuming larger and more demanding roles in the governance of universities. In reality, only a rather small number of faculty members on a particular campus are inclined to spend the time and energy needed to carry out the tasks of governance. Faculty members by and large prefer to let the administration manage the institution with the understanding that administrators will be held strictly accountable for the results of a pattern of decisions over a reasonable period of time. Some of the most able, productive people on the faculty make it quite clear that their other roles preclude their participation in governance activities, even their attendance at traditional faculty meetings. The majority of faculty members limit their participation to opinions, questions, and responses about their individual salary increases or to current topical issues. But such matters are neither the main business of productive faculty work in the university nor the major tasks of institution governance. The best and brightest faculty members are absorbed, as they must be, in loyalty to their disciplines, in creating and transmitting knowledge to the community, in professional associations and organizations, and in instructing and guiding their own students.

Certainly, educators should ask aloud whether some of the more obvious forms of apparent participation in governance—such as the many ad hoc committees and faculty action panels—lack significant participation by the most productive faculty people. If the committees and panels fail to draw these people into their ranks, what does that say about these manifestations of faculty governance? I make the distinction between effective forms of faculty governance—not usually good copy for the campus daily, but dogged work month in and month out—and the kind of faculty governance we have heard a great deal about since the upheavals of the late 1960s. If we put the distinction in our minds, we should, I believe, encourage and support effective faculty governance, but limit our participation in the other variety.

In conclusion then, let me restate these concerns. The contemporary concept of faculty governance is too limited and is inaccurate in portraying faculty participation, too often, as an outgrowth of the storms and controversies of the late 1960s. That kind of faculty governance may become more meddlesome than productive. In any case, it has largely been avoided—maybe boycotted—by the best and most productive members of the faculty. What those of us who are concerned with leadership for higher education need to do is to recast our attitudes about the kind of faculty governance that constitutes effective participation. The faculty can strengthen its hand in governing the university today by two principal means.

First, it should support and strengthen those among the faculty who have been designated to work with the boards of trustees and the entire community. A faculty member named to higher levels of administration should have the attitude, "Support me, help me with all your confidence, otherwise let me go back, willingly, to my teaching and scholarly research."

Second, the faculty can strengthen its hand in governance by focusing its involvement on key matters of decision and by a deeper, more meaningful commitment to the tough issues in governance rather than through broader and more superficial participation in diverse committees and organizations.

Developing Faculty Leadership

JOE E. ELMORE

QUALITATIVE IMPROVEMENT in the learning experience is being impeded by today's circumstances of the so-called steady state, with its necessity for carefully conserving scarce resources. Change and improvement cannot be incremental; net additions to regular programs are increasingly difficult to support and to justify. Improvement must come from within the institutions and their resources; compared with additions, such changes are more fundamental and harder to accomplish.

This widely recognized situation has far-reaching implications. It shifts the focus of responsibility for improvement from planners to practitioners, from administrators to faculty, or at least to administrators together with faculty. But how to facilitate and evaluate programs to develop faculty responsibility and leadership becomes a basic question facing American institutions and their administrations. The style of leadership needed calls upon and orchestrates leadership from members of the faculty. This style of administration has not recently been stressed, and the present climate in higher education increases the difficulty of the task. Administration has been busy developing management systems and learning the techniques, no doubt for some good reasons. Human relations within institutions of higher education have become increasingly bureaucratic, perhaps also for some understandable reasons. Relations have become more formal and ritualized; the atmosphere of collegiality has deteriorated. Relations between administration and faculty are often marked by hostility and distrust. Demoralization, disenchantment, fragmentation, and alienation are words used ever more frequently to describe higher education.

It is not surprising, even if it is regrettable, that one response has been a conviction that *anything* institutional is *necessarily* inimical to the individual. More and more people seem to have given up hope that institutions can possibly provide a healthy locus for human endeavor. There has been a growing hostility to structure and form in the name of individuality. According to this view, institutional structures inevitably reduce people to things unless they rebel or withdraw into some private diversion. One's function is separated from one's person, and the gap widens between the professional and the personal aspects of life. As relations in colleges and universities have become more and more formal and devoid of rich humanness, as competence and the possibilities of leadership have become defined more and more by title and role, as encounters in academic professional work have become more stylized and stultified, many people have rebelled, often with gusto, or have sought escape into some private sphere. The rationales for rebellion and withdrawal, with their strong anti-institutional and romantic bias, call forth rationales for more rigid structure and accountability. The dialectic is vicious. To be obliged to choose among dehumanization, rebellion, and privacy is a destructive course.

This atmosphere is clearly not conducive to the development and exercise of leadership. The context suggests that any consideration of leadership should give primary attention to the campus environment. Environment includes structure and organization, policies and systems, but also human sensibilities, rhetoric, philosophies, oral traditions, and myths. A college or university is a complex network of many factors that comprise the whole organism—a web of personal, professional, and organizational relations; of traditions, loyalties, and convictions; of places, purposes, and pressures. One cannot do justice to the integrity of the environment or to the fully human individual if any of these factors is left out. We in the academic community need to give sustained, perceptive, and balanced attention to analyzing colleges and universities as environments. The health of higher education depends in part on resolving the inhuman dialectic from which we suffer. It also depends in part on recovering the integrity and wholeness of our environments. Leadership development depends partly on creating an environment in which its members can be fully human.

An environment conducive to faculty leadership welcomes and values the initiative, the imagination, the energy, and the ideas of faculty members. It is a climate that summons up their talents and interests and is cognizant of their individualities. The human resources in a college or university constitute a reservoir of talents and potentialities; the challenge facing administrators is to liberate them for our educational aims. The college community needs to create a climate in which a person with the talent, imagination, and skill for leadership can make a contribution. It needs to learn to give as much attention to evoking and nurturing that leadership as it does to planning systems, cost-benefit analyses, and efficient organization.

Overcoming departmentalism

It is not my intention to idealize the faculty, nor have I forgotten the importance of discrimination and judgment. No climate can remove the necessity for tough choices or all the difficulties that ensue once choices have been made. No climate can make a good leader out of a ding-a-ling. Not all faculty members have a talent for leadership, but many do in a variety of ways. Their leadership is not of a single style or type or in one area. One thinks of groups of faculty members that have developed cross-disciplinary programs and courses, wilderness programs, systems of faculty evaluation; of faculty members who have persuaded their colleagues of the advantages of new calendar arrangements; of those who have analyzed the budget and led the way in devising means of saving money; of faculty members who have created designs for flexible science laboratories and laboratory equipment. The point is that if there is a climate hospitable to faculty leadership, that leadership will emerge and will strengthen institutions of higher learning.

An environment conducive to faculty leadership will also be marked by the habit of taking an institutional perspective and assuming some responsibility for the entire institution. The habit will be encouraged when faculty members are engaged in the affairs of the entire institution, when there is open access to information and materials, when there is honest, vigorous give and take about major institutional decisions, when the stake that faculty members have in their institutions is recognized. The academic community will have to reverse the trend toward loss of collegiality, and in many institutions it will need to overcome the rigidity of departments.

To ameliorate departmentalism, some institutions have found it helpful to rotate the chairmanship in departments, to structure and give significance to a variety of collegial occasions, to support cross-disciplinary teaching and research and team teaching. Faculty can be grouped for many purposes in ways other than by departments. Budgets can be set up to lessen departmentalism. Librarians often see educational issues from the perspective of the entire institution and, particularly if they are respected by their colleagues, can convince their colleagues of the importance of this perspective.

Strategies will vary among institutions, but wide consultation and administrative openness to faculty members' input are crucial. Also crucial is simple recognition of the faculty member's stake in the institution, not just in his or her unit. Loyalty to an institution and the habit of taking an institution-wide perspective cannot be developed overnight, but there are environments that encourage those traits.

Finally, the climate conducive to faculty leadership is one in which sharp, rigid distinctions between faculty and administration are lessened. There must be a division of labor, of course; but must the division of labor lead to a stratification of faculty versus administration? Titles and status by position should be deemphasized; the highest value should be placed on ideas, persuasiveness, and effectiveness in realizing educational goals. The best policies and programs will not be made because people have been given a position, a title, and authority; they will be made by people who have good ideas, an ability to formulate and articulate them persuasively, a sense of timing, and a skill in organizing ever-widening groups to implement them.

Most important, whatever the organization and structure of a particular institution, relationships should not become routinized and ritualized. Probably all of us need periodically to be involved in fresh patterns of relationships, to have new and different experiences, and—to put it in a more homely way—to mess up our neat organizational patterns. In many cases it is helpful if administrators teach and if teaching faculty assume administrative responsibilities part time on a rotating basis—as associate academic deans, associate deans of students, as directors of this or that program.

Real differences exist between being a faculty member and being a member of the administration. But have we educators not exaggerated the differences, forgetting that both faculty and administrators are educators and human beings? We sentimentalize if we cover up the differences, but we also do violence to each other when we forget our commonness as educators and as human beings, and when we relate to each other as stylized puppets, playing whatever role is assigned to us.

Faculty leadership for improvement

The academic community must develop ways for faculty members to assume responsibility for faculty evaluation. Evaluation has become a bad word, suggesting the collection of data which the administration uses to decide whom to keep and whom to let go. Faculty development has also become a bad term in many places, connoting what the administration does *to* the faculty. In defense of the administrators, it is indispensable to collect good data from a variety of sources and to develop fair processes for making difficult, consequential personnel decisions. Moreover, the art of making discriminating judgments about people—whoever is involved by whatever process with whatever data—is probably a no-win game these days. But many institutions have used evaluation primarily for decisionmaking (so-called summative evaluation), forgetting or ignoring that evaluation is also formative. It is diagnostic, too, and it is a necessary part of the improvement process. Of particular importance, faculty members need to assume leadership and responsibility for evaluation for qualitative improvement.

For example, Earlham College has developed a system of assessing the work of tenured faculty on a rotating basis every five years. Such a program need not undermine the tenure system if the purpose is clearly improvement and if faculty members assume leadership in the process. When it is the year for a tenured faculty member's work to be assessed, he or she chooses three colleagues to constitute a committee. Usually two of the colleagues are outside the person's department. The committee meets with the faculty member and develops a plan for the year in the light of the faculty member's interests and concerns. A folder of evaluation materials is collected, consisting of a self-evaluation, colleague evaluations, and letters from students and former students. Course evaluations are also assembled. At the conclusion of the process, the committee writes a summary report, which the dean shares and discusses with the faculty member. The aim is the development of a five-year plan for improvement, together with the determination of the ways the college can support the faculty member's plans and goals for the future. After a little more than a year of operation, the system seems to be working well.

Faculty members can exercise leadership by working with each other on the improvement of teaching and learning. After trying various ways to develop consultancies across institutions, last year Earlham appointed one of its own faculty members as consultant on teaching on a half-time basis. The person was chosen after wide consultation with teaching faculty. Faculty members are free to seek the consultant's assistance on their own initiative. The consultant's work is completely separated from the decision-making process for salary, contract renewal, or tenure. He or she does not tell the dean or the faculty affairs committee with whom he is working and he has no money to disburse. He or she is a colleague, friend, and helper and works with faculty members in any ways they mutually decide will be beneficial. During the first year of the program, almost one third of the Earlham faculty took advantage of the consultant's services. In the judgment of an outside consultant, the program is working very well. The administration intends to rotate the consultant every two years. Within a decade a number of people will be experienced in this kind of endeavor.

This fall Earlham also appointed a faculty member to work about half time with colleagues on instructional development, exploring the best ways to organize material for learning and the best ways to structure learning experiences. The two consultants will work closely together, the one mainly on teaching and the other on learning. It is too early to say how this program will work out, but I think the potentialities are good.

Both programs help lessen the unhealthy split between professional and personal development. The consultants are primarily concerned with assisting faculty members in their professional activities, particularly teaching and learning, but they often find they cannot separate a faculty member's personal situation from his or her professional work. The consultants are not psychotherapists; yet as colleagues, they are sensitive to the personal dimensions of their colleague's work.

To encourage faculty leadership, an institution must provide funds to support faculty members' activities for improvement. Funds for sabbatical leaves and attendance at professional meetings are important but insufficient; support is also needed for other activities that contribute to improvement. It is important for faculty members to be involved in the supervision of these funds and to have flexibility in their use consistent with institutional and programmatic objectives. Workshops, both inter-institutional and intrainstitutional, both departmental and interdepartmental, can be useful. Teams of faculty members who work in the summer to develop new courses or to revise old courses and curricula can contribute to program improvement. Often a faculty member needs support for a new experience or a new challenge to break out of a routine. And many faculty members need support from the institution for research or study in their subjects. Faculty members are not simply teachers; they are scholars and teachers of *something*. They need support to expand their knowledge, deepen their insights, sharpen their disciplines, and renew their love of their subjects. As indicated above, funds are needed to support the activities projected by tenured faculty members in their five-year plans. While the uses should be flexible, the group in charge of the funds should be aggressive in seeking out faculty members to discuss ways in which the institution might support their work and should coordinate grants with institutional priorities.

Another desirable move is to set aside institutional funds for program development. Each institution needs an internal foundation. Under present financial pressures, large sums probably cannot be allocated to this purpose, but even a small fund can be effective in the development of faculty leadership. Earlham is in its fourth year of having an internal foundation to make small grants to both administrative and teaching faculty members for initial costs of new programs. The funds are supervised by a group of faculty, students, and administrators. Most of the grants are small—no more than $4,000—but I have been impressed by the number of significant changes achieved. For example, effective intensive language programs in French and Spanish were begun with support from the internal foundation. The entire mathematics curriculum has been restructured, and instructional materials for the new courses have been produced. Programmed materials to assist students in working through their career development plans have been written. Funds have also supported efforts to teach students better organizational skills with the aim of improving student organizations. The internal foundation has contributed to the development of faculty leadership, and it now has high priority in our budgetary decisions.

Style and aims of leadership

Because there is a fundamental separation between faculty and administration in higher education today, members of both groups have come to associate leadership with the administration alone and are thereby missing the leadership potential within the faculty. Leadership in a college or university is a matter of cooperation and collaboration in a collegial environment. It cannot be reduced to a simple dichotomy of administration and faculty or of structure versus caring, the political versus the personal, policies versus trust, programs versus attitudes. Leadership is a complex human activity which is violated by such simplicities and is too complex to be reduced to one or two factors. Reductionism of this sort is unrealistic and is probably one reason why higher education is given to cycles of faddism and disappointment. We place great hope in one emphasis or technique or program, only to be disappointed before we go on to another. Leadership is a matter of data and consciousness, of power and persuasion, of decisiveness and diplomacy, of policies and personalism, of hard actualities and soft myths and traditions.

In an institution, not only the students learn and grow; it is also the faculty and the administration. To give students optimum opportunities for learning and maturation, the institution must concern itself with the development of the faculty and administration, for teaching and learning are activities that extend beyond classroom and curriculum. Educators teach by their style. Institutions teach by style too—by the ways they organize themselves and pattern relationships, by their decision-making processes, by the nuances of their rhetoric and the form of their conceptions. Alfred North Whitehead once remarked that style is the ultimate quality of mind; in the same sense, style is the ultimate quality of our campuses.

The style of a place, its climate and total environment, should be the focus of our concern. The possible effects of the leadership of any one person are quite limited. Every administrator who has been at his task for long will agree with the confession one administrator has made:

> I find that I can sometimes facilitate, but rarely create; that I can sometimes wind or unwind red tape, but rarely cut it; that I can sometimes urge, but rarely command; that I can somtimes sympathize, but rarely cure.[1]

We in the academic community shall be disappointed if we expect a messianic leader to rescue us and bring us to the academic holy city. But cooperative, collaborative efforts in a collegial environment can provide the leadership we need. The challenge is to develop leadership from a significant number of faculty members and administrators to nurture human resources and to achieve integrity. The academic community needs to institutionalize ways of sustaining a climate of nurturance. It needs flexible structures that will permit diverse approaches, in recognition that rigid, standardized forms stultify humanness. It needs to overcome the cleavages that fracture its integrity. It needs many leaders, voluntary and self-generating, who are welcomed by their colleagues in a system of mutual support concerned to achieve institutional goals.

1. "Confessions of an Academic Administrator," *New Republic*, July 27, 1974, p. 18.

Achieving Broad-Based Leadership

JESSE N. STONE, JR.

THE PROBLEMS CONFRONTING INSTITUTIONS of higher education have become too complex to allow administration to remain limited to the president and a small cadre of top administrative officers. Higher education in America has entered an era in which its leadership must be broadly based. It must be so broadly based, in fact, that it accepts input from all sectors of the academic community for improvement of the health of these institutions.

Although growth in enrollments is predicted to decline in the next score of years, they have already brought to campuses representatives from every sector of American life, with their varying aspirations. At the same time the institutions are being challenged by a plethora of problems, among them inadequate finances, demand for public involvement, liberalization of policies in recognition of women's rights, and faculty demands for collective bargaining. All of these occur at a time when the institutions are becoming focal points of public scrutiny and when administrative prerogatives are eroding.

One may readily conclude that faculty members expect to play a larger role in all aspects of institutional operations, not limiting their interests to teaching, research, and public service, but extending them to financial and physical plant planning and management, governance, student affairs, and public posture as well.

Indeed, a larger role is expected of them. How, then, to make the most of the leadership that faculty members can provide is a question of great moment. I am confident that among faculties there are people who can augment the leadership at their institutions. In fact, resolution of all the problems that must be addressed by the institutions cannot be achieved without faculty participation. Of inestimable value are the experiences and successes that faculty members of long tenure have gained from their special interests and their long tie to the educational enterprise as well as the vitality and commitment that youthful faculty members bring to the institution. To ignore their potential is to deny a readily available resource. But adequate use of that resource has not been made.

Deterrents to leadership development

There are several impediments to making the most of faculty leadership. Three of the most significant are: (1) the notion of a division of labor which requires increased specialization; (2) the decline of the service concept in higher education, which regarded service to and for others as a means of improving the individual and collective well-being; and (3) the greater infusion of politics into academe during the 1960s.

Division of labor has led to increased efficiency in the academic community. But the concomitant specialization has too often also led to limited involvement, an isolation of professionals within their disciplines where learning, the expansion of knowledge, and individual growth and development occur. In the 1970s, when greater accountability is being called for and pressures on institutions are mounting, even further cleavages within the academic community are in the offing. The growth of the administrative arm has generated new fears among faculty members. To a large extent, faculty members have been isolated from the process of discovering solutions to the many problems facing institutions, especially problems common between the institution and the larger society.

Division of labor often breeds bureaucracy, and bureaucracy gives rise to authority. And authority is often the cause of credibility gaps that make it difficult to develop faculty leadership.

As higher education became a major enterprise in the 1960s, the service concept diminished. By the service concept, I mean that concern with the individual and collective well-being of those who compose the institution. Faculty involvement with basic survival in an environment where the cost of living is constantly rising unfortunately militates against the service commitment in all aspects of the institution. The outcome, of course, is faculty energy spent in support of faculty rights, often with service to students and institutions given a lower priority.

Most faculty members abhor the need for assigning such a high priority to their individual and specialized interests, but the public disenchantment with higher education in general and the constant demands to improve quality and efficiency make it only natural for faculty members to exhibit these kinds of concerns.

During the past few decades, as government has played an increasing role in higher education activities, public institutions have experienced increased political pressures. Administrators have long dealt with such pressures, but they are relatively new to faculty. With the news media giving detailed accounts of the behavior of state legislatures in regard to higher education, preparing scenarios on the deliberations of governing boards, and generally involving themselves in nontraditional ways in the problems and activities of academe, faculty members are somewhat bewildered and resentful.

Political pressures and government involvement in higher education have had an adverse effect on the ivory tower notion of the professoriate, have diminished professorial prestige and status, and, to a large extent, equated educators, who have put in long years of successful research and study, with blue collar workers.

Given these varying sets of circumstances, how does one proceed to make the most of faculty leadership to enhance the role, scope, and mission of American higher education as well as restore the service concept?

Cultivating faculty perceptions of the institution

In the first place, let me make some suggestions. In each institution, a perception must be developed in which each member views the institution in its entirety. Gone is the day when a faculty member can limit his or her activities to teaching, research, or public service. Everyone in the academic community must be sensitive to the demands for change that affect the institution. Everyone in the academic community must be sensitive to the financial stress that affects the operation of the institution. Everyone must be sensitive to the newer demands posed by a more diverse student body, in which the students seek to pursue the goals they have set for their lives. The successful exercise of any delegated authority is dependent on such a sensitivity.

The problems that university administrators are called on to resolve must stretch our imaginations to the fullest. We need advice that leads to the solution of our problems. We need that input and those actions from the faculty that may assist discovery and employment of techniques to deal with deficit spending, with increasing enrollments, with healing the wounds resulting from student dissent, with curriculum expansion, with faculty salary increases in a tight budget, with parking, and so forth. These are problems that affect every person at the university and whose force reaches beyond the immediate university community to the governing board, to state government, and to the various university publics. They condition how the various publics view the university, and they influence the posture the publics take toward the university. To see the university only as it goes about the business of teaching and learning is, therefore, not enough. It must be seen also as a social agency and as an expression of state government, as it seeks to provide a much needed service for the people.

Success in encouraging and perfecting this type of leadership may well depend upon three qualities: (1) display of mutual respect by faculty members and administrators; (2) complete openness on the part of administrators about the problems affecting the interests of faculty members and the university as a whole; and (3) the president's skill as a leader capable of inspiring faith, competence, and trust, as well as a belief in the ability of presidential leadership to address faculty needs and interest.

Presidential initiatives toward leadership

Faculty members and administrators each perform basic, essential services in the higher education process. They must cooperate and complement each other, and each group must carry on its duties and responsibilities as an integral part of the whole. Presidential leadership must be willing to recognize openly the value of total faculty participation in university leadership. The expression of the faculty's considered opinion, continuous faculty development, and participation in governance, budget preparation, and even the development of spending priorities must be recognized as appropriate avenues for faculty participation in leadership. Presidential leadership must strive to establish a relationship in which there is mutual respect for accomplishments, even as it insists on faculty and administration fulfilling their responsibilities to each other and to the university and its publics.

Just as the administration is involved with various publics, today's circumstances bring faculty members in contact with various publics, both inside and outside the university. Organizations such as the American Association of University Professors, labor unions, political organizations concerned with educational funding and pay for educators—these are but a few of the types of organizations and publics with which faculties have contact. The proliferation of ideas and information requires presidential and administrative leadership to be open in a way quite different from that which has prevailed in the past. Openness is not only designed to obtain support, but is also required to eliminate false rumors, notions, and concepts that can impair the enthusiasm of faculty members to produce fully.

Every college and university president today must be concerned both with the welfare and well-being of his university and with the image of the university as a fully productive, quality-oriented institution. Each president must recognize the changes in the presidency itself, changes that no longer set a president apart from other members of his institution and that no longer permit his pronouncements to enjoy their earlier weight and force. Presidential leadership, it seems to me, begins with the understanding by the president that leadership in any higher educational institution is a job too big for one person acting alone, no matter how energetic, how competent, or how experienced. Hence, a partnership for leadership with jurisdiction carefully defined and delegation wisely made is essential. The president must be able to sell the partnership idea and must himself be visionary, intelligent, and able if he is to inspire confidence and gain support.

At Southern University we have initiated a policy that encourages personal communication between the president and the faculty members.

The faculty members are invited, on a departmental basis, to the president's home for coffee. They are eager to share ideas about their department's needs, strengths, and weaknesses. These encounters have been a valuable learning experience. As a result I have been able to address many university problems more expeditiously. Most important, perhaps because the groups were small, I came to know faculty members in a way not possible had I met only with the faculty as a whole.

It is only when viewed as a partnership that leadership in higher education can become truly united and effective. Partners working together for the common good can stimulate an effectiveness felt far beyond the walls of any good institution and even beyond their own years in the institution. The vision of people working together can inspire hope, imagination, and dedication. Our institutions and our youth need more than the vision, the imagination, the hope, and the dedication; they need the practical application of men and women in higher education working together for the success of these institutions and of youth.

3. DESIGNING NEW PERSONNEL POLICIES

Policies as Reflectors
of Institutional Goals

CHARLES R. LONGSWORTH

NEW PERSONNEL POLICIES should be designed in response to changing institutional goals. They should also take into account the needs and expectations of the institution's personnel, the need to maintain balance among conflicting demands, and the obligation to assure some consonance between the practices of the institution and societal standards and legal requirements. More frequently, however, new personnel policies are designed in response to a personnel crisis that threatens the institution's stability and demands an immediate response.

Perhaps nothing has stimulated the forced draft of new personnel policies more than the threat of staff or faculty to unionize. In general, colleges and universities have been slow to create formal mechanisms for redress of personnel grievances and for other procedurally clear and institutionalized responses to personnel needs. Rather (at least in many private institutions), an atmosphere of benevolent paternalism has prevailed, either as a remnant of nineteenth-century practices or simply in the honest belief that if the managers are sufficiently paternalistic and sufficiently benevolent (and perhaps enlightened), the institution and its personnel will be better served by the kind of individual attention that such an approach implies.

Fortunately or unfortunately, such paternalism is disappearing rapidly under the pressure of the federal government and the paucity of benevolence (and enlightenment).

Many institutions install formal grievance procedures but only after there have been prolonged organizing efforts and union votes, which management usually has fought with great energy and determination. Immediately thereafter, management has initiated the design and installation of a grievance procedure. Management has thus been humbled, has learned some lessons, and is frightened into action.

Those who have had the experience of being frightened into designing new personnel policies realize, of course, that our colleges and universities are labor-intensive organizations with traditionally defined relationships among faculty, administration, and staff. These relationships, which depend to a high degree on the integrity, good will, scrupulousness, and intelligence of the participants, are assumed to be based on a different (and higher) expectation of humaneness than the relationships assumed to prevail among the various levels and classifications of employees in other forms of corporations.

Whether or not these ideas of collegiality and gentility are still widely shared and whether or not they best meet the needs of the students and the people who work together in such service is somewhat beside the point. The fact remains that colleges and universities are service organizations, dependent almost entirely on people and the relationships among them, and it is of vital importance that institutions design and maintain personnel policies that best serve the needs of their people.

Goals of personnel policies

Whether personnel policies and practices are formal or informal, they must be as consistent, equitable, ethical, and legal as they can be made. They must take account of, and comply with, all applicable laws and be as humane as possible. This is the standard.

The principal goal for the design of new personnel policies is to further or attain institutional objectives. If, for example, the institutional objective is to maintain a core faculty and to supplement it as needed to achieve educational or financial flexibility, policies will be designed to attract part-time people. They will include careful attention to fringe benefits, leave policies, office and secretarial assistance, and so forth. If, on the other hand, the goal is to have a full-time, long-term faculty of a stable size with continuity as a principal objective, then tenure, retirement, and leave policies will all be designed to favor long-term affiliation with the institution and to discourage part-time and short-term appointments. Or again, if the institution always wishes to seek appointment and promotion from within, personnel policies will probably include opportunities for further education and training and notifications of job availabilities that favor consideration of internal over external candidates.

The second consideration is the educational impact of personnel policies. Often educators forget how much their students learn by the examples set in the institution's daily life. Many students enter college with little idea of the world of work and the ways in which the lives of working people are organized, fulfilled, or, in some cases, shattered by the personnel policies of employers. Insofar as students become interested in and acquainted with the employees of the institution and its policies, they begin to realize the assumptions that are implicit in the minds of those who have designed and administered the personnel policies.

For example, if all the secretaries are women, all the part-time faculty are women, and all the dormitory cleaning is done by women, whereas most of the full professors, the tenured professors, the president, deans, and department chairpersons are men, it seems to me there are only two possible conclusions for a student to draw. One is that men are superior and women are inferior, and, therefore, the positions held by the members of each sex and the status they enjoy are simply reflections of a very hard but unavoidable fact. The other is that the institution is ignorant of the law, indifferent to the history of sex discrimination, unaware of the ways in which talent is distributed and talented women can be recruited and employed, or indifferent to the educational impact of the example it is setting. Either way, the inference is likely to be that the institution's behavior represents the assumptions of its leaders, and students (unless they are very independent-minded) are being given examples that burden rather than enlighten them.

New policies in practice

Hampshire College was formed in the period 1966–70 and had the opportunity to design personnel policies that reflect the institution's goals without compromises attributable to prior practice or policies and without the imperatives of an operating situation. Hence, it enjoyed a rare opportunity to establish, in an unhurried environment, policies that were consistent with its goals. The two principal institutional goals that were central in Hampshire's considerations were greater egalitarianism and flexibility in faculty composition by age, rank, and interests.

The new policies were designed initially by a faculty-administration planning group. As the college has evolved, however, the planning has followed a rather consistent pattern. Identification of a need for change or opportunity to initiate change has been determined by the administration in consultation with the most affected persons and with the trustee compensation committee, which retains the responsibility to support administrative recommendations to the full board of trustees. A committee made up principally of representatives of the most affected group of employees develops proposals for policies. Proposals are refined in consultation with the administration until there is agreement to go to the trustee compensation committee or alternatively to the entire membership of affected persons whose endorsement is sought (this step may follow endorsement by the compensation committee). Thereafter, approval is requested from the board of trustees. Thus, each policy or policy change results from consultation, endorsement, and approval on the part of persons most affected and the persons with the responsibility for approving or administering the policies.

The goal of greater egalitarianism has been manifest in a number of ways, all of which have benefited the college. Fringe benefits, including eligibility for sabbatical leaves, were awarded on a proportional basis for anyone working half time or more who would be eligible if they worked full time. Retirement benefits, life insurance, tuition-support payment, and other fringe benefits are awarded to all classes of employees without distinction.

Hampshire's planners assumed that a faculty contract system, developed to encourage faculty growth through regular evaluation and review and to maintain flexibility, could be designed to protect academic freedom and yet result in a gradual faculty turnover that would minimize rapid growth in the instructional budget without a concomitant increase in teaching resources.

The policy originated in 1968 in the deliberations of a group composed of administrators and faculty members. The group was charged with establishing the faculty-institutional relationship. The committee began its work by examining the current status of tenure, its deficiencies and advantages, and the disjunctions between tenure in theory and in practice. At the time the deliberations began, there was growing interest in public and private education in experimenting with alternatives to tenure, and there was a proliferation of articles pro and con. Although several of the participants in the planning had come to Hampshire from tenured positions at other institutions, they became interested in examining the question anew. Ultimately, the committee proposed an experimental contract system as an alternative to tenure. The contract system was installed in 1969 and has governed the relationship between all faculty members and Hampshire College since the college opened in 1970.

The attempt to create a system other than tenure for defining the relationship of faculty to the college grew out of several premises of Hampshire's planning. The first is Hampshire's assumption about the role of the teacher. Hampshire was designed to reduce reliance on the concept of course and subject matter as the basic building blocks of educational progress. The consequences of this viewpoint have profound implications for the role of the teacher. Emphasis on academic advising, bibliographic skills, examining ability, breadth of interest and concern, and a willingness to learn supplants the emphasis on specialization that characterizes American higher education. This emphasis, in turn, puts a premium on the adaptability of the faculty member.

A second critical point was the realization that Hampshire College could not afford to develop a faculty with a majority at senior ranks (and salary levels). It was assumed (and decreed, therefore) that budgets would be established on the basis of a presumed distribution of faculty by rank and that the ratio would be maintained (one full professor: two associate professors: four assistant professors).

Faculty employment and evaluation system

Hampshire has now completed six years of experimentation with a faculty contract system. Emphasis should be on the word experiment, for we set out on no crusade to slay the Goliath, tenure. Rather, we set out idealistically and, I think, courageously to see whether we could develop a faculty employment and evaluation system that would foster growth in individual faculty members; that would enable the institution, which was new and uncertain about its future, to maintain greater control over the composition of the faculty, both in special interest and rank; that would, over the long term, build a fine teaching faculty from which some successful members could and would move in time to other good positions; and that would help the institution survive financially.

Faculty members are hired on contracts of a defined term of three, four, or five years, with responsibilities defined by a candidate's proposal accepted for funding by the college. Renewals are offered seventeen months before contract expiration, after an evaluation by colleagues and students and recommendations to the president by the school dean (Hampshire has no departments) and the college-wide and powerful committee on faculty reappointments and promotions, which is composed of five faculty members, two students, and the dean of the college, ex officio. The committee operates on the assumption that Hampshire appoints able people who can do well in its particular environment and generally do, aided by frank evaluations, which help reveal weaknesses. Further, the committee assumes that persons who do not find Hampshire congenial to their particular interests and talents will recognize the incompatibility, as the college recognizes it, and will move on to other positions with Hampshire's help and blessing. New institutions are idealistic. Since June 1971, 101 faculty members have been evaluated, with the results shown in table 1.

TABLE 1: *Faculty Evaluation and Contract Renewals,*
Hampshire College, 1970–71—1975–76

Year	Number of Candidates	Contracts Renewed	Contracts Not Renewed
1970–71	9	8	1
1971–72	24	23	1
1972–73	16	15	1
1973–74	10	8	2
1974–75	16[a]	13	3
1975–76	26	20[b]	5
Total	101	88	13

[a] Two more persons decided not to stand for review.
[b] One person withdrew candidacy.

A number of deficiencies in the policy were revealed early, and modest corrections were made. As we have gained experience, however, it has become clear that there are fundamental problems, which suggest, at least, that the design of policies involving evaluations of people must not rest on noble assumptions about human behavior, that it is very difficult to elicit frank and penetrating appraisals of human beings. We began to experience an increasing disinclination on the part of faculty members to evaluate each other and a tendency to shift responsibility to the president, whom faculty members publicly proclaimed to be "all powerful," while, in private, thanking their stars they could so elevate him. For example, at one point I turned down a unanimous recommendation for reappointment, and the dean who had forwarded it from his faculty said, "You did the right thing!"

Although our difficulty in achieving honest, penetrating, and even negative appraisals is not unique—the society seems disinclined to value elitism in any form—the absence of a tenured cadre of senior faculty whose evaluations of younger persons can be made with the comfort of personal security exacerbates our problem. Even the ablest of our senior people are sensitive to the fact that they, too, will be evaluated again and that there are opportunities to "get even."

The faculty has nevertheless continued to support the contract system and has worked hard to make it succeed. The senior faculty leadership, as it evolved, was most committed to it as an alternative to tenure, and Hampshire made clear and encouraging progress in the selection, evaluation, training, and retention of an outstandingly able faculty in very difficult circumstances: an institutional self-image that created high expectations; a cooperative environment (The Five Colleges, Inc.) in which Hampshire had to manifest an intellectual ambience acceptable to some highly self-confident neighbors; the teaching of able, bright, and independent students.

By 1975–76, it was clear that the experiment needed a close look. In June 1976, I appointed a faculty task force to examine our contract policy and report its sense of the experiment's problems with an eye to beginning a full-scale review and, subsequently, formulation of new proposals for defining the fundamental relationship between the faculty and the college, assuming that perpetuation of the contract system in some form was one possibility.

The committee found a number of fundamental problems, although it did not, as a consequence, recommend that the contract policy be abandoned. The committee's findings, in sum, were:

1. The most striking and worrisome conclusion from the discussions is that the contract system and the reappointment policy and procedures

have the over-all impact of lowering the quality of the faculty. Re-appointment was felt to be most difficult for both the best and worst candidates for reappointment. The general tendency, therefore, is not to identify, support, and promote excellence, but rather to encourage mediocre performance and favor the median strata of the faculty.

a) The very good people tend to become threats to all the others. They raise the ante for everyone; in a system in which everyone votes on everyone else's reappointment, they are penalized for their "rate-busting" behavior.

b) In addition, the current system discourages hard, negative judgments. This is especially true at the school level, where negative judgments tend to be avoided and cases passed up the line where the CCFRAP (College Committee for Reappointments and Promotions) or the president will make the hard, negative judgment.

2. The current system also has an adverse impact on the faculty's quality by diverting inordinate faculty time and energy from teaching, advising, scholarship, and other forms of professional development. The involvement of so many faculty members in the review of more than twenty of their colleagues a year seriously drains important resources from the principal educational functions of the college.

3. Although the reappointment process is supposed to provide opportunities for faculty growth and for the identification of problems and their correction, the current system functions neither as a support nor as an incentive for faculty development. It does not foster the development of the faculty as a whole because of the avoidance of hard, discriminating judgments and the bias toward median faculty performance. It also does not support faculty development on an individual basis. It rarely contributes to the improvement of a faculty member's capacity to perform well in and contribute to the Hampshire system. To the extent that the requirements for excellent performance in the Hampshire system are peculiar to Hampshire, it does not contribute to faculty member's marketability in the external world.

4. The vague criteria for performance and the exaggerated definition of faculty responsibilities create a sense of paranoia among the faculty members in regard to reappointment. This has a generally demoralizing and draining effect, which further impairs the quality of the faculty.[1]

It is my observation that these are the fundamental weaknesses of Hampshire's contract system. The fatal temptation at this point may be the inclination to try to correct the apparent deficiencies of a system designed to facilitate a critical kind of human interaction by tinkering with the process rather than recognizing that human imperfections and fallibility are most revealed in such circumstances. The major question to

1. Report of the Hampshire College Reappointment Task Force, July 19, 1976.

be asked is whether the Hampshire College faculty will ultimately be better served by staying with a system which, despite its problems, has served reasonably well, or whether it can better achieve its aims through a more tenurelike system. Neither will bring full satisfaction. Neither will avoid the pains and anxiety of deciding the professional fate of others, unless mediocrity is to prevail.

Thus the stage is set for an interesting debate, and the faculty will have a central role, as will the president and trustees, in determining what new policy or policies to adopt or how to continue the old policies, possibly with changes.

Our experience, it seems to me, is a healthy one and the case interesting. The faculty, as the most affected, and the administration and trustees are struggling in good faith to maintain institutional goals and to protect the faculty and satisfy their needs. A major departure in personnel policies produces unknowns and sometimes leads to wholly unpredictable and usually highly educational experiences.

New Policies for the Part-Time Faculty

THOMAS W. FRYER, JR.

PART-TIME FACULTY in American higher education are today employed in such numbers that the practice constitutes a new dimension in the educational programs and professional relations of institutions. Universities have traditionally employed a class of part-time faculty called teaching assistants (TAs). The nonstatus of these persons is assumed to be a proper rite of academic passage, and their sometimes less than masterful teaching performance is thought an appropriate trial in the travails of the expendable undergraduate.

In community colleges, on the other hand, TAs are not widely used, and class distinctions among teaching faculty (such as academic rank) are far from universal. Institutions pride themselves on the "quality of instruction." The part-time instructor is the community college's second-class citizen, however, and the fact that in at least sixteen states there are more part-time than full-time instructors[1] may reflect a serious inconsistency in a philosophy that espouses excellence in teaching.

1. John Lombardi, "Part-Time Faculty in Community Colleges," Topical Paper Number 54 (Los Angeles: ERIC Clearinghouse for Junior Colleges, December 1975), p. 12. This monograph provides the most comprehensive bibliography available.

The California community college experience is instructive in suggesting trends and areas of need for new personnel policies. During the 1974–75 academic year, part-time instructors outnumbered full-time instructors by 40 percent.[2] Statewide there were 14,273 full-time instructors, while 20,027 part-time instructors from off campus provided teaching services. (This latter number does not include 7,505 full-time instructors teaching an overload for extra compensation in the same institution.) Stated in other terms, 28 percent of the full-time equivalent teaching positions in regular community college courses were filled by part-time instructors from off campus.

The use of part-time instructors is common in most disciplines. In some instructional areas, more than 50 percent of the instruction is conducted by part-timers. Those academic areas with the highest concentration of part-time instructors include business and management, 49.9 percent; public affairs and services, 58.2 percent; home economics, 46.8 percent; apprenticeship, 64.8 percent; computer and information science, 44.9 percent; and law, 53.9 percent.

Nearly one third of the part-time instructors from off campus are either not employed elsewhere or are employed elsewhere only part time. Approximately 13 percent, or 2,565, are completely unemployed except for their work in the community college.

The new professional

There appear to be three separate categories of part-time faculty: full-time faculty members at the community college or other educational institutions who teach part time for extra compensation; those who are employed full time elsewhere, typically in business or industry and who do not wish a full-time faculty position; and persons who see themselves as teachers and wish to enter the teaching profession on a full-time basis, but can find employment only part time.

The third group includes a new professional who has appeared on the scene in American higher education in the last ten years—the permanent part-time teacher. This new person has emerged as a result of the declining growth rate in higher education, the enormous surge in evening and off-campus programs and the concomitant growth in part-time and adult students, the resource squeeze, the radical alteration in the academic labor supply from a seller's to a buyer's market, and the achievement in

2. Donald H. Sewell et al., "Report on a Statewide Survey About Part-Time Faculty in California Community Colleges" (Sacramento: California Community and Junior College Association, January 1976), p. 5. This excellent report is the basis of most of the numerical data for the California situation contained in this paper.

post-World War II America of a degree of affluence and welfare assistance unthought of twenty-five years ago.

Permanent part-timers, as defined here, do not constitute the majority of the part-time faculty, but are the most vocal and aggressive in the group. This part-timer is also, perhaps, the most exploited and thus attracts, perhaps deservedly, the most attention. The California experience has implications beyond local boundaries.

A most troubling issue raised by such extensive use of part-time faculty is that of compensation. Institutions have found it expedient to use part-time faculty because, almost universally, these persons are paid lower salaries. This economic incentive has driven colleges toward part-time faculty utilization as a survival technique. In California, particularly in the late 1960s and early 1970s, before the passage of revised community college finance legislation in 1973, large urban districts were able to balance their budgets *only* through the expanded use of part-time faculty.

In some cases hiring freezes were applied. These freezes broke up full-time positions, upon the resignation or retirement of faculty members, into a number of part-time assignments. The reconversion of these part-time positions into full-time contracts proves difficult from both fiscal and personnel perspectives.

Salary issues have energized, yet exacerbated problems in, institutional relationships with the part-time faculty. The emerging permanent part-time faculty member has a personal idea of proper compensation. In each of the last several years the California legislature has seen bills introduced to require paying part-time faculty on a pro rata basis.

It is difficult to estimate what equitable compensation rates are because the complete assignment of a full-time faculty member is often not clearly spelled out, thus making it difficult to determine exactly what a full-time faculty person is being paid for; and on a statewide basis there is no uniform number of total hours per week a full-time instructor is expected to work. One analysis concludes that part-time faculty members in California community colleges teach nearly 40 percent of the instructional workload, for which they are paid 20 percent of total faculty salaries.[3] If it is assumed that full-time instructors are paid on the basis of a fifteen-hour workweek, it would cost more than $90,000,000 to increase the pay of part-time instructors to a level commensurate with that of the full-time faculty in California community colleges. Assuming a thirty-hour full-time faculty workweek, the cost would be more than

3. Chuck McIntyre, "Current Data on Part-Time Teaching and Finance" (Address at California Community Colleges Conference on the Part-Time Teacher and the Community College, Inglewood, California, January 28, 1976).

$35,000,000 statewide.[4] Thus far, legislation requiring pro rata pay has not been successful.

Judicial developments

Perhaps the most interesting and relevant development in the area of part-time faculty employment is found in the courts. The landmark case, *Balen* v. *Peralta,* was rendered by the supreme court of California in mid-1974.

H. Pat Balen, currently president of the board of trustees of the Peralta Community College District, was hired in 1965 as an hourly instructor to teach speech in the evening program at Laney, one of the Peralta colleges. He was continuously rehired to teach the same class semester after semester for a total of four and one-half years. Balen was given oral notification during the 1969 fall term that he would not be reemployed in the spring semester 1970, a timing which, for whatever reasons, coincided with Balen's attempt to organize other part-time faculty members purportedly to protect their interest.

Balen's complaint contended that by law he ought not to have been discharged without notice and hearing; that even if he were classified as a temporary employee, the statute authorizing such a temporary classification was unconstitutional; and that his discharge was politically motivated in violation of the First and Fourteenth Amendments to the U.S. Constitution.

The state supreme court, reversing lower court rulings, held that Balen was properly classified in a status entitling him by statute to "pretermination notice and hearing" and that because Balen had been denied such notice and hearing, it was "unnecessary to reach his constitutional claims."

This case is of national significance in part because the California court relied on the *Sinderman* ruling (*Perry* v. *Sinderman* (1972) 408 U.S.) from the United States Supreme Court in reaching its major conclusion that

> the essence of the statutory classification system is that continuity of service restricts the power to terminate employment, which the institution's governing body would normally possess.[5]

The California statutes on part-time employment are notoriously confusing. The Balen case, for example, was thrown out of the superior and appellate courts based on judicial interpretation at those levels of California law.

4. Sewell, "Report on a Statewide Survey," p. 10.

5. H. Pat Balen v. Peralta Junior College District (1974) 11 Cal 3d, 821.

Most community college districts have acted on the premise that persons employed from outside the community colleges on a part-time basis are classified as "temporary" (and therefore not entitled to hearings in the event they are not rehired) if they are employed to teach fewer than 60 percent of the hours considered to represent a full-time teaching assignment.

This so-called 60 percent test was added to the California education code in 1967. Subsequent legislation introduced a new test, the "75 percent rule," which seems to define a "temporary" employee as any person serving fewer than 75 percent of the days of the academic year, without reference to a minimum number of hours.

The California education code, four fat volumes of turgid obscurantism, is riddled with internally inconsistent, confusing, and in some cases apparently mutually exclusive provisions, which involve the employment of part-time instructors.

The courts themselves are bewildered. The Los Angeles County Superior Court, in a December 1976 ruling in a part-time faculty tenure case (*California Teachers Association* v. *Santa Monica Community College District*), began its "Notice of Intended Decision and Memorandum Opinion" as follows:

> The Court asserts with confidence that only one clear principle may be gleaned from this case; the Education Code provisions dealing with temporary teachers must stand as man's masterpiece of obfuscation. . . . Applying the tools of statutory construction so lovingly crafted by appellate courts over the years leads only to the conclusion that the sections of the Education Code which must be interpreted are a hopeless muddle with direction signs pointing simultaneously and successively north, south, east and west.

There are 70 community college districts operating 103 community colleges, each with its own complement of harassed souls trying to operate legally. With the rapid accretion of case law superimposed on the ever-changing catastrophe of the code, chaos reigns supreme.

A new criterion for permanence

In the *Balen* case, however, the state supreme court simply transcended the law, which seemed to define "temporary" in terms of degree or level of contact with the institution and settled on the concept of *continuity of contact* as the controlling criterion, offering the opinion that

> because the . . . temporary classifications are not guaranteed procedural due process by statute, they are narrowly defined by the legislature, and should be strictly interpreted.

The court continued:

> plaintiff's continuity of service would seem to indicate the necessary expectation of employment which the legislature has sought to protect from arbitrary dismissal by its classification scheme.

The decision further offered the following comments on the concepts of probationary employment:

> The probationary plan envisions a two-fold purpose: It allows the new teacher sufficient time to gain additional professional expertise, and provides the district with ample opportunity to evaluate the instructor's ability before recommending a tenure position. A part-time instructor . . . generally serves under conditions comparable to those of his full-time counterpart; thus there is no reason for differentiating between their statuses for the purpose of attaining probationary classification, nor has the legislature directed us to do so.[6]

Based in large measure on the *Balen* case, another Peralta case (*Peralta Federation of Teachers, Local 1603, AFT* v. *Peralta Community College District*) in the Alameda County Superior Court ordered in 1975 that tenure be granted to seven employees who had been employed on a part-time basis for three consecutive years, and that probationary status be granted five others who had entered their second consecutive year of employment.

Parenthetically, this same ruling held that a rational and legal basis *did* exist for paying temporary employees a lower rate than regular or probationary employees. Not unexpectedly, the college district is appealing the granting of tenure, and the union is appealing the denial of pro rata pay.

It is interesting to note that in this Alameda County Superior Court action, the Memorandum of Intended Decision actually states:

> on July 1, 1971, Edward A. Walker became tenured as to 40% of a full-time teaching position; that on July 1, 1971, Dr. Virginia Franklin became tenured as to 31% of a full-time teaching position; that on July 1, 1971, Gertrude Y. Fator became tenured as to 50% of a full-time teaching position.[7]

Again, the significant element in this court decision is that tenure in part-time teaching assignments is defined by the court in terms of *continuity of employment creating the expectation of reemployment*. In their relations with this class of teaching personnel, institutions should be mindful of this emerging judicial interpretation.

6. Ibid.

7. Peralta Federation of Teachers v. Peralta Community College District.

A blossoming crop of cases petitioning for tenure for part-time faculty is now before the courts all over California. The question of an employee's receiving tenure in two or more school districts, an inevitable result of granting part-time tenure, has not been addressed by the California courts; but there does not appear to be a statutory prohibition against a faculty person holding tenure simultaneously, including tenure in two full-time positions, in separate school districts. The code does prohibit an individual from achieving tenure in two positions in a single district.

Collective bargaining

Collateral to the court activity, California's new collective bargaining statute, the Rodda Bill, enacted in 1975, provides:

> A negotiating unit that includes classroom teachers shall not be appropriate *unless it at least includes all of the classroom teachers* employed by the public school employer [emphasis added].[8]

This provision, which has not yet been interpreted by California's Educational Employment Relations Board (EERB), has enormous significance for the bargaining process in community colleges. A strict constructionist approach would hold that each and every classroom teacher, whether a part-time teacher of one class on an occasional and irregular basis or a full-time tenured faculty member, had equal status and weight in bargaining. This interpretation would vest in the part-time faculty sufficient voting power, at least theoretically, to control the bargaining process.

Another interpretation of the passage, however, could accommodate the definition of a class of "casual" teachers, utilizing National Labor Relations Board precedents, and might exclude from the bargaining process part-time persons who are employed irregularly, below a certain percent of full-time employment, or both.

At this juncture, it is not clear which approach the EERB will take. Hearings in two community college districts have been held, one selected as representative of a single-college district, the other as representative of a multicollege district. Whatever the specific outcome, it is clear that part-time faculty will play a major role in collective bargaining in California community colleges.

Faculty organizations have been changed radically by the part-timers. Full-time faculty members, once dominant in organizations that opened their doors to part-time faculty primarily as a device to increase

8. Article 6, "Unit Determinations," Section 3545(b)(1).

membership, now find themselves in the curious position of being outnumbered and outvoted in these same organizations.

Union leaders, who have often been selected from the ranks of the full-time faculty, are powerless to change this, even if they wish to, because they must relate to a new constituency that is predominantly part time in character. In some cases, entirely new faculty organizations, asserting their primary interest in the full-time faculty, have emerged as reactions to the trend.

The part-time faculty in California community colleges presently is organized in a 2,500-member organization called the California Association of Part-Time Instructors (CAPTI). Comparable organizations have emerged in New York City and the state of Washington.[9] CAPTI looks toward expanding its organizational horizons beyond the community colleges into the California state college and university system, where a large percentage of part-time faculty members are likewise employed, and perhaps beyond the borders of California as well.

Wider implications

What are the implications of all this for other institutions in other states? First, whether or not the fact is realized by the employing institution, it is entirely possible that persons teaching on a regular and continuous part-time basis are accruing permanency if the matter finds its way to judicial determination. There will undoubtedly be wide variation among the states, but the question is one that bears immediate legal review at the institutional level. The "it can't happen here" attitude is likely to yield unpleasant surprises.

In order to prevent an ever-increasing number of part-time faculty members from achieving tenure, some institutions will consider requiring an actual break in service of at least one academic term just before the individual reaches the length of service in which full-time faculty members achieve continuing employment rights.

Second, to the extent that institutions employ, whether accidentally or on purpose, permanent part-time faculty members, it is professionally incumbent upon the employing institution to deal with these persons on a professional and equitable basis. (Equitability does *not* necessarily mean 100 percent pro rata pay and benefits.)

Part-time faculty members are often the victims of systematic academic and institutional discrimination. They are frequently assigned by the senior departmental faculty members to the large, undesirable classes at the inconvenient times of day. (Ironically, this tends to make part-timers the most productive faculty group on campus.) In many cases these

9. Lombardi, "Part-Time Faculty," p. 6.

persons are prohibited from participation in departmental affairs. In California community colleges, it was found that 70 percent of the colleges offer active in-service development programs for full-time faculty, while only 37 percent of the institutions report comparable programs for part-time faculty.[10]

When taken with what many part-time faculty members see to be their invidious wage situation, these facts give rise to a kind of righteous indignation in the new class of permanent part-time faculty. Eventually a price, and usually a *higher* price, will be paid when a group of persons perceives itself the victim of an unjust system.

Suggestions for designing new personnel policies

How should institutions properly use and relate to part-time faculty? Following are a few brief, purely practical suggestions, based in part on four assumptions: (1) present conditions, in the making for more than a decade, will not be unmade overnight; (2) the use of part-time faculty purely as an economic expedient, or merely to accomplish academic grunt work, is *not* appropriate or legitimate; (3) in states where collective bargaining exists, much of what is desirable will have to be bargained rather than granted; and (4) a full-time career commitment by a faculty member involves more than the total of the constituent classroom teaching assignments he may have.

1. The instructional program should be planned so that part-time faculty members are employed for limited and specific purposes:
   a. to provide special competence not available on a full-time basis;
   b. to provide for reasonable expansion and contraction of the educational program based on actual, rather than planned, enrollments; and
   c. to provide necessary service flexibility in off-campus activities.
2. A policy guideline should be adopted in each institution governing the maximum extent to which instructional services will be provided by part-time persons. Depending on the curriculum of the particular institution, probably not more than one fourth to one third of the total instructional program should be conducted by part-time faculty members. Technical and highly specialized occupational curricula require greater utilization of part-time faculty members than the liberal arts. The newer, nontraditional institutions, because of the special nature of their programs, will probably use part-timers considerably beyond the suggested limits.
3. A planned development program should be provided for part-time faculty members. It should include orientation to the insti-

10. Sewell, "Report on a Statewide Survey," p. 12.

tution, department, and curriculum. The program should consist of both individual and group experiences, and part-time faculty members should actively participate in its design. Information should range from the basics of mail procedures, pay dates, and payroll matters, through descriptive data concerning the college's population, institutional philosophy, and grading guidelines. A faculty handbook should be published for part-time faculty members.

4. Part-time faculty members should be invited and encouraged to participate in the affairs of their academic departments and areas as well as in institutional committees.

5. In principle, part-time faculty compensation should recognize that a teaching assignment involves more than time in the classroom.

6. Part-time faculty members who are compensated by the credit- or contact-hour should be paid for their participation in institutionally sponsored development activities.

7. A full range of support services and facilities should be provided for part-time faculty members. These services should include office space, audiovisual and textbook assistance, timely duplicating capability, and information concerning student referral locations for such matters as registration, financial aid, and counseling.

8. Specific training should be provided administrative personnel to deal with the special situations of part-time faculty members, including especially appropriate means of handling the aggressive pursuit by many part-timers of full-time employment. Among the greatest frustrations suffered by part-time faculty members are the disappointments occasioned by their perception of broken promises, such as, "You'll get the next full-time job that opens up in the department"—a promise that should never have been made or implied in the first place.

These suggestions are presented as neither reparation nor panacea. Until, however, educational institutions begin to establish more adequate policies for part-time faculty members, policies that regard these persons as ends as well as means, as professional colleagues in the important work of colleges and universities, courts and legislatures will continue increasingly to make policy externally—a highly undesirable alternative.

New Policies for Changed Institutions

DONALD E. WALKER

THE CONTINUING GROWTH of unionism is major evidence that old personnel policies are not working well. Let me focus on the growth of unionism and on the reasons that academic administrators should be welcoming it as a positive development rather than a pathological threat to the academy. To do so, however, we need to look at the kind of world for which we are going to design new policies. The basic question is, Are we to design new personnel policies to minimize the inevitable concatenation of disasters, or are we to design new policies for a changing university whose role will be even more significant in a changing world? The answer to that question has implications for strategy.

Too frequently, I think, our counsels to one another in the academic world have been on the pessimistic side. G. K. Chesterton reports that a little girl once gave him the definition, "An optimist is a person who looks after your eyes, and a pessimist is a person who looks after your feet."[1] There may be allegorical wisdom in the definitions. Our pessimism has been designed to look after our feet and to tell us only where to look for another foothold. What we need is more attention to our eyes, the vision of where we are going.

There is a mood of pessimism in higher education today, a feeling that even if we are not threatened with the ruin of all bright things, then at least the period of our greatest usefulness to the society is past. Our country is in a preferred position in the family of nations in large degree because of our commitment to education, and particularly higher education. To hold that position in a world that is moved and shaped by expertise requires a continuing high level of commitment.

We are in a populist, neo-Jacksonian revolution. Those who have been disadvantaged in society are demanding to share the material benefits and opportunities of that society. All social classes are demanding to be involved at all levels in the decisionmaking processes that shape our nation. It is a truism of a democratic society that improvement is the mother of discontent. This should not be cause for despair. Rather, it symbolizes the vitality of the society and the wellspring of its creative thrust, not imminent decline. In the democratic society, the historical response to populist challenge has been to open the doors to opportunity in a vigorous strategy of interaction with the demands of the wider society. The role of higher education in a challenging milieu cannot be pas-

1. *Orthodoxy* (London: John Lane Co., 1909), p. 199.

sive: it must shape a response to the challenges. That response must both fit the needs of the society and preserve the integrity of the academy. Creative change in a democratic society is a dialectical process. The feeling that new personnel policies are needed on campuses reflects the society's populist, neo-Jacksonian thrust. Universities and colleges can no longer leave their personnel policies to the Old Boys' Club, with its informal, personal vagaries, for it and other private elites are all under attack.

The demands for change come to us in the academic community in a pincers movement. We are, on one side, increasingly confronted with a plethora of state and federal agencies subjecting us to their changing agendas as they in turn respond to demands in the society. The other jaw of the pincers is the internal demand for more decisionmaking at the grass roots level and for greater numbers of affected persons to participate in that process.

Educators are faced with demands that what goes on inside the university be made comprehensible to outside agencies and constituencies. Funding agencies not only require that the university adhere to their rules of reporting expenditures but also increasingly tend to demand that we allocate funds like a bureaucratic governmental agency and practice similar personnel policies. When colleges and universities respond with endless explanations of their unique qualities, the explanations appear to be self-serving evasions to preserve the Old Boys' Club way of doing things.

Maintaining integrity

The wave of participatory concern has its own reasonable demands, in my view. People should be involved in decisions that affect their lives. This wave of participation carries with it the demand for involvement and also the demand that decisions meet the canons of due process, not merely in the legal sense, but in the common-sense notion of fairness. If the university is to meet these demands realistically while preserving its own character, it must develop a position of its own: There are counterclaims that must be presented to groups on and off the campus if the dialectical process of democratic change is to be constructive. The university cannot simply be the inert anvil hoping to wear out more hammers. In meeting the demands for legal parameters in personnel policies and for participative and fair decisionmaking, the university must fight for the right to act to preserve the integrity of its unique mission. Legal systems designed for other agencies are not always appropriate to the academic community. Accounting procedures that fit other organizations do not always fit colleges and universities.

In addition to having the right to solve problems in ways that preserve its values and unique qualities, the university must demand that (within the constraints of democratic due process) professional academic judgments be left to academics. Within these constraints, the universities must have the freedom to preserve that subtle cement of the academy—the spirit and atmosphere of collegiality. What is collegiality? George Angell, director of the Academic Collective Bargaining Information Service in Washington, D.C., defines collegiality or, as he calls it, "colleagueship" as having four components: friendly relationships, shared governance, common goals and aspirations, and mutual aid in time of need.[2] This definition is as comprehensive as any.

How, then, does the union fit this picture of personnel policymaking? First, some of the good news. The union model is a familiar model of defense for organizations and groups of people when they are under pressure or attack in the society. People retreat easily to familiar models of defense. The machinery is there. It is understood and accepted by the democratic society. Furthermore, it is acceptable to external authority figures who demand comprehensible explanations and accountings from campuses. A trivial illustration: I was confronted by a legislator about reports he had received concerning some campus altercation. "Are those kooky professors acting up again?" he asked. "You don't understand, Representative," I replied. "We have a union contract at the university. We are just working out some problems with the union." The legislator's manner changed to one of sympathetic and slightly alarmed comprehension. "You mean to say you have union problems? You poor bastard!" At least the model was one he could understand and sympathize with.

Now a bit of bad news. The industrial model of collective bargaining does not fit the academy. Such a statement has become almost bromidic in discussions of unions on campus. It is nonetheless true. "The industrial model is conflict-oriented, growing out of a pessimistic opinion of man and an almost Darwinian view of conflict resolution: survival of the strongest."[3] There is a tendency to meet all issues by confrontation, confrontation that sometimes results in impasse. But the industrial union model tends to direct attention toward such tangible and arguable values as wages and hours and working conditions, the latter defined in narrow terms such as number of students in a classroom and the square footage of office space to be assigned to each faculty member. Given the short-

2. Speech, June 7, 1976, at a conference at Boston College, Boston.

3. Donald E. Walker, David Feldman, and Greg Stone, "Collegiality and Collective Bargaining: An Alternative Perspective," *Educational Record,* Spring 1976, p. 119.

comings of this model, it is little wonder that campus collective bargaining has been referred to as "a bad idea whose time has come."

If, then, in the "real world," forces drive us toward revised personnel procedures, if the union model is readily available and will be more used in the future, and if the industrial model of campus collective bargaining will not adapt well or hospitably to campus environments, then we must ask: Is there a more useful model of campus collective bargaining? Is there a collective bargaining model that can address some of the requirements caused by the new pressures on personnel procedures and still preserve the values campuses must insist on if realistic, workable, and humane personnel procedures are to be maintained?

The university as a pluralistic democracy

There are such models. I propose a basically familiar but neglected one. Suppose the university were perceived, not as an industry, but as a type of pluralistic democracy. Suppose the contract be viewed, not as a hard legalistic document to focus and direct conflict, but as a kind of constitution, designed to solve problems of responsible people in a cooperative and procedural fashion. Universities have many of the characteristics of pluralistic democracies. Power is widely shared in a university community. The students have power: they have demonstrated at least the capability of "shutting the joint down." Faculties, too, have power: they own their own "tools of production" and are the ultimate shapers of the "products" of the institution.

The university cannot operate without the faculty's cooperation and willing support. As James Norton, chancellor of the Ohio Board of Regents, has pointed out:

> There is no way you can tackle the problem of quality on a campus without the support of the faculty. The faculty is similar to a police department. These are what we call "reverse discretion hierarchies"—the person with the most discretion in enforcement of the law is the patrolman on the beat. The same thing is true, of course, in higher education. The inviolate unit in which discretion is total is at the bottom. So we must have the understanding, the cooperation and the initiative of people working at that level.[4]

So power is shared by students and faculty. In addition, support personnel on a campus have the power to determine at least the effectiveness and ease with which routine affairs will be transacted. This group is increasingly more self-aware and better organized.

4. James A. Norton quoted by H. L. Enarson in "The Occasional Search for the Public Interest," *AGB Reports*, March–April 1975, p. 25.

If the union contract reflects the real dispersion of authority and power in the academy, things certainly may get no worse and may in some instances improve. In many universities, for example, if a faculty member is denied tenure or promotion, the de facto decision has been made by his colleagues, regardless of what managerial legalistic terminology cloaks the act. His colleagues have decided he is unworthy. Under the traditional administrative structure, if the individual feels he has been erroneously judged, he must appeal his colleagues' decision to an administrator, who then makes a recommendation to another administrator, who discusses it with someone "higher up." This process generates, instead of solutions, disagreement among administrators, who by common consent are the least qualified to make the decision. After all, who can possibly pronounce on the skills, ability, and performance of a chemistry professor, except members of the chemistry department? This arrangement produces a "flue effect," in which the heat moves up the chimney and the matter lands on the president's desk or before the board of trustees. Suppose alternatively that the real character of dispersed authority were recognized and written into a contract so that a faculty member allegedly aggrieved by colleagues could appeal to a counsel of peers in his own college. Should he be turned down at this level, he could then appeal his case to a council of colleagues at the university level. Should this remedy fail, then he is out of business. This arrangement does not preclude appeal to the board of trustees and the courts.

The dispersion of authority and power in colleges and universities makes the pluralistic democracy a more realistic model than traditional models. A second characteristic also argues for its workability. Universities and colleges tend to be self-regulating and homeostatic. On the best university campuses, there is a delicate equilibrium of people and structures. When not outrageously abraded or tampered with, campus constituencies have enormous capacities to solve their own problems. In the best universities, most of the decisions are made by a process of adaptation, accommodation, assimilation, compromise, with, in the nice phrase of Thomas Lewis, "resistable forces always meeting movable forces."[5] Here too, the model of pluralistic democracy fits the social reality of the university better than does any other.

The basic faith of the university goes back to the creed of Madison and Jefferson, that ordinary people operating within reasonable structures can make decisions as wise and realistic as a managerial elite. There is much wit and wisdom in a faculty and a student body. Procedures and

5. *The Lives of a Cell: Notes of a Biology Watcher* (New York: Viking Press, 1974), p. 60.

arrangements that release and use this potential will be the most successful and make the best "fit" for universities in our time.

Under the pluralistic democracy model, the faculty contract can be treated in many ways like the constitution of a democratic state rather than a traditional labor-management agreement. Appropriate structures can be built into the document that are low in conflict susceptibility. Whereas a labor contract, which runs inviolate to the end of the contractual period, under the model suggested here, meetings between union leadership, administration, and trustees can result in codicils of agreement, mutually subscribed to, which make the contract more workable.

The principal prerequisite for the type of contract philosophy and management proposed is a climate of trust between contracting parties. Trust is a delicate membrane, difficult to nurture and preserve. It requires active cultivation by all parties and open communication. In a university community, it is not what people know that hurts; it is what they do not know—what they suspect. Good open communications, regular informal meetings, and a healthy respect for the legitimacy of the concerns of others are prerequisites. Trust must be reciprocal: it is critical to the development of a contract and administrative style that facilitate the solution of problems. Once such a contract exists, the fairness of its personnel procedures will reinforce and extend the atmosphere of trust among campus constituencies.

"Fair enough," it may be argued, "but what about collegiality? Is collegiality not destroyed by the bureaucratic, impersonal nature of a union contract?" It could be, but I know of no reason why it *should* be. For one thing, collective bargaining often comes to a campus because collegiality is at a low ebb. Collective bargaining is wrongly perceived as the cause, rather than the effect. It may be well to recall the basic nature of collegiality. Dictionary definitions are skeletal; collegiality cannot mean simply a guild system of masters, journeymen, and apprentices, nor can it be confined in a climate of Old Boys' Club decisionmaking. The collegial spirit is a kind of freemasonry of the mind. It assumes that academics have more in common than the issues that separate them. It assumes that the values supporting the search for truth, knowledge, wisdom, and objectivity constrain men in such a way that they are able to resolve their differences amicably and creatively. Collegiality is a spirit. That spirit, like rare wine, can be carried in vessels of different configuration.

The collegial spirit requires most consistently systems in which professionals have a major role in making the decisions that affect their colleagues and the climate in which they work. This requirement is compatible with the collective bargaining model.[6]

It is not my view that collective bargaining is right for every college and university. There are campuses where collective bargaining generates problems of its own. Trouble develops, for example, when administrators see collective bargaining as alien tissue grafted onto their administration. They resist a symbiotic acceptance of the phenomenon and its incorporation into managerial style. Many colleges and universities now boast that the collective bargaining model is inappropriate for them. So it may be. There is, however, the correlative and usually unspoken assumption that collective bargaining will only work in institutions with low standards of academic excellence. That assumption, by the way, has taken some battering in the light of events in the last year or two. There may be more surprises down the road. It is the contention of some authorities in collective bargaining that by the 1980s, 60 percent or more of at least the public colleges and universities will be organized on some basis. Furthermore, I think that rather than rejecting the collegial model of collective bargaining out of hand, we should consider it as a readily available response to a questioning and sometimes battering society. Sorely pressed academic communities will increasingly retreat to collective bargaining. Rather than regarding collective bargaining as some sort of transitional purgatory, perhaps it should be seen as adaptable under ideal conditions to the finer traditions of even the best colleges and universities.

6. This paper draws on Donald E. Walker, David Feldman, and Greg Stone, "Collegiality and Collective Bargaining: An Alternative Perspective," *Educational Record*, Spring 1976, pp. 119–24.

Encouraging Private Support

MAURICE B. MITCHELL

THE PROBLEMS of encouraging voluntary support for higher education—fund raising, as it is bluntly called by the practitioners—seem so obvious as to make creative contributions to existing practices quite difficult. It is a rare institution that approaches the matter without substantial experience—sophistication—in the bread-and-butter areas of development. Alumni, the corporate sector, the government, friends, parents, trust officers, lobbying in the field of philanthropic taxation, and foundations (domestic and foreign) beckon, and we must be practiced in our wooing.

Every university has alumni boards, parent support groups, booster clubs for everything from the library to the gymnastic team, presidents' clubs, publications, graduate school alumni groups, and homecoming weeks.

Some universities seem to do a better job than others. Success in fund raising is rarely a matter of superior talent, although the development experts would have us believe otherwise. The day-to-day tasks of development, carried out with vigor and conscientiousness, produce the substance of the voluntary support received by higher education. All too often, however, the successful situations seem to result from traditional patterns of acceptance, from the idiocy of intercollegiate athletic enthusiasms, or from some emerging trend that has attracted a new clientele and created a sense of renewed growth and excitement. Even new growth and excitement, which seems to be a product of imagination and leadership, are difficult to sustain and most often rest on a single leader or transient funding situation.

That there are traditional patterns of acceptance for a chosen few is beyond argument. Many of us suffer from a recurring dream about the Yale alumnus. We see him taking the single letter he receives in the mail from the silver salver of his uniformed butler. He slits the envelope with his diamond-encrusted letter opener. A message falls out from the official at Yale who permits its alumni to make contributions. The alumnus reads the first sentence and discerns that Yale needs money from him. Quickly he calls for his checkbook and sends off a large sum. Then he dutifully reads the rest of the letter to find out how the money might be used.

My version of this dream blends into reality: Some of the replies from alumni and alumnae contain lightly smothered oaths, usually adding up to the news that no further gifts will be forthcoming until the institution rids itself of its dratted chancellor. It is small comfort to report that writers of such intemperate threats are usually found to have contributed $16.00 during the twenty-seven years since they were graduated.

This kind of emotional giving is the special asset of a relatively few institutions. The rest of us know that we do many things much better than the traditional, status-blessed few, but we also know that we must work twice as hard to achieve half the results. It is a great tribute to most of my colleagues that they are dedicated enough to accept the burdens and face these realities.

I shall pass over the matter of intercollegiate athletics as a fund-raising or respect-producing instrument, noting only that I do not believe this activity produces either of these results. In the first place, present-day intercollegiate athletics are incompatible with the purpose of a college or university. This incompatibility results in a shameful degradation of the operations and integrity of the institution. Further, the claims about profit-able intercollegiate athletic programs and great gifts for the benefit of the whole institution from admiring fans are usually based on bookkeeping and other practices reminiscent of O'Henry's gentle grifter.

Innovative educational programs must be viewed with great care before they are assumed to be financially important sources of increased support. It is certainly true that an institution of higher learning benefits from experience with innovation in curriculum and process. But there is a danger that some of these programs may be inspired solely by a desire to keep up with the market. While attempts to keep up may sound laud-able, another view of such programming might identify it as simply faddish and superficial. Still, the university is so often seen as antiquated in its view of the contents of curriculum that some of these novelties are worth encouraging. Integrity in the evaluation process is the key here.

Reviewing development activities

What is troubling, however, is the tendency to assume that gifts, grants, and contracts—even new physical facilities—received in support of these programs represent some sort of financial triumph or that they add up to important contributions to the financial health of the institution. Some do, of course. But many troubled financial officers have noted that eager scholars and administrators are all too ready to overlook or mini-mize some of the elusive cost factors in these projects. Overhead, for one.

"A little more water in the pump" is an economic theory that has drained many college coffers. Shared faculty costs is another. Often the shared faculty costs result in costly overloads or even more costly additions to the size of the faculty: The project just grew too fast or turned out to be too large to handle with existing staff.

Income from these special efforts is frequently considered to be an addition to the university's total of contributed income when, in truth, it often should be more properly considered a loss. Again, there are exceptions, and the matter should create much discussion, policy formulation, and enforcement.

Any institution seriously interested in increasing its flow of funds from voluntary outside sources should review its basic development activities at regular intervals. These reviews should include careful scrutiny of all items of voluntary income with regard to the cost of acquiring the funds and discharging the obligation incurred.

Such costs will surely include actual expenses for special projects of the kind referred to above. They might also include such items as the cost of administering financial aid; most of us have elaborate and costly units for dispensing financial aid. Should scholarship funds be taxed in some way to cover the cost of handling them? It seems a fair question, and there must be many others like them. Without such scrutiny, it may be that many kinds of voluntary assistance are actually overstated. Indeed, the reporting and record-keeping functions are themselves worthy of study. Even at this late stage, many gifts are credited four or five times— to the alumnus or alumna, to the class, the college, the major department fund.

A few other development activities have always had particular significance—for example, the relatively new practice of establishing private foundations for fund-raising purposes at state-supported institutions of higher learning. I am outraged by this process. At a time when the Congress is scrutinizing tax encouragement for philanthropic gifts, we must exercise the greatest care to avoid the use of such tax exemption privileges for cynical purposes or in an indefensible manner. Yet these foundations are an obvious device to circumvent the limitations on tax exemption growing out of educational support.

If the state-supported institution finds that it cannot obtain legal approval for some special building or program and if the state legislature, assigned the task of allocating taxpayers' money, does not approve, does the institution yield to the wishes of the taxpayers? No. It turns to its foundation—a cynical and dangerous organization indeed, with the privilege of allowing tax deduction to those who make gifts. The private foundation accepts gifts, tax deductible, from generous donors for the purposes already denied support by the taxpayers. The state's residents must now pay higher taxes to offset the loss of tax income from the generously treated donors!

Effect on the state

To make matters worse, let us suppose that these tax-deductible funds are used to acquire property that is then given to the university—perhaps an athletic facility (possibly one of those select clubs for special fans), or a distant conference center at some pleasant resort. Not only has the project been financed against the will of the legislature and at the further expense of the taxpayers, but the state now is saddled forever with the continuing cost of maintaining and running the facility.

In Colorado, where the state constitution forbids any taxpayer aid to independent institutions or their students, this kind of competition for voluntary funds is more than exasperating: There are more taxpayer-supported agencies with private foundations out seeking private funds and more fund-raisers from these sources than from private sources. But the threat and the hazards of this practice are universal; in the end, the state institutions may be the greatest sufferers, although the hazard to all who benefit from tax exemptions for legitimate educational purposes is far greater than is generally recognized.

Many private sources of funds—the corporate sector prominent among them—will not give to state-supported institutions. They believe that they give generously through their taxes. Yet the impression is spreading that the back-door tax exemption offered by these foundations is beginning to erode an important source of voluntary support for independent institutions of higher learning. Despite the generally favorable outcome of the new Tax Reform Act, special tax treatment of gifts for educational purposes is far from assured in the future. Every board of trustees, every alumni group, and every university administration should be briefed at regular intervals on the state of the university's tax situation. The final tax reform act of this series has yet to be written. No constituency or development project approaches in importance this single privilege of obtaining, as a matter of right, tax credit for gifts to schools.

Finally, I should comment on that moment of truth in attracting voluntary support: the major institutional campaign. Although no institution can afford to let up in its incessant search for continuing support for current operations, it is the big drive that gives it a chance to refresh, refurbish, and replace its physical plant; to erase, at least in part, the damage done to faculty salaries by continuing inflation; to catch up on library needs; to freshen up its programs, add a little to its annual income from endowment, expand scholarship funds, and so on.

The University of Denver has just come to the end of phase one of such an endeavor, and it is a most stimulating time. Its last fund drive occurred in the early 1960s, when a campaign to match a $5 million Ford Foundation grant with $10 million in locally raised funds was undertaken. These funds were used for faculty and program improvements, and they have long since been depleted.

I have a certain resistance to the big campaign—perhaps a fear of the institutional nakedness that comes when the effort falls short of the goals—but our time has surely come. Much of the university's physical plant is worn out, and the First and Second World War temporaries have lost their nostalgic charm. The conversion of student housing to academic space provides faculty members with a lot of bathrooms but does little for university income, and the scattering of academic units through many buildings is increasingly costly. Financial aid funds, once deemed adequate, now fall well below current needs, and we lose more of the most priceless objects—gifted students—than we should.

At the end of a self-examination in connection with an accreditation procedure, we decided to make a serious study of the university's goals and mission in the 1970s and beyond, the last such effort being more than fifteen years old. For almost a year the deans and vice chancellors met with the chancellor and with selected visitors and advisors. The findings produced by these discussions were then shared with faculty and students and finally with the board of trustees. At this point, we decided to consider a major capital campaign and retained a nationally known consultant in an advisory capacity. The trustees accepted involvement with much interest, and for more than a year all groups have engaged in a most comprehensive study of attitudes toward the university in its community, its needs, and its potential for fund raising.

When the needs were finally identified and priorities established, we began to see the size of the campaign. The amount to be raised was, it seemed to us, staggeringly large. We knew that others, including some of our trustees, would share these feelings.

To validate our findings and to give credence to our needs and to our ability to use the campaign proceeds to meet those needs, we made an unusual move. We retained a firm of public accountants to audit our campaign and its expressed needs in advance. Their final report will be an assurance to contributors that the university has matched its hopes with financial reality. This verification may be an important asset as we move forward.

We have also produced, after extended debate, a statement of the university's case for support. Never before have we refined and clarified our objectives and our raison d'être so sharply. If we decide not to proceed beyond this point, we will have had three great benefits from this process: an audited confirmation of our needs and our ability to describe them accurately in fiscal terms, a better informed board of trustees, and a re-statement of who we are and what we hope to be.

Soon we will make the final decision to proceed beyond phase one with a project that may determine our way of life for the rest of this century. Many benefits of the search for increased voluntary support are realized before the first check is cashed.

The Future of Voluntary Donations

EDWARD D. EDDY

WHEN A COLLEAGUE recently confronted the prospect that his institu-tion's multimillion dollar capital campaign would be phased out several multimillions away from its final goal, he observed, "Realism is recog-nizing a flat tire when you have one."

There has never been, and there will never be, any dreamy magic in the solicitation of funds—only hard work, common sense, and plenty of conviction and faith. Indeed, the next ten to twenty years will be, with-out doubt, the most challenging in the history of voluntary giving to higher education. Without faith, the words "most challenging" may be translated to read "most discouraging."

Let us review quickly the familiar grounds for discouragement in the decade or two immediately ahead. The foremost problem is the en-rollment decline—at least by one third, they say. In Pennsylvania the projected enrollment for private colleges and universities by the early 1990s will decline by a mere 51 percent. What will emerge, of course, is the "age of the academic gimmick" in two models: one to attract the student to the campus and one to attract the money to maintain the campus. The fight for funds will be almost as unseemly as the scramble for students.

All these fluctuations will be taking place in a nation that has changed its priorities, replacing higher education with such concerns as inflation, crime, and health. The dominant interests will be those of the dominant population: the baby-boom children who passed through our colleges in the late 1960s and early 1970s and who will be in their middle age by the mid-1980s. They will want the philanthropic and tax dollars to flow toward medical care, social agencies, recreation, and adult education. Their voices will be heard on corporate and foundation boards and in legislative halls.

Meanwhile, on the college campus, student consumerism will be enjoying a period of unparalleled ascendance. When the student has the choice—of college, curriculum, and faculty member—the prestige of privilege evaporates. It is not the status one gains, but the job one gets that will determine the amount of the alumni contribution. It is not the warm feelings about the good times one had while growing up, but the career start one was given that will determine the amount of bequest. In a delightful and frightening article in a recent issue of *New York* magazine, Tom Wolfe describes the "Third Great Awakening" as the "Me Decade."[1] Because of our affluence the center of attention has become the self. One suspects, therefore, that the consumer student may well become the somewhat selfish alumnus, who measures what he gives almost entirely by what he got.

Add to this challenge the likelihood that an increasing percentage of college-bound students will be women and those from minorities who begin their adult life generally with debt rather than capital. They will be able to do better as earners and givers than they have in the past, but not immediately. Their contributions will be longer in coming and more deliberately bestowed—providing, of course, their collegiate experience was a positive one.

Finally, we will be challenged—and discouraged—by the continuing assault on the idea of charitable giving. At the present time, the federal government seems to be leading the charge through a wide variety of approaches: discouraging, if not preventing, the big gift; cutting down on the discretionary funds of foundations while offering little real incentive to corporations; and harassing the public and now the private colleges with rules, regulations, and reams of quibbling questionnaires. We do not know where the present onslaught regarding charitable deductions will end, but it is likely to be a continuing threat. Our elected and appointed officials make speeches on the necessity of private enterprise while, in legislation and regulation, they limit the wherewithal and force a public shape to the private institutions.

Increased alumni gifts

The future of voluntary donations for higher education thus will not be an easy one. If we are willing to recognize a flat tire when we have one, let us examine what is possible, or, at least, advisable. My own intuition is that alumni and alumnae will continue to offer the most con-

1. "The Me Decade," *New York,* August 23, 1976, pp. 26–40.

sistent and best potential for voluntary giving over the next decade or two. We know that giving to annual alumni funds, according to the Council for Financial Aid to Education, has risen for the fifth straight year in number of donors and average size of gift. We know that charitable giving through bequests and other deferred gifts has grown dramatically during the past twenty years and is likely to continue to grow. In 1950 all charitable bequests in the United States came to $274,000,000. By 1972 they had increased ten-fold, to $2.7 billion, with higher education's share totaling $300,000,000. This accounts for one third to one fourth of the total individual gifts to higher education.

Giving will not be prompted so much by sentiment as by "performance realization," which is the current jargon for delivering the goods. The college or university that deserves and gets the most from its graduates will be the one that did the most for them. Individual gifts will continue to be prompted largely by individuals, be they faculty members, presidents, deans, trustees and their friends, or fellow graduates. But perhaps now the career counselor will emerge as one of the major stimulants to "treasured memories" and "unfilled obligations."

Corporate giving will continue as a mixed bag: some extraordinarily enlightened and some insignificant and self-serving. As an officer of a women's college, I have had the amusing opportunity over the past sixteen years of watching the corporate world struggle with the difficult (for them) question of support for women's education. Many corporate officers have been through the cycle of amusement, shock, annoyance, and finally acceptance of the women's movement. An increasing number of corporations, such as Westinghouse, Alcoa, and Jones & Laughlin, are really taking hold of both the ideas and the obligations. But generally, from this experience, I would have to conclude that the American corporation will not become during the next ten years the mainstay for the survival of the American college. Fundamentally, university administrators have done a poor job of educating corporate officers in what we consider the raison d'être of the questing—and questioning—mind. They are suspicious of us, and we are fearful of becoming their servants.

The prospects for foundation giving are far less clear-cut. Foundations, corporations, and, to some extent, alumni and other individuals, increasingly will engage in the practice of "selective survival." By that term, I mean to imply that they will narrow their choices in order to concentrate their funds on those institutions which, according to their standards, they hope will continue with some strength. The choices may be based on geography, on type, on past relationships, or on support for some arbitrary number of institutions. Whatever the number, the donors will be accused of elitism, to which they will probably plead guilty. It is their choice.

What we have said about alumni contributions will apply also to other sources of giving. The process of deciding will be marked by greater sophistication and by the desire for relevance to all of higher education, rather than merely by the desire to maintain that pretty campus in that sweet little town.

Let us look, for example, at the matter of total institutional financial health. Certainly more people in important places know more today than ever before how to judge the fiscal condition of colleges and universities. We have talked so much about deficits that everybody now is an expert deficit-watcher. (We are better educators than we realize—or want to be!)

The one point of agreement among foundation officers seems to be that they do not intend to allow good money to follow bad. They do not expect to make grants to balance budgets, but, rather, in those areas where their funds might make a difference—a difference in program, in quality, perhaps in facilities, but not a difference in balance versus deficit. "They want to give where the money will count." It seems highly doubtful, therefore, that either foundation or corporate funding will ever be used extensively for basic institutional support, including enlargement of endowment. These sources may provide the icing on the cake (which helps to draw the sweet-toothed student), but not the plate on which the cake rests.

There may also be a trend, already under way, toward support of tradition rather than innovation. Lip service will continue to be given to "bold new approaches," but realistically the funds will be allocated mainly to the kind of innovation that is intended to preserve or strengthen the traditional.

The "we decade"

Support will come for the programs or projects that possess high leverage for the institution while also being relevant as well as useful to more than one campus or group. Though foundations, corporations, and individuals may have particular interest in one or a handful of institutions, they will want and expect those institutions to undertake more than the solution of their particular problems. They will want leaders not of Tom Wolfe's "Me Decade" but of the "We Decade"—and this will come just at a time when most educators and institutions could not care less about their neighbors. One of the contributions of voluntary giving from foundations may well be that the donations will help keep higher education together rather than allowing it to split apart—as it now seems destined to do.

Everybody knows there is trouble ahead. Colleges and universities must be ready to show any potential donor how that institution plans to weather the drought. The present and the future must be made a continuum; otherwise, they will be adversaries. At Chatham College we are making an attempt this year at thoroughly realistic long-range planning in order to sort out our own options and be prepared with a solid case for encouraging good money to follow good intentions. As we look ahead into the 1980s, the past seems a feeble guide. We may have accomplished a lot in the past ten years, but that does not mean that the next ten will be comparable or as easy.

We need to know what lies ahead so that we can chart not only our future but a good case for our future. We are asking a group of expert forecasters to help us to make this approach. In a series of lecture-discussions this fall, we are examining such factors as the economy, population trends, the climate for philanthropy, changing social values and ideology, changing motivation in youth, the role of government, and occupational opportunities for college-educated women.

Among those involved in this program are Earl Cheit, Max Lerner, Juanita Kreps, Kenneth Boulding, George Cabot Lodge, and Ralph Huitt. Colleges, universities, and anyone in our area interested in higher education have been invited to participate. We are convinced that change is already upon us and that we ought to try to understand and control it, not merely respond to it. The college or university without this approach to the future is a risky investment for voluntary gifts from any source.

Perhaps the best and most helpful way for me to attempt to summarize the emerging pattern of voluntary giving would be to pose ten questions. Let me role play. I am now Mr. Foundation Executive. We are talking about the sharing of my money—and you seem to think that you might deserve some. OK, then, please answer as concisely as possible these questions:

1. Does your institution have a clear, realistic, and well-articulated "mission"? Does it really know where it is going, how it will get there, and whom it should serve?

2. How well informed are the trustees? How frequently do they meet, for what length of time, and for what purpose? May I see the agenda and the minutes for the last two years? How many trustees are genuinely involved in the discussion and action?

3. What kind of leadership is provided by the top administrative officers? Would you say that they are educators or principally managers? What is the evidence that they have a vision beyond their own time of service? Or, conceivably, are they engaged mainly in writing chapters in the institution's history?

4. What is the quality of your back-up team? Is it a team, or a collection of individuals hung together on an organization chart?

5. What percentage of your faculty members have tenure? What is their average age? What has your college done to protect itself from too much tenure?

6. What mechanisms do you have and use to evaluate the various facets of collegiate life? Do your faculty members pay any attention to student and peer evaluations of teaching? Are consultants brought in— and listened to—on the management level?

7. Assuming a strong concern for quality in the classroom, is there any concern for the education that takes place outside the classroom? To what extent do people on your campus care about the priorities and values of students, and to what extent do they consciously help students to sharpen their ability to make intelligent decisions?

8. Are flexibility and adaptability prized within the institution so that, as conditions outside the campus change and as student motivations are modified, the institution can respond intelligently without destroying its integrity? Or is everyone anxious to preserve and defend? What mechanisms exist to cope effectively with change?

9. What is the long-term financial base for your college? Could its appetites perhaps be larger than its cooking capacity so that it will always feel and look underfed? Have you evolved a sensible, realistic plan for viability over the next fifteen to twenty years?

10. What is your record for effective use of past foundation grants? Would this grant really make a difference, or will it be lost in the continuing struggle to replace the floor boards?

Well, thank you, Mr. President. Those were most interesting answers. By the way, did you notice that you drove into the parking lot with a flat tire this afternoon?

The College Endowment Funding Plan

FREDERICK D. PATTERSON

A FUNDAMENTAL PROBLEM of higher education, and of small colleges in particular, relates to the difficulty of obtaining the funds required for basic operations. The rise in educational costs because of productivity increases in the economy, the competition for students and well-prepared personnel, as well as inflation, must be met by increasing revenues from public and private sources. Moneys from these sources are most often contributed for special-purpose projects and are intended to be spent over a short period of time. This type of aid, while it improves the variety of activities available, does not ease the financial problems of institutions. Indeed, such funding often augments the problems because restricted, short-term funding invariably contributes to new, higher levels of ongoing expenditures. In short, both federal and private assistance *tend to create permanent programs, but provide only temporary financing.* Thus, colleges and universities end up with an additional program expenditure built into the budget.

The College Endowment Funding Plan (CEFP) is an attempt to deal with the problems confronting institutions while, at the same time, accommodating the wishes of the donors. It is an aid mechanism, new for institutions, which relies on monetary and investment procedures currently in use. The CEFP recognizes the need of colleges and universities to provide for basic current support *and* for the future. Its goal is the creation of endowment at a level capable of providing a substantial part of these revenues. Endowment, by becoming a significant part of the income of institutions, can help those institutions meet current and future revenue needs. This goal is urgently desirable in view of the forces affecting the level and the growth rate of their expenditures.

The CEFP begins with a college or university, public or private, that has raised a sum of money. In most cases, the money will be in the form of a restricted gift for current use with a short expenditure period. The CEFP is a means of ensuring that funds to support the specific project chosen by the donor will be available after the end of the initial gift period. This outcome is achieved through income resulting from the investment of gift and loan moneys and by the creation of an endowment. In the case of a gift for endowment, as opposed to one for current use, the plan can also be used. Here its role is to increase the impact of such a gift by creating an endowment larger than the gift alone would have produced.

In either case, the result is achieved by leveraging the gift money with borrowed money.[1] The combined gift and loan funds are then invested at a favorable interest spread—that is, the rate of return on the investment is higher than the interest on the loan. Over the years, the earnings from this investment enable the institution to provide current budget support and to meet the loan payments of interest and principal. After the loan has been retired, the institution owns the investment, which

1. Borrowed money substitutes as a challenge grant and makes unnecessary the search for matching gifts.

then represents an endowment whose future earnings can be used to provide a continuous flow of revenue.

The functioning of CEFP

A hypothetical case will illustrate the operation of the plan.[2] It is a simplified version of the CEFP, intended for purely explanatory purposes. Other economically realistic variations are possible.

In this example, it is assumed that a restricted gift of $1,000,000 is raised by an institution with the stipulation that 10 percent (to be taken from earnings each year) of the gift be spent annually—that is, $100,000 a year for ten years—for the support of a specific project chosen by the donor. In addition, a $500,000 grant is received from a public or private source as an endowment building component. The purpose of the grant is to assure required income to the operating budget, thus enabling loan income, above costs, to help provide capital accumulation for endowment.

On the security of the gift, a twenty-five-year loan of $3,000,000 is obtained at 8 percent interest. The combined moneys from the program gift, the endowment component, and the loan are then invested at 9 percent. During the loan term, the annual earnings from this investment are used to pay the interest due on the loan and to provide $100,000 for program support (budget income), as stipulated by the donor. Beginning in the sixteenth year, the loan principal is repaid in ten equal annual installments.[3] Earnings remaining each year, after all obligations have been met, are reinvested at the best obtainable rate consistent with investment security. Yearly obligations include taxes on earnings, secured from borrowed moneys. Earnings on gift moneys are tax free.

By the end of the loan term a total of $2,500,000 has been spent on program support, thus extending the funding of the program beyond the ten-year period specified by the donor. After the loan has been retired, the institution owns the original investment of $4,500,000 plus more than $1,500,000 in additional funds. This end sum represents an endowment that will generate a flow of future earnings, thus alleviating some of the pressures for additional revenues.

Thus the plan satisfies the wishes of the donors and assists in meeting the needs of institutions for current and future income. In the case

2. For a complete explanation and analysis of CEFP, see Frederick D. Patterson, *The College Endowment Funding Plan* (Washington: American Council on Education, 1976). The present paper is adapted from chap. 2, and table 15 presents the detailed figures for the hypothetical case here described.

3. Arthur D. Little, "Public Policy Study of the CEFP," Report to the CEFP Planning Committee and for the National Commission on the Financing of Postsecondary Education (September 30, 1973), pp. 33–34.

of a restricted gift for current use, program support is ensured beyond the expenditure period as an endowment is being created. A gift for endowment is also increased through the CEFP, inasmuch as it produces a larger fund capable of generating additional revenues.

The results produced by the CEFP are achieved by simply combining acceptable procedures into a mutually supporting and interacting arrangement. The funding mechanisms on which the plan relies are neither new nor unique in college finance. They include: use of private gifts; "matching" funds; the "challenge," or incentive concept of matching the results of fund raising from private sources; long-term loans for use by educational institutions; creation of institutional capital through a process of prudent investment; use of endowment income to meet interest payments and to pay off loans; and use of endowment income as part of an institution's educational and general income.

What is new and unique about the CEFP is the manner in which these basic elements of educational finance are packaged. In addition, the structure of the CEFP is such as to permit flexible variations and trade-offs among its component elements, including: the relative size of the loan and the gift contribution; the term and payback schedule of the loan; the source of borrowing; the size and source of the endowment building component; the rate of interest paid on the loan; the rate of return on the investment; the type of investment chosen and the risk involved; the amount, scheduling, and use of budget income taken from the investment earnings; and the relative size of the endowment fund produced after the loan is paid off.

Changes in aid patterns to permit endowment building

The discussion thus far has emphasized that the CEFP can achieve the two purposes of funding—to provide current income and to build an endowment within the existing framework of higher education finance. As the example illustrated, only in the pattern of restricted aid for current use are some changes necessary in order to achieve the purposes of the plan. They are needed to meet the specific level of current income expenditures required by restricted gifts.

A careful study of various combinations of gift and loan funds in relation to the level of endowment produced was made by J. Peter Williamson, who determined that the expenditure period of the program gift should be approximately ten years. Current gifts for restricted use are most often given for shorter periods, usually three to five years. It will therefore be necessary to alter the expenditure requirement. Several major contributors have expressed willingness to change the time span of their gifts. It is expected that others will also do so in view of the favorable effect that such a change will have on endowment building. Specifically, by lengthening the expenditure period, a smaller sum will have to be spent annually for budget income, which allows the accumulation of a larger investment.

The other change, also involving restricted gifts for current use, is the requirement that a portion of the gift or grant (one third of the total, in our illustration) be earmarked as an endowment component. The essential characteristic of this portion of the total gift is that the college is not required to spend any of the income earned from borrowed funds for program activities. Instead, all of the income from this portion of the gift is used to pay interest and help retire the borrowed moneys from investment accumulation. Its role is to assist in endowment building, and it is thus called the endowment building component. It can be provided by either public or private donors.

Thus, for the endowment component to have the greatest impact it must be contributed in a lump sum at the beginning of the investment period. Invested together with the program gift money and the loan, it enlarges the size of the investment fund and its earnings. Various analyses of the plan have indicated that the size of the endowment component should be half that of the program gift. If one donor makes both contributions, one third of the funds will represent the endowment component and the rest will be for program support.

The endowment building component, a predetermined amount contributed in one payment, replaces the annual payments that would otherwise be required to subsidize the interest rate on the loan. It is believed that donors—public and private—will be willing to make a single grant in this manner in view of its desirable contributions to endowment building. Moreover, it is compatible with present patterns of assistance from these sources. Endowment component grants are for a specific and well-defined purpose and are given once, rather than on a continuing basis. The value of such grants is greatly enhanced by combining them with funds from other sources.

CEFP contributions to institutional financing

In addition to ensuring that the new level of expenditures, resulting from restricted gifts, can be met without additional contributions, the CEFP can have a long-term impact on the financing of higher education institutions. Over time, the repeated inclusion of restricted gifts in CEFP will result in the accumulation of a substantial endowment. As a result, an increasing portion of an institution's revenues will come from endowment earnings. Such a revenue pattern can compensate for the productivity gap faced by colleges and universities. By placing a greater emphasis on endowment income, institutions realize productivity-related gains in their revenues, which counteract the effects of the rising level of expenditures.

In addition to the problems of obtaining funds for basic operations and of closing the widening gap between revenues and expenditures, the CEFP addresses itself to another question that each type of institution must face in its fund-raising efforts: namely, how to obtain money from both private and public sources without undesirably modifying its major thrust of control. Private institutions in seeking public funds wish to obtain them under conditions that will leave them autonomous, free from political control. On the other hand, private moneys to public institutions should not lessen the states' responsibility for major support of basic operations. Money from private sources for public institutions can best be given and managed through the foundations now being developed by many public institutions.

The CEFP, by relying on existing funding mechanisms and procedures, does not alter the basic thrust of institutional support. The plan is a funding device that any institution can use to eliminate the adverse effects of restricted gifts (from any source) by counteracting the negative forces affecting their expenditure. The CEFP aim is to strengthen institutions fundamentally by making them economically viable through endowment.

The plan attempts to assist specifically colleges and universities that have limited or no endowment. Only institutions having endowment earnings below a certain level per student may wish to participate for the CEFP can have its greatest effect on the institutions with the greatest need.

For public colleges and universities, the aim is to create a source of funds to complement those received from the state. Private moneys help meet that part of the cost of education not covered by appropriations, which affects the quality of education but is not included in the "cost of education" as that term is defined.

For private institutions, the CEFP's objective is to seek endowment earnings of about $1,000 per student. This amount, when combined with unrestricted income from other sources, *should* equal 60 percent of the cost of education per student. The remaining cost of education would be provided by tuition and fee charges.

The choice of $1,000 in endowment income and its relation to other revenues is based on the education costs of small private colleges. The average cost of education per student is approximately $4,000. The aim is to ensure that no more than 40 percent of that amount, or $1,600, is provided from tuition, with endowment accounting for almost half of the other revenues. Thus, assuming that 5 percent of the endowment is used in the budget, an institution with an enrollment of 1,000 will need an endowment of $20,000,000 in order to provide $1,000 per student. It is expected that the *rate of return* from endowment investment will be greater than 5 percent and that the portion of the earnings not spent will be reinvested. Even $500 per student in small private colleges would help significantly.

For private institutions, reduction of pressure to accelerate the rate of tuition increase is especially important. Since private colleges and universities as a group have traditionally received most of the philanthropic support, .the CEFP enables them to increase the impact of these funds and to reduce their dependence on tuition increases. Moreover, recognizing the unequal distribution of endowment among institutions, the plan encourages participation by those colleges and universities that have endowments per student below a certain level.

For public institutions, adoption of the plan will help provide quality education beyond that permitted by state appropriations. Although most of them receive relatively little private support, the existence of the plan may provide an incentive for alumni and other donors to increase their contributions.

Indeed, it is the goal of the CEFP to *diversify as well as enlarge* the revenue base of private and public institutions to minimize the adverse effects that may result from changes in any source of funds. The aim is to preserve the diversity among colleges and universities and the quality of their programs so that students may have improved access to quality education at costs they can afford. After all, "Excellence in education is not merely a matter of limiting admissions to select students, providing conventional academic programs and upholding traditional standards. Rather, excellence is providing varied kinds of education that are relevant and helpful for persons of many different backgrounds, abilities, and aspirations."[4]

The CEFP as a concept manifests a unique set of important advantages:

1. It is a method of institutional assistance, the most fundamental kind of support that ensures the survival of institutions and enhances the contribution of other noninstitutional programs, such as student aid.

2. It is a method of creating revenues which does not alter or compromise the fundamental character of colleges and universities, public or private.

4. Howard R. Bowen, "The Effective Use of Financial Resources," a speech presented at the AGB National Conference on Trusteeship, April 30, 1974 (Washington: Association of Governing Boards, 1974), p. 19.

3. It provides a continuous flow of budget income to the institution in predetermined amounts and over a specified period.

4. At the same time it is a means of capital formation, achieved through the establishment and investment of endowment funds.

5. Endowment funds, in turn, ensure a future flow of unrestricted revenues that will help institutions meet part of the rising expenditures.

6. Most important, while satisfying the revenue needs of colleges and universities, the CEFP also respects the wishes of the donors. It operates within the established framework of higher education finance and relies on proven funding mechanisms.

7. Private donors are provided with an additional incentive to contribute through the matching and leveraging of their contributions. A gift for current use will not only support a specific program but will also help build an endowment fund; an endowment gift will eventually create a larger fund.

8. Because of the CEFP's inherent flexibility (in the variety of possibilities for packaging its elements), an institution can design the plan to suit its educational objectives, budgetary requirements, and the financial environment within which it operates.

9. The plan also allows arrangements that include governments, either through the granting of the endowment building component or the loan. The impact of government (federal or state) contribution is greatly enhanced by the leverage and yield of endowment funds.

10. Moreover, the CEFP, as an institutional endowment building method of support, is compatible with the current pattern of government assistance. By creating a stable flow of current and future income, the CEFP complements the specific pattern of federal aid and the basic support of public institutions by the states.

11. As a less direct but equally important effect, institutions will be encouraged to develop and exercise their own private fund-raising capabilities in order to be able to participate in the plan. They will also have an incentive to formulate long-term institutional development plans to help convince donors of the importance of their contribution. Moreover, the increasing importance of endowment will encourage colleges and universities to provide more effective financial management of their portfolios and budgets.

12. Finally, by enlarging the base of institutional support, the CEFP reduces the pressure for drastic tuition increases. The benefits will accrue not only to the students who are able to pay but also to those in need, who will then require less financial aid. Institutions also benefit because fewer students will need assistance and lower amounts of aid per student will have to be provided.

Institutional Response
to Students' Rights

ALFRED L. MOYE

To EXAMINE ADEQUATELY the ethical and legal aspects of student rights, one should consider the practices and policies of higher education institutions before 1961, when the decision in *Dixon* v. *Alabama* extended the constitutional rights of due process to students. Since that decision several other cases have reaffirmed the constitutional guarantee of due process. These decisions influenced the development by most colleges and universities of codes of conduct outlining the rights and responsibilities of students in nonacademic matters. The student rights movement gained momentum in 1967 when five national organizations drafted the Joint Statement on Rights and Freedoms of Students. This statement, also endorsed by other professional groups, was intended to establish a model that institutions could follow in conforming with the minimum elements of due process.

In retrospect, most people would agree that the application to students of the principles of due process makes eminently good sense. Why, then, did it take court action to convince the leadership of higher education that it was necessary to extend these rights to students? The answer to that question would unlock one of the mysteries of higher education. While we in the higher education community are often at the vanguard in research and discoveries, we seldom exercise the leadership in matters of social justice that society expects from us. We seem to be unable to legislate ourselves. Once we are told what is acceptable and unacceptable, we proceed to do the minimum to comply with the law.

An example of our inability to respond voluntarily is illustrated by the Privacy Act of 1974. A colleague told me that during the period of unrest in 1966 at his institution, membership rosters of so-called subversive student organizations were given to the House Un-American Activities Committee. There seemed to have been no prior evaluation of the ethics or value of such a move. Now the law (Privacy Rights of Parents and Students) prohibits disclosure of such information.

The framers of the Joint Statement of Rights and Freedoms of Students were obviously aware of the need to protect student records when they incorporated the following section into the statement:

> Institutions should have a carefully considered policy as to the information which should be part of a student's permanent educational record and as to the conditions of its disclosure. To minimize the risk of improper disclosure, academic and disciplinary records should be separate, and the conditions of access to each should be set forth in an explicit policy statement. Transcripts of academic records should contain only information about academic status. Information from disciplinary or counseling files should not be available to unauthorized persons on campus, or to any persons off campus without the express consent of the student involved except under legal compulsion or in cases where the safety of persons or property is involved. No records should be kept which reflect the political activities or beliefs of students. Provisions should also be made for periodic routine destruction of non-current disciplinary records. Administrative staff and faculty members should respect confidential information about students which they acquire in the course of their work.[1]

Yet until the Buckley Amendment was passed, many institutions were maintaining superfluous materials in files and sharing much of it with people who should not have had access to it. In 1972, when I assumed responsibility for student affairs at the University of Pittsburgh, one of the first moves I made was to destroy the student records maintained in the vice chancellor's office. I doubt if early conformity to the Joint Statement would have stopped the enactment of the Privacy Act of 1974; early recognition of students' rights to privacy may have made the enactment less traumatic, however.

Guidelines for academic integrity

The Joint Statement also contains a section on due process in the classroom. Yet few institutions make any attempt to provide students a mechanism for redress of grievances against faculty, nor do they attempt to influence the faculty in matters relating to assigning grades, meeting classes, being prepared, setting standards for evaluation, and so on. At the University of Pittsburgh we have adopted *Guidelines on Academic Integrity,* which details the expectations, rights, and responsibilities of faculty and students. The document reaffirms an earlier policy statement on the subject of academic integrity and establishes basic principles and guidelines to be followed by faculty and students.

1. Faculty should meet and students should attend their classes when

1. *AAUP Bulletin,* December 1967, pp. 365–68.

scheduled; faculty should be available at reasonable times for appointments with students and both parties should keep such appointments; faculty and students should make appropriate preparations for classes and other meetings; students should submit their assignments in a timely manner; and faculty should perform their grading duties in a timely manner.

2. The general content of a course or other academic program should be described with reasonable accuracy in catalogues or other written documents available to students. The content, objectives of, and standards for evaluation (including the importance to be assigned various factors in academic evaluation) in a course should be described by the faculty member at the first or second class meeting.

3. Integrity of the academic process requires that credit be given where credit is due. Accordingly, it is unethical to present, as one's own work, the ideas, representations, or words of another, or to permit another to present one's own work without customary and proper acknowledgment of sources. The limits of permissible assistance available to students during a course or an academic evaluation should be determined by the faculty member and described with reasonable particularity at the first or second class meeting, or well in advance of an evaluation, so as to allow for adequate student preparation within the permissible limits.

4. All academic evaluations should be based upon good-faith professional judgment, in accordance with applicable standards; factors such as race, color, religion, sex, national origin, political affiliation, and activities outside the classroom that are unrelated may not be considered in matters of academic evaluation, academic assignments, or classroom procedures, nor shall reasoned views expressed by students during the course of study adversely prejudice any student.

5. University records, which shall contain only information reasonably related to educational purposes, shall be considered a matter of privacy not to be released except with student consent, or as may be required by law; provided, however, that any student shall be permitted to review his or her own personal record, except for its confidential contents (such as the recorded comments of counseling personnel).

6. The faculty of each school shall establish rules implementing these principles, and procedures pertaining to the investigation and redress of grievances.[2]

There have been several cases adjudicated each term under the code. The real advantage of the guidelines, however, is the deterrent effect on arbitrary and capricious behavior by faculty members. Likewise, it has enabled faculty members to address the issue of student misconduct without fear of legal reprisal from the student.

2. *Guidelines on Academic Integrity,* University of Pittsburgh (January 1975), pp. 3–4. For a more complete discussion, see Moye, "Meeting Student Demands: An Example of Voluntary Response," *Educational Record,* Spring 1977, pp. 191–200.

Although no legal mandate to establish an academic integrity guideline exists, we felt it was absolutely necessary to extend the elements of due process to students in the academic arena as had been done for nonacademic affairs. We predict that there will eventually be legal action to force the same on all institutions. Our policy, however, is to try to predict critical issues and respond to them before they become problems and to take action because action is the right course. We established an office of veterans affairs before it was fashionable or financially profitable to do so because we thought it was necessary. In the proposal to establish the office of veterans affairs, we indicated that it was our intention to add to that office an advisor for the handicapped, a move that was accomplished two years ago. We recognized the need to serve this minority class and proceeded to do so. We have also committed $60,000 a year for renovations to upgrade the physical plant to accommodate wheelchairs. We have not eliminated all architectural barriers on campus, but we have made significant progress. More important is the lead time we have given ourselves: As the federal government establishes standards on this issue, we will be either within compliance or near it.

Although internal and external pressures were applied as a result of our actions, we did not block the attempt of the gay students at Pitt to organize, nor did we try to influence the decision of the committee on student organizations, which grants official recognition to student groups. In responding to pressure groups, we simply reaffirmed the rights of students to freedom of association, inquiry, and expression. At a briefing conference last fall on student rights, a lawyer from a prominent university suggested that gay students need not be recognized. He related to us the success his institution had in thwarting the attempt by these students to gain recognition. This response was totally irresponsible and represented the kind of behavior that results in federal legislation to force us to grant inherent and constitutional rights to diverse segments of our society. In this sensitive area, the opposition still speaks out strongly, but it will not be long before state and federal authorities will legislate the rights of sexual minorities.

The foregoing may suggest a predisposition against government intervention in campus affairs. There are times, however, when government regulations can be an ally. Four years ago, the University of Pittsburgh integrated the marching band over the protest of alumni and students. I do not recall any reference to Title IX at that time, and I suspect we were not fully aware of the act. We opened the band to women because we believe it just. Had there been as much discussion of Title IX then as there has been recently, we would have had a legal basis for initiating change and saved ourselves time and effort in trying to convince the various constituencies of the correctness of the decision.

With regard to Title IX, we monitored the development of guidelines from the Department of Health, Education, and Welfare to respond to them and to be prepared to comply as quickly as possible. We have been amazed to find that in many areas we met or exceeded the limits of the law. This compliance was true even in many athletic areas, with the exception of granting full athletic scholarships to women athletes, and this deficiency has since been corrected. Title IX did not generate the hand-wringing at the University of Pittsburgh that seemed to take place on many campuses. We have reviewed our practices to determine the extent to which we discriminate against women. This review included formation of a student affirmative action committee to investigate policies and practices of student organizations to ensure that they do not overtly or covertly discriminate against women and/or minorities.

Another area of concern in this regard is that of the university's paying membership fees to clubs that discriminate against women or minorities. This does not affect student rights, but it does reflect institutional attitudes. Apparently many institutions have not evaluated their policies regarding male-only clubs as reported in a recent article.

> The Labor Department is studying whether federal contract holders, including universities, violate a federal executive order when they pay the membership fees and expenses for employees to join private clubs restricted to members of one sex.
>
> Various women's groups in the past have criticized the practice of academic institutions or associations paying the fees of top executives for membership in male-only clubs.
>
> Earlier this year, James D. Henry, Associate Solicitor of the Department of Labor, said in response to a question from the Treasury Department that his office believed that "payment by the contractor of membership fees and related expenses for employees to join sex-segregated organizations" was an employment practice which had a discriminatory impact on women. He said it also constituted a "company-sponsored activity or program" from which members of minority groups and women are not to be excluded under regulations covering the executive order that bans sex bias in employment by federal contractors.[3]

I have a strong feeling that correction of this injustice will be far more difficult than building an athletic program for women.

In an effort to reaffirm explicitly the board of trustees' commitment to the principles of freedom of the press, we presented to the board for

3. "Labor Department Reviewing Fees for Male-Only Clubs," *Chronicle of Higher Education*, July 12, 1976, p. 8.

approval a charter for the student newspaper, *The Pitt News*. The charter stated:

> The Board recognized the necessity for a strong, editorially independent campus student press free from censorship while providing a communications medium for its readers and an educational experience for the student publications staff.

Many colleagues advised the administration to sever all ties with the paper by incorporating it as independent, thus freeing the university from any liability. It was our feeling that forcing independence on the paper at this time would have been tantamount to destroying it. One cannot predict what relationship the university administration will have with future editorial staffs, but the present staff has shown an increased sense of responsibility. Furthermore, a board of directors oversees the operation of the paper and is free to recommend withdrawal of the charter for cause.

Another sensitive area of conflict has been the rights of student athletes accused of criminal misconduct. Last fall three of our football players were accused of assault following an incident outside a local restaurant. When the incident was reported in the local media, there was an outcry to suspend them from the team immediately. The young men and the university suffered considerable vilification and abuse by outside observers long before the case was brought to court. The university's posture was that the students should be presumed innocent until proven guilty; consequently, we did not interrupt their status as members of the team. When the case was heard, they were vindicated by the judge's decision. In fact, the judge himself said he "felt the case should not have been treated differently than any other simple assault case and wouldn't have if it hadn't involved prominent football players."[4]

Student participation in governance

In recognizing the right of students to participate in university governance, we have established several avenues by which students may become involved. The chancellor's student affairs advisory committee, which is composed of the presidents of all major student groups, meets monthly with the chancellor to discuss issues of concern. The agenda for these meetings can be set by the students or any administrator who wishes broad input into decisionmaking. Advisory committees exist for most areas, and student representatives sit on the board of trustees and every senate committee. When it became apparent that a tuition increase was inevitable in 1976, student leaders met regularly with the vice chancellor

4. *Pittsburgh Press*, April 9, 1976.

for planning and budget to review the budget and help establish the priorities that were used to determine budget cuts. Although the tuition increase was opposed, the opposition was mild compared to the reactions to tuition increases on other campuses. We believe that open dialogue and involvement helped defuse a potentially volatile situation. Again, we view this type of input into decisionmaking as a student right. Recognizing that support for higher education is not going to increase dramatically in the near future, we intend to involve students earlier in the budget process so that they will be even better prepared to participate in future difficult decisions.

The reduction in the age of majority to eighteen years in most states grants the students the right to make contracts, including contracts for educational services. Thus, the age of the student as consumer is a concept that has arrived. Although most institutions do not have formal or easily recognized contracts, we administrators will find ourselves establishing legally enforceable contracts in the eyes of the law by our own statements of educational policies and rules. A good example is the case of a student consumer at a Connecticut university who sued for a tuition refund for a course that she claimed had been worthless. Educational consumerism will probably result in more court cases.

The consumer movement in this country is twenty-five years old. There are four basic rights listed in the 1962 Kennedy Consumer Bill of Rights: the rights to choose freely, to be informed, to be heard, and to be safe. A fifth right was added by President Nixon in 1969: the right to redress.

The specifications for the Guaranteed Student Loan Program illustrate that the federal government is aware of the new status of students as consumers in the educational marketplace. The law requires: (1) a fair and equitable refund policy, which shall be made known to the student before his initial acceptance for enrollment at the institution and before each academic year in which he enrolls thereafter; (2) each institution to make an effort in good faith to present each prospective student with a complete and accurate statement about the institution, its programs, faculties, and facilities; (3) each institution preparing students for a particular vocation or trade to include in its literature information regarding the employment of students enrolled in such courses, vocations, or career field. Such information shall include data regarding the average starting salary for previously enrolled students and the percentage of such students who obtained employment in such positions.

The existence of a subcommittee on educational consumer protection in the Federal Interagency Committee on Education is a warning that unless we seriously adopt the student-as-consumer philosophy, we will be legislated to do so.

Recognizing the consumer movement and attempting to sensitize the university community to the concept of student consumerism, we are, with the help of students, currently writing our own consumer rights statement, entitled "Standards of Fair Practice," which augments existing guarantees to students contained in such documents as the code of conduct and the academic integrity guidelines. When completed, the statement will be promulgated throughout the university. The scope of the statement is too broad to be included in its entirety here. It will include statements of honesty in advertising; complete and timely notice of deadlines for applications, course changes, standards, and criteria; penalties and sanctions resulting from failure to comply with rules and regulations; fair and equitable treatment resulting from institutional error or oversight; retroactive changes in institutional policies and standards; and the expectation that the institution will honor contractual agreements and comply with state, federal, and local laws, ordinances, and statutes.

While it may be important for the University of Pittsburgh and every other institution to consider a statement on the student as consumer, it would be helpful to have organizations such as the American Council on Education and those groups that collaborated on the Joint Statement on Rights and Freedoms of Students to join forces again to produce a national model on student consumerism. In the absence of a proactive stance from the higher education community, my worst fears will be realized, and the federal government will present a set of guidelines to which we can respond only after the fact.

This discussion began on a pessimistic note that related the rights of students to past practices and policies of institutions. It will end on the more optimistic note that universities have learned to respond more appropriately to students. The examples cited here have concerned some of the positive steps taken at the University of Pittsburgh, but I would submit that it is far from unique in its responses and that many institutions' efforts equal if they do not exceed those at Pitt. It would be desirable to have all institutions determine for themselves the norms that govern their organization and internal workings without external pressure or intervention and to be assured that these norms guarantee the rights of students from both ethical and legal standpoints.

A New Focus for Administrators

GEORGE B. VAUGHAN

THE ISSUES FACING HIGHER EDUCATION today are so numerous and complicated that any listing of them would, at best, be arbitrary. Educational administrators today find themselves confronting affirmative action, the threat of declining enrollments, the role of the federal government in higher education, limited budgets and unlimited challenges, rising costs, collective bargaining, and any number of amendments, rules, and regulations. Coupled with these concerns is a certain public disillusionment with higher education so that it behooves the individual institution to define its mission in reference to its obligations to students, faculty, and the society. These broad issues often send forth ripples that affect the smallest and most isolated of our college campuses; they further serve to convince the campus administrator that the domino theory is alive and well in the field of higher education.

Emerging from the issues at the national and local levels is an awareness that the relationship of the college to its students is changing and that these changes constitute new obligations to students. It is perhaps debatable whether higher education indeed has *new* obligations to students or whether certain obligations have been regarded in the past as being of minor importance. The question of whether the obligations are new or simply have lain dormant for some time is academic. The point is that various forces are at work within the higher education community which have created a new awareness of the obligations an institution has to its students. The new awareness permeates much of what institutions of higher education do as they strive to meet the legal and ethical demands now exerted on them.

A quiet revolution: the student as consumer

Several issues faced by higher education today are closely related to the role of the student as a consumer. The National Student Education Fund refers to that segment of changes in higher education related to the role of the student as a consumer as "a quiet, but important, revolution in postsecondary education."[1]

As one writer notes, "The introduction of a consumer perspective

1. Mary S. Carlson and Chip Berlet, ed., *The Options Handbook: Communicating with Prospective Students about Postsecondary Educational Options*, Information Needed by the Student, no. 1 (Washington: National Student Educational Fund, 1976), p. 5.

into postsecondary education has been at once confusing, challenging, and welcome."[2] Another source states that "educators, government officials, and the general public all agree that students should have the best possible information in order to choose the type of education they wish to pursue."[3] In relating the student as a consumer to the law of supply and demand, another writer points out:

> the classical theory of the marketplace . . . assumes that consumer demand is rational and well informed. If students are ill informed or misled in their choices of institutions and programs, the system will fail to perform "efficiently."[4]

If the consumer issue is at the base of certain issues that call for new obligations to students—two examples that indicate the consumer issue is much more than a passing fad are actions on the part of the Veterans Administration regarding class attendance, and the concern of the Department of Health, Education, and Welfare regarding the regulations covering the Guaranteed Student Loan Program—what will be the role of the administrator in regard to this issue?

Certainly, the role of the administrator will change as the federal government emphasizes the rights and responsibilities of students receiving federal financial assistance. Apart from the legal implications of the student consumer movement, however,

> consumerism represents a renewed concern for an issue that is compatible with the educational mission of all institutions—that of assuring that institutional policies and practices are fair and responsive to student needs.[5]

The view from a small campus

The following are specific examples of the view afforded the chief administrator of a small, comprehensive, publicly supported community college. While the view might be more limited than the seemingly Olympus-like view afforded the administrators of our major colleges and universities, it is also true that the issues faced by the chief executive of a small campus are just as important to that campus and its students as

2. Elaine H. El-Khawas, "Clarifying Roles and Purposes," in *Promoting Consumer Protection for Students*, ed. Joan S. Stark, *New Directions for Higher Learning*, no. 13 (San Francisco: Jossey-Bass, 1976), p. 45.

3. Joan S. Stark in *Promoting Consumer Protection for Students*, p. vii.

4. Robert H. Davidson and Joan S. Stark, "The Federal Role," in *Promoting Consumer Protection for Students*, p. 10.

5. Elaine H. El-Khawas, "Consumerism as an Emerging Issue for Postsecondary Education," *Educational Record*, Spring 1975, p. 131.

are the issues faced by the larger institutions of higher education. In considering examples from a single campus, it seemed appropriate to use examples of new obligations to students that not only fit into the national movement, but that also relate to the college's own mission. Obviously what is feasible for one campus may not be appropriate for another. Each institution of higher education, however, should evaluate what constitutes new obligations to students on its own campus in regard both to its own mission and national trends and interact positively with those obligations.

Mountain Empire Community College (MECC), which just completed its fourth year of operation, is located in the extreme southwestern portion of Virginia. The college, which serves a population of approximately 88,000 people spread over 1,400 square miles of mountainous land, is a member of the Virginia Community College System. Like most public community colleges, MECC serves the people of its area by maintaining an open-door admissions policy, low cost, a comprehensive program, and accessibility. While the problems faced by MECC in its attempts to serve its constituents are not unique, some of the solutions arrived at are perhaps worth sharing. The following illustrations are some of the ways MECC has attempted to ensure that it has complied not only with the legal but also with the ethical considerations involved in meeting its ever-changing obligations to students.

Two years ago, the president and dean of student services at MECC determined that the information provided to students by the college was not adequate. Meanwhile, it was discovered that the Fund for the Improvement of Postsecondary Education (FIPSE) was prepared to fund a national project dealing with "Better Information for Student Choice." FIPSE selected eleven institutions and four resource agencies to participate in this project. MECC was one of three community colleges chosen to serve as a demonstration institution. As a result of its sensitivity to the role of the student as a consumer, and with financing from FIPSE, the college began to gather information that would serve as a basis for more adequately meeting what was determined to be its legal and ethical obligations in the area of student information. Included in the new information packets developed by the college is an information brochure on each of the college's curricula. Each brochure includes statistics or the cost of the individual program, the placement of graduates, job satisfaction of graduates, employer satisfaction with graduates, starting salaries, employment opportunities, and the availability and types of student financial aid. As a result, both prospective and enrolled students will have a clearer idea of what to expect and what not to expect from their educational experience at MECC.

Given MECC's location, where distance is often measured in time rather than miles, accessibility for many students meant that they would have to travel from two to three hours a day in order to attend their "local" community college. Transportation appeared to be a key factor; moreover, for a number of those students traveling up to fifteen hours a week, it appeared as if the time factor made attending MECC a questionable investment. Clearly the college had an ethical obligation to seek ways of making the college more accessible.

In order to meet this obligation to its students, MECC embarked on a bold educational adventure. Through funding from the Appalachian Regional Commission, the college obtained five specially equipped buses designed to allow students to take individualized courses while traveling to and from college. The buses, with their thirty-two student stations, have "flip-down" desks, reading lamps, earphones, cassette-player recorders or cassette players with a filmstrip viewer, as well as electrical outlets and compartments for books and supplies. General equipment includes color video receivers, slide projectors, cassette players, a stereo cassette player, AM/FM radio, restroom, and a microphone for the traveling instructors. In essence, the buses are well-equipped learning laboratories designed to permit individualized instruction while traveling to and from the college, thereby allowing students to use time that is normally wasted. The experiment is bold, and although at this time its success is somewhat limited, the concept represents an exciting approach that one college is using to meet its obligations to its students.[6]

MECC's mission calls for service to its area that goes beyond offering programs designed for the recent high school graduate. In attempting to determine its obligations to the total population, the college surveyed the majority of the heads of households and spouses in the homes in its service area. The surveys revealed that many adults were interested in attending college, but often were not interested in the more traditional college courses. The surveys also revealed that most adults preferred to attend classes in the evening. These facts, coupled with the knowledge that family ties are still strong in many rural areas, led the college to develop programs that would appeal to the entire family. As the situation demands and finances permit, the college offers baby-sitting, bus transportation on the buses described above, and family counseling to encourage the tradition of family education. As a result, MECC has designated three nights a week as "Family College Nights." Classes are offered (both

6. For further reading on this project see George B. Vaughan, "Learning in Transit at Mountain Empire," *Community and Junior College Journal*, June–July 1974, pp. 54–55; and "Busing—Community College Style," *College Management*, October 1974, pp. 20–21.

credit and noncredit) for children as young as eight years of age and for adults of any age. One of the students enrolled in the Family College Nights program is an eighty-seven-year-old grandmother. She has earned seventeen credit-hours and audited courses amounting to another twenty-eight credit-hours. Her courses are in such diverse fields as pottery, philosophy, and music.

The family approach to education, which is conducted through MECC's division of community services, has been highly successful as both a concept and as a practical means of generating students. This past year, more than 25 percent of the college's total credit enrollment was generated through the community services division; the majority of these people were enrolled in the Family College Nights program. Moreover, the program has helped change the minds of a number of people who had never considered attending college as a viable choice and has helped promote lifelong learning among many rural families served by the college.

As pointed out earlier, a major part of the community college philosophy is to provide a program of community services for the people it serves. While "community services" is a concept that is somewhat ill-defined and differs from college to college, it usually consists of a combination of credit and noncredit courses as well as any number of seminars, lectures, and other types of service functions. What community services normally does not elicit is a strong commitment on the part of regular teaching faculty to this important function. MECC felt that those students served by the community services program were as important as full-time students and that the college had as great an obligation to those students as it did to the students enrolled in the regular college programs. The administration determined that since the college's mission was to serve all of its students (as exemplified in the Family College Nights program) and that since the heart of the college's instructional program is its full-time faculty, then a portion of all faculty members' time should be devoted to the community services function. This has been accomplished by assigning approximately one fifth of each faculty member's time (exceptions were made in certain technical programs because of the large number of contact hours involved in the regular program) to the community services division. This action has been a major step in integrating the regular teaching faculty into the community services program. Moreover, this concept has provided the vehicle for those students enrolled in the community services program at the college to receive the same quality of instruction as the regular students.[7]

7. For a detailed discussion, see Vaughan, "A President's Formula: Involving the Entire Faculty in Community Services," *Community College Review*, March 1975, pp. 48–52.

The chief administrator's role

In attempting to deal with the many complex issues facing higher education today, there is a tendency on the part of many chief administrators to become so involved with the issues on a philosophical plane than they rarely make contact with the students. It must be quite a shock for the chief administrator to discover, only when the Veterans Administration auditors arrive on campus, that students are receiving veterans' benefits while not attending class. The following, while limited in scope, are considerations that might be taken into account as chief administrators evaluate their new obligations to students.

The first and perhaps the most important step a chief administrator can take is to sensitize himself to the fact that both legal and ethical obligations to students are changing. This sensitization process does not mean that the chief administrator must become familiar with the intricate details of such things as the Buckley Amendment or the rules and regulations regarding the Guaranteed Student Loan Program. But the chief administrator of even the smallest institution must have other administrators who are familiar with the details of new and revised regulations. In turn, these staff members must provide chief administrators with information that will sensitize them to changing trends. As chief administrators become more sensitive to their new obligations to students, it should become clear that they, as professional people, have an obligation to present prospective students with as much accurate information as possible and to fulfill the institution's implied and stated mission.

If the chief administrator does not take positive steps to acknowledge the institution's new obligations to students, it is likely that even more rules and regulations will be forthcoming from federal sources. One writer closely in tune with student thinking regarding the new student rights that are emerging from current issues states that institutional administrators are interested in consumer protection in postsecondary education because "they are concerned about the growing regulation of institutional activities, including affirmative action in hiring and treatment of students, record keeping, public disclosure of information, government-mandated admissions, refund and financial aid policies."[8] If the higher education community does not take voluntary action to serve students and society more capably (and remember that society is paying more and more of the cost of higher education and is therefore a consumer in the truest sense),

8. Layton Olson, "Consumer Protection in Postsecondary Education," in *The Options Handbook: Communicating with Prospective Students about Postsecondary Educational Options* (Washington: National Student Educational Fund, 1976), p. 11.

it is highly probable that outside agencies will put forth more rules and regulations that will force compliance.

Chief administrators can read and use certain publications that will help them become more aware of and meet new student obligations. The suggestions offered in these publications, if followed, will go far in bringing institutions into line with what constitutes good practice in meeting both legal and ethical responsibilities to students.

Finally, chief administrators must remember that they are ultimately responsible for seeing that their institutions are complying with the various rules and regulations, implementing the institution's statement of mission, and doing the many things that will help ensure that new obligations to students are being met. With this in mind, the issues facing higher education today quickly leave the lofty pinnacle of philosophical thought and become the day-to-day concerns of all of us who have assumed the responsibility of serving as the chief executive officers of colleges and universities.

6. BALANCING STUDENT RETENTION
AND ACADEMIC STANDARDS

Accommodating
the Nontraditional Student

PHILLIP E. JONES

IMPROVING educational opportunities for the nation's talented, economically disadvantaged, and educationally segregated populations became the focus of attention of many colleges and universities as a result of the National Defense Education Act of 1957.[1] In order to serve the educationally and economically disadvantaged, many institutions began to work toward developing compensatory programs and services. Their purpose was to minimize the financial and academic impediments faced by many minority/low income students in traditional, competitive, predominantly white institutions of higher education. The faculties and administrations of undergraduate programs in these institutions soon found themselves operating in a new area with few effective sources of prior experience to help them in dealing with the educationally and economically disadvantaged.

Systematic methods to admit, finance, and provide extra academic assistance to large groups of disadvantaged students were used during the early 1960s. Programs to serve the educationally and economically disadvantaged and to maintain the academic standards of the institutions began to appear during the 1960s as the result of student protests, increased social awareness, and federal financial support. The assassination of Martin Luther King, Jr., on April 4, 1968, gave additional momentum to these programs. Many institutions approached the structuring of programs in a piecemeal fashion, however. Writers generally concur with Helen Astin's observation that there were very few efforts before 1968 to design programs that integrated institutional commitment with well-defined plans for recruitment and admissions, followed up by diagnosis and orienta-

1. E. W. Gordon, "Programs and Practices for Minority Group Youth in Higher Education," *Barriers to Higher Education* (New York: College Entrance Examination Board, 1971).

tion.[2] Very few efforts were made to adjust the institutional processes through specially designed curricula, counseling and tutoring, work-study and financial assistance, staff selection, and evaluation and follow-up.

Basic assumptions about the deficit model

Institutional attempts to balance student retention with academic standards generally take the form of compensatory programs that are based on a deficit model of education.[3] The deficit model operates on the presumption that institutional processes and definitions of academic standards, or outputs, need no modification. Instead, students with nontraditional characteristics are enrolled, and the processes are supplemented for the students through compensatory programs. In the deficit model, students with nontraditional characteristics are required to offset their educational and economic deficiencies through compensatory programs and to meet traditional academic standards for completion of the educational program.

Within the institutions, the learning processes, or curricula, are based on criteria for selection that exclude many black and other minority students. There is little flexibility in the institutional processes to consider any advantages the students might bring to the learning environment and to consider the environmental learning differences of minority students. The onus of educational redress for these disadvantaged students in higher education is on the students themselves.[4]

Functional components of institutional programs to balance student retention and academic standards are based on acceptance of the deficit model of higher education. Five assumptions must be made to accept the functional components of the programs:

1. There are students who, because of insufficient educational backgrounds, have educational disadvantages in higher education institutions that historically have had fewer such students.

2. These students have the learning potential to matriculate in the institutions in which the disadvantaged have not matriculated in significant numbers.

3. Traditional academic programs, standards, curricula, and teaching methods have changed very little to accommodate the needs of educationally disadvantaged students.

2. *Higher Education and the Disadvantaged* (Washington: Human Services Press, 1972).

3. Roosevelt Johnson, *Black Scholars on Higher Education in the 70's* (Columbus, Ohio: ECCA, 1974).

4. Ibid.

4. These students can succeed in traditional academic programs and can meet traditional academic standards in regular curricula, and they can do so under the same teaching methods as traditional students.

5. Adequate academic, financial, and personal support can be provided to balance retention and maintain academic standards for the students to succeed.[5]

By establishing compensatory programs, institutions seek to ameliorate the impending academic difficulties of students with different input characteristics by supplementing their conventional curricula. The desired outcomes are not modified. Special efforts are necessary to produce the desired outputs from inputs other than those traditionally defined. Hence, institutions provide support in the form of services rather than through innovations in the traditional academic programs, standards, curricula, or teaching methods.

The programs provide supplemental processes in the educational system to assist students in bypassing some of the characteristics which ensure that academic standards are not compromised. If one accepts the assumption that the students have the potential to succeed, then development of a system to help the students bypass these obstacles is necessary because the institutional processes have not been modified, and the output criteria remain unchanged. The bypass system must provide adequate support for removing or minimizing any learning impediments the students may encounter. The system must also be strong enough to provide the students a reasonable opportunity in which to perform and to complete the institutional processes. The "reasonable opportunity" is predicated on accepting the assumption that the students will perform on an academic level commensurate with the traditional academic standards of the institution after impediments resulting from their previous educational environments have been removed.

If the institutional response to the disadvantaged is a deficit model approach and the students are expected to meet high academic standards, then the institutional processes to remove the disadvantaged students' deficits must be well developed and effectively administered. The administrative structures of compensatory programs must serve to institutionalize the supplemental processes. Institutionalization is necessary for the students' different characteristics to be considered as integral components of the higher education system and not as the by-products of an institutional ad hoc deficit model program.

5. Phillip E. Jones, "A Descriptive Analysis of the Administrative Structures of Selected Educational Opportunity Programs" (Ph.D. diss., University of Iowa, 1975).

Implications of equal educational opportunity

Compensatory programs established to provide equal educational opportunities are a legitimate function for higher education institutions. The expansion of knowledge should extend to all people in a democratic society, and development of this concept is a legitimate research, teaching, and service objective in the institutions. Greater insight into the disadvantaged student and improved teaching methods are needed to extend the institutional boundaries to include historically disenfranchised racial and economic minorities. Institutional student input procedures require reestablishment of admission criteria to include the learning experiences of students from de facto or de jure segregated educational systems. New insights must be gained by both the disadvantaged and traditional students entering the institutions, as well as by faculty and administrators, to enable an exchange of knowledge.

The establishment of equality of opportunity components is a massive and complex task in higher education. Educational institutions respond in microscopic ways to macroscopic societal problems. Because of the massive societal complexities in creating equality of opportunity in higher education, federal and institutional resources will be necessary to administer compensatory programs until the concept receives broad acceptance.

Starting funds for new programs from federal and state sources should help institutions make broad responses to the needs of the disadvantaged. The problem with heavy reliance on federal support for compensatory programs is the difficulty of making the transition in the budgeting process from special appropriations to recurring appropriations. The time required to institutionalize equal opportunity programs will be lengthened if institutions rely on federal funds for their development. If balancing student retention and academic standards is considered an essential part of the institutional process, and not merely an ad hoc demonstration project existing at the behest of the federal government, the programs must be firm components of institutional base budgets. The need to be in the base budget is especially applicable to programs in institutions that do not rely heavily on federal funds for institutional operations, but do rely heavily on federal funds to administer their equal opportunity programs.

Changes in institutional processes are complicated by the institutional definitions of outputs. Equality of opportunity does not mean lower academic standards for students with nontraditional characteristics. Black and other minority students must be held to high standards for academic development. There are, however, problems in defining high academic standards. In a deficit model system, advantaged students often demonstrate learning difficulties. The built-in rejection mechanisms in deficit model systems reject advantaged as well as disadvantaged students. The same bypass processes that support disadvantaged students also help other students. The difficulty in the problem of maintaining high standards is not in the definition of academic outputs but rather in the definition of institutional processes that operate to eliminate advantaged as well as disadvantaged students.

In a study of twenty compensatory programs in large, predominantly white universities, I found that the students entered the institutions with high school academic averages and ranks in class comparable to those of other students. The students were defined as disadvantaged largely on the basis of admissions tests. The study showed that the students stay at the institutions and graduate with academic averages as strong as their high school averages when they entered the institutions.

The Salisbury Experience

NORMAN C. CRAWFORD, JR.

ACADEMIC STANDARDS are in the eye of the beholder. While one person may view standards as relative, others may view the same standards as absolute. At Salisbury State College, we undertook a critical reexamination of the ultimate academic standard—the high school graduation grade-point criterion—and its subsequent effect on the admission and retention of students.

The educational philosophy of Salisbury enabled it to come into its own. To understand fully the changes we have experienced, let me examine some comparative statistics for September 1969, the year before we initiated our new policies and practices, and September 1976. In 1969, the college enrolled 965 full-time students and 227 part-time students. In each of the last seven years our enrollment has increased by an average of 400 students. In 1976, more than 4,000 students were enrolled, including 2,800 full-time students. The faculty has grown from 61 to 155; of that number, 124 have joined the staff since September 1971. The minority enrollment has grown from three full-time students in 1969 to an estimated 350 in 1976. The college has conferred more baccalaureate degrees in the last five years than during the first forty-five years of its history.

Challenging the traditional graduation standard

The story begins when our relatively small faculty acknowledged that for us the real meaning of accountability was that we should be able to justify, both educationally and intellectually, all our policies and procedures. As we began to reexamine our policies, it was apparent that many were punitive in nature. Why else would we deny a student the opportunity to drop a course after a specified date during the semester? Was not the loss of time and money sufficient penalty for failing to complete a course? When a student failed a course, was it not sufficient penalty that he or she made no progress toward the degree? Did we need to insist that the student repeat the course (even if it was not required) in order not to have the *F* count against him or to demand an even higher level of performance from him in his other courses—that is, *A*'s and *B*'s until he had raised his cumulative average to 2.0 or *C*? If a student who wrote poorly at the beginning of an English composition course wrote better than average at the end of the term, shouldn't he receive a *B* (the same grade as one who wrote good themes in the beginning and showed no significant improvement)? Shouldn't we award a degree on the basis of accumulated competence (degree credits of *C* or above) rather than requiring a *C average* on all work? We discarded the *D*'s and *F*'s of transfer students but retained a kind of academic penance for the *D*'s and *F*'s of students in our own college.

Discomforted by our inability to defend the cumulative grade-point average as the most appropriate academic performance criterion for graduation, we decided to change the graduation requirement from a grade-point average to 120 semester credit-hours of *C* or better. In essence, we had made the decision that our degree should certify an accumulated competence rather than a satisfactory average on all work attempted within our institution. The significance of that rather simple challenge of the traditional academic standard for graduation has been overwhelming. Many in our college would say that we first saw the light when we made that change. Admittedly, a few might still suggest that making the change was our first mistake. All agree, however, that our first decision has caused a ripple effect which is sparked with excitement.

Changing the grading system

After we changed the graduation requirements, it was obvious that we needed to reevaluate the grading system. If one needed 120 hours of *C* or better to graduate, what did *D*'s mean? We concluded that *D*'s did not signify acceptable competence but represented a minimally satisfactory exposure. We decided *D*'s could be used to satisfy requirements outside the student's major field. For example, an English major could get D's in laboratory science general education courses without having to take additional science, but would still need 120 credit-hours of C or better to graduate.

We then asked, what do F's mean? If a student was no longer held to a cumulative grade-point average requirement for graduation, the answer could only be that F's signified neither competence nor minimally satisfactory exposure. The student, for one reason or another, simply had wasted his time and money and had made no progress toward graduation. That being the case, someone asked, should we continue to label this a "failure"? We concluded that most F's were not, as the public had generally assumed, an academic evaluation that a conscientious student's efforts were unsatisfactory. More often than not, in our experience, an F represented that the student had not turned in work to be evaluated or that the student had been immature, uncertain of his identity, unsure of why he was in college, or, perhaps, even had a bad teacher and would not play the game. It did not take long for us to agree that it was more appropriate simply to call this absence of certifiable competence "no credit." It really would not have made much difference if we had continued to label it "failure." We could call it whatever we liked, as long as a student needed only 120 hours of C grade or better to graduate. What difference would it make, other than to our conscience and integrity or to the student's future attitudes toward learning and the academy?

Consequences of the innovations

There is no longer a deadline after the close of registration by which a student must drop a course without penalty. If the student drops a course during the drop-add period, the course never appears on his record. If he fails to complete the course satisfactorily, for whatever reason, he receives a grade of *N,* a nonpunitive, nonjudgmental grade, meaning simply that he did not receive credit.

Disadvantaged students, without special, expensive remediation programs, are succeeding at a high rate. Even with remediation, these students generally perform poorly during their first college semesters and are normally subject to academic dismissal. Under the traditional grade-point average requirement, it is virtually impossible for disadvantaged students to accumulate enough A's and B's to attain the required average. Our experience has shown that these students, given sufficient motivation and good teaching, begin to earn a majority of C grades or better in their third or fourth semester and achieve the required accumulated competence (120 semester hours of C or better) in nine or ten semesters. We believe that it is in the interest of society and of the individual student to turn out winners in ten semesters, rather than losers in three.

Many people have said, "You know, I've really thought about going back to college, but I just don't think I can get back into the swing of it." We found that when we told people that there was nothing to fear, that the worst they could do would be to try, and for one reason or another receive no credit, many of these people began to come back. Formal educational institutions, especially our colleges and universities, have so conditioned the public to believe that learning is a succeed-or-fail situation that many are afraid to try. We have been astounded by the number of more mature individuals who seek our services once they are convinced they have nothing to fear.

We have virtually eliminated any reason for "grade-grubbing" by students. When the cumulative grade-point average is no longer the ultimate criterion for success or failure, grades of *C* or better are of equal value. Students no longer need to appeal to a faculty member for a higher grade in an effort to offset a poor grade elsewhere in their record.

Our new procedures seem to be relatively free of semester time constraints. We know and accept that people learn at different rates, and yet we have doggedly held to the assignment of a final measurement of student learning to coincide with the end of the semester or quarter. Theoretically, our system enables the student to demonstrate his competence at any time and to receive credit for it at that time.

Students are no longer motivated to go through the motions of learning simply to fool their professors into giving them some grade other than *F*. We have all experienced panic at the end of the term when we recognized that we were hopelessly behind in some of our courses. Fear of receiving *F* grades became our primary motivation and, if smart (or dumb) enough, we copied someone else's homework assignments or slapped together book reports on books we had never read, only to give the appearance of having done the work and to avoid the penalty of an *F* grade. We are beginning to find that our students no longer play this silly game. It appears that instead of going through this pretense they resign themselves to accepting No Credit—an accurate, fair, nonjudgmental grade—often with a commitment to repeat the course in the next semester and to do it right. In short, we have eliminated the gamesmanship, the artificial motivation to beat the system.

We are now able to say (with credibility) that our institutional commitment is to help people succeed. Most colleges espouse this goal in their literature, but we feel that we have policies reflecting this commitment that back up our literature. Many of the top-notch faculty members recruited to the college in the past five years profess that it was the institution's demonstrable commitment to these values that most influenced their recruitment. They felt our policies facilitated good teaching and learning in contrast to the traditional practices and policies of other institutions, which may be perceived as impediments. We believe that, given good teachers, virtually all conscientious and well-motivated students will be able to experience some measure of success. What is "success"? By what academic standards shall success be judged?

Academic standards

I have suggested that academic standards are viewed by some as relative and by others as absolute. Unfortunately, in academe we usually view standards in relative terms. We see standards as separating winners and losers. The average student becomes our standard and, by definition, those students better than average become our successes and those students below the average become our failures. Given this interpretation, the only way to prove that we have academic standards is to show our losers. For many, the normal curve dictates the standard, and we create the self-fulfilling prophecy that some of our students must fail.

In my judgment, the only appropriate academic standards for institutions of higher education are absolute. They are measurable behavioral objectives, formulated from the informed consensus of competent professionals in the disciplines in which we provide instruction. They include measurements such as correctly answering items on the College-Level Examination Program (CLEP) subject-matter standardized examinations, typing sixty words per minute, solving certain types of mathematical problems, and so on. The real quality of our institutions can only be measured by how successful we are in developing these competencies in our students. An institution cannot justify manipulating the balance between academic standards and the retention of students. It establishes appropriate and professionally defensible academic standards and then measures its effectiveness by the number of students it helped to be successful in achieving these standards.

Hope for the future

One of my assistants suggests that every thing we have done at Salisbury in the past six years reminds him of an artichoke: You do not really know what is there until you have stripped away all the leaves and get down to the heart. We have found that the heart is not programs, grades, standards, degrees, but learning.

The term "learning" is one that all educators should use to describe their primary activity. I sense that it projects something very different from the word "education" to our students, their parents, and to our government representatives. Subtly, it suggests a personal activity, rather than something that is done to you. One can find many dissenters to the suggestion that all persons should be "educated." Perhaps this dissent is best summed up in the criticism that too many people go to college. But what governor, what legislator, would deny that each person in our society should have the lifelong opportunity to learn?

The benefits of learning do not accrue solely to the individual. Society benefits from an educated citizenry, and all persons should be encouraged to improve themselves by learning throughout their lives. To provide this encouragement, learning must be viewed as nonthreatening, not a win-or-lose situation. Too many people elect not to try to learn rather than risk failure, and society is the loser. The quality of learning that takes place only from fear of failing has little sustaining value. Learning can and must be a positive, pleasant experience, from which a rewarding sense of accomplishment is derived.

We have too long told many who seek admission that they are not good enough to have the opportunity to learn in our institution. We have told those who are fortunate enough to be admitted, "Look around. Half of you will not be here four years from now." It is understandable that many of those who have graduated from our institutions have done so with little respect for formalized education.

If there is one thing we do, inevitably, it is to influence the attitude of every student toward future learning. Higher education is no longer the darling of our society. The conclusion is inescapable that our traditional institutional practices have had a negative influence on the general public's (electorate's) attitude toward formalized learning.

We compete for funding with poverty and welfare, health problems and medical care, crime and the judicial/penal system. These three natural competitors for the tax dollar are highly correlated with low educational level. We must dedicate our efforts to try to convince our society to invest its limited dollars in the cure (education) for these illnesses rather than in the treatment of the symptoms.

All educators should consider whether the Salisbury experience might benefit their own institutions. They should consider first whether an accumulated competence criterion might be more educationally defensible for their college or university than the present requirement. The implications could be revolutionary, for they force one to consider many other aspects of the educational program. It might be that, as leaves of the artichoke fall away, learning is found to be the heart.

Effective Education for the Unprepared

FREDERICK S. HUMPHRIES

ONE OF THE GREATEST CHALLENGES facing American higher education is effective education of those students who come to higher education inadequately prepared for collegiate curricula.

> Today we expect more of education. We are now trying to evaluate colleges on the basis of their skill in educating students rather than for their skill in selecting students. People are beginning to talk about "value added" and about the process of teaching and learning. Even that quaint old word "pedagogy" is making a comeback. The task of education, as we see it now, is not to select those who will be successful but to make successful those who come.[1]

It is not surprising to learn that those students who score in the eightieth percentile or higher on the Scholastic Aptitude Test (SAT) or American College Testing (ACT) are more likely to complete the collegiate curriculum than those whose scores are below that level. What is surprising, though, is to have a high proportion of students from among the lower 50 percent completing the collegiate curriculum. For many complex reasons, minorities tend to occupy the lower strata in disproportionate numbers upon entrance to college. This paper will not focus on the complex reasons for this imbalance, but will concentrate on what must be done to educate effectively students who are poorly prepared on entering college.

Identifying effective education for poorly prepared students as a major problem in higher education is not meant to detract from the equally important concerns of planning educational programs that recognize the broader inadequacies of compartmentalized education, knowledge proliferation, overemphasis of higher education on career specialties,

1. K. Patricia Cross, "New Forms for New Functions," in *Lifelong Learners— A New Chronicle For Higher Education,* ed. Dyckman W. Vermilye, Current Issues in Higher Education 1974 (Washington: American Association for Higher Education, 1974), p. 87.

and the erosion of general education requirements. It is recognized that higher education must plan curricula that include: (1) the reestablishment of a value-oriented liberal arts curriculum; (2) educational programs that teach problem identification as well as skills and technical knowledge; (3) a curriculum that not only imparts knowledge but teaches "learning how to learn" and demonstrates the interrelatedness of knowledge; (4) educational activities that teach students to make decisions with the full knowledge of what informs those decisions as well as the consequences that flow from them; (5) courses that enlighten and examine the relationship between and among humans and that tend to foster rather than undermine better human relationships; and (6) courses that accentuate student strength and build confidence. These challenges must also be addressed in any curriculum that purports to address the education of handicapped students.

The problem

Tennessee State University is a medium-sized, multipurpose, land-grant university, which offers associate, baccalaureate, and master's degrees. The university consists of seven schools—a joint school of allied health with Meharry Medical College, a school of education, a school of arts and sciences, a graduate school, a school of agriculture and home economics, a school of business, and a school of engineering and technology. The university has a faculty of approximately 300 members, a student body of 5,500, an administrative staff of 50, and a professional and supportive staff of approximately 650 persons.

Tennessee State University, historically a black institution, is faced with the problem of desegregation. The student body is 85 percent black and 15 percent white and other. A quick look at the demographic data relating to the student body will give some indication of the planning necessary to provide an appropriate and effective educational program. Our students come largely from the state of Tennessee, with only 20 percent from other states and twelve foreign countries. Our out-of-state students consistently come from major metropolitan areas—Washington, D.C.; New York; Chicago; Detroit; Cincinnati; Dayton; Birmingham; Atlanta; Houston; Denver; and Los Angeles.

Approximately 60 percent of the student body receive financial aid. The university typically dispenses $4.7 million through the student financial aid program. Many students are the first in their families to attend college. These students are typically deficient in reading, writing, and arithmetic skills. A deficiency in conceptualization, especially as it relates to social science disciplines, has become apparent. The student's aspirations, however, are of the highest order. Many want to pursue, on completion of their undergraduate work, graduate and professional opportunities. Tennessee State University is located in Davidson County, in which there are approximately 500,000 residents. There are 76,000 students in the metropolitan school system, and 4,500 teachers administer the Davidson County school system. Highly technical industries are located in and around the county. Several major corporation headquarters as well as a large banking industry are located within the county. To serve this community adequately, Tennessee State University must plan to serve the professional development needs and postgraduate aspirations of the teachers and to develop modern, up-to-date courses that address the continuing educational needs of a highly technical, business-oriented community. Yet we are cognizant of the need in higher education to present a healthy balance in the curriculum of ethics and humanism.

All first-year students entering the university are required to take the ACT and Sequential Tests of Educational Progress (STEP) tests. These tests indicate that the majority of entering freshmen have limited conceptual, analytical, and reading skills. The freshman ACT scores ranged from six to twelve points below the national norm in the years 1973–75. No doubt the ACT scores indicate a less than adequate preparation by the secondary and elementary schools; nevertheless, the students' inability to perform at expected levels presents a tremendous burden for the teaching faculty at the university.

The ACT scores indicate that our students are below national norms in English, mathematics, social studies, and natural sciences.

The solution

The university has not lowered its standards of excellence and expectation but has designed many different strategies to help the students overcome academic weaknesses that have their genesis in the high schools, in the elementary schools, and in the impoverished environment. These programs include: an experiential learning program, interdisciplinary activities, a social science laboratory, a writing clinic, a reading center, a mathematics laboratory, and a media center.

Conventional wisdom holds that remedial programs or development programs must be conducted under conditions in which participation in college-level work is reduced. The logic is that full participation for the deficient student in a college curriculum at the freshman level is sure to result, at worst, in academic failure or, at best, in poor academic performance. Consequently, it is not unusual for students engaged in remedial programs to take a reduced load. Tennessee State University has experimented with this philosophy as it relates to reading. Our present policy is that a student participating in the reading development program may not take more than twelve regular college-level hours. Our data now point toward a reexamination of this philosophy.

For many students attending Tennessee State University, discipline of the mind and perseverance in the pursuit of knowledge are characteristics that must be developed. In the fall of 1977, we will be rejecting conventional wisdom. All freshmen will be allowed to take the normal fifteen credit-hours. They will be scheduled, if needed, into reading classes, the writing clinic, and the mathematics clinic in addition to the regular load. We will be guided by the principle that the related skill development programs will be used as study and work sessions to develop the appropriate study habits and discipline required to be effective in the college-level environment. The material used in the clinics will be closely associated with the classroom activities of the normal college-level courses. Assignments will not be given in the development skills program. Assignment of work outside the classroom will come from the collegiate curriculum only. The thrust of the remedial programs will be to develop discipline and to provide the skills necessary for the college curriculum.

The approach to effective writing will go beyond the normal activities of the freshman English composition courses or the writing clinic. We have an experimental plan that establishes teams of teachers from the disciplines of English, history, and psychology to coordinate their requirements for term papers for freshman students. A consistent format is required for each term paper and will be assured by the coordinated activities of the departments. This coordinated effort should establish a continuous, consistent demand for the display and development of expository writing skills. The goal is to obtain a range of four to six excellent term papers from among the three disciplines in a fashion orchestrated by the teachers. The program will continue into the sophomore, junior, and senior years and requires close cooperation among the faculty members. The English teachers act as resource persons for the faculties of history and psychology.

In a similar way, we are attempting to sensitize the faculty, other than those teaching reading, to the normal reading difficulties of our students. The reading faculty becomes a ready resource for the teaching faculty. Our goal is to equip each faculty member with at least enough knowledge to recognize (1) the reading level required of assigned textbooks; (2) the process by which assigned textbooks can be evaluated for reading levels; (3) words that are beyond the perimeters of the comprehension level of the student in a given class; and (4) activities that will allow teachers to solve word problems or enhance conceptual development.

Again, the goal of this approach is to involve the entire faculty in rectification of the reading deficiency. In executing this approach, we expand the role of the faculty in the university. Each faculty member must now assume some responsibility for the students' reading. We repeat this pattern in mathematics, but we are just beginning our efforts with the faculty of mathematics and the natural science departments. The process is similar to that explained above.

Mathematics laboratory. The low scores on the mathematics section of the ACT in part result from the fact that 60–70 percent of our entering freshmen have had only business mathematics in high school, with no exposure to algebra, geometry, and trigonometry, which are on the ACT. With such limited preparation, approximately 50 percent of the students taking freshman mathematics in the university fail the courses.

To remedy this problem, the university will expand its tutorial efforts into a well-conceived mathematics laboratory to eliminate mathematical deficiencies and to enrich the mathematics background of those students who enter the university already prepared in mathematics. Specifically, the mathematics laboratory programs will include

- practice in the basic skills—multiplication, division, fractions, percentages, algebraic manipulations;
- heuristics—exercises that develop problem-solving abilities and individual creativity in mathematics and demonstrate a view of mathematics other than numeration;
- computer-assisted instruction—to develop logic, teach advanced mathematical concepts, and to present drill and practice; and
- evaluation—test instruments that demonstrate progress and diagnose weaknesses.

The program of the mathematics laboratory is geared to serve an estimated 250 students. Each student will each month receive a minimum of ten hours of individual attention, sixteen hours of group tutorial aid, and three to five hours of computer-assisted instruction.

Writing clinic. A major barrier to academic success and career attainment for poor students has been communication, especially written communication. At Tennessee State University in 1973, 73 percent of the entering freshmen scored between one and fifteen on the ACT English unit; in 1975, 78 percent scored in this range, an actual increase of 7 percent. A score of fifteen is approximately five points below the national norm.

The purpose of the writing clinic is to help students who enter college without the requisite written composition skills to express their ideas effectively in a college-level style and to develop a positive attitude toward writing. To achieve these ends, the clinic uses both individual and group instruction. The clinic identifies the students' weaknesses by analyzing the students' responses to a usage test. Instruction and materials are based on strengthening the students' weaknesses as illuminated by the analysis.

The writing clinic is essentially a series of thirty-minute writing sessions. These programs focus on the operation of the basic skills of composition (punctuation, sentence structure, grammar, diction, style, logic, and organization) in the production of sentences, paragraphs, and compositions.

Reading center. Sixty-five percent of the freshmen entering Tennessee State University scored below grade ten in comprehension and vocabulary skills òn the STEP reading section. A language arts improvement project, which began with Title III funds, was established at the university in 1968. One purpose of this project was to assess the reading deficiencies of entering freshmen and to provide a program of skill enrichment as needed in the areas of vocabulary, comprehension, and rate of comprehension. After evaluating the progress of the language arts improvement project, the university established a reading center that serves a twofold purpose: to help students acquire skill for independent learning of all the materials required in their subjects; and to employ the efforts of teachers in various academic disciplines to show the learners what is required of them and to do it in such a way that they develop an understanding of the process as well as the content to the extent of their capabilities. The first step in the program is to assess the weaknesses of the students in the areas of vocabulary skills, comprehension, and speed of comprehension. Students functioning at tenth-grade reading level or below will be required to enroll in reading courses in the center for academic credit. The instructional materials for these courses will be designed for use in both individual and group instruction to improve the students' overall reading abilities.

Media center. To reinforce the efforts of the writing clinic and the reading center and to help all the departments develop personalized learning experiences for their students, the university will establish a modern instructional media center. It will have equipment for use in a short-term audiovisual lending library for faculty and students of the university. The media center will train students and faculty in the use of a technical videotape recording service for instructional use. In addition, the center will provide the faculty with professional and technical resources to design and produce instructional materials.

It is our hope that the media center will be the "man for all seasons" in the academic life of Tennessee State University. It will house practice instructional material, programmed instruction on all academic courses offered, and material that allows even the best student to be challenged.

The materials will be tailored to the learning style of the individual student.

Social science laboratory. For the last three years freshmen entering Tennessee State University have consistently scored lower in social studies than in any of the other major components of the ACT. An analysis of the data suggests that our students have not developed the conceptual and analytical skills to function at the expected college levels. Our approach to resolving this deficiency was to develop a social science laboratory. The social science laboratory will be equipped with an instructional computer, various types of simulated societal games (economic, political, educational, social, and civic), and other instructional materials used in the social sciences and related areas. The social science laboratory will afford students and teachers, through role playing and interaction with the computer, a classroom situation in which they can replicate on a small scale the function of various aspects of society. The specific purposes of the social science laboratory are to improve the overall quality of instruction at all levels; to develop new and modified courses in the social sciences and related areas; to develop new teaching strategies in the areas of social sciences, communication, and psychology, using the computer and simulated societal games; to involve students and faculty in the social sciences and social research; and to facilitate intrainstitutional cooperation consistent with the objectives of courses, departmental programs, and resources of the center. In brief, the social science laboratory will enhance, enrich, and facilitate the development of the interdisciplinary career program at the university.

Interdisciplinary activities. In addition to the above support programs, the university has planned a series of curriculum efforts to enhance, enrich, and facilitate learning from an interdisciplinary perspective.

We are aware that disciplines themselves represent arbitrary but convenient divisions in the totality of knowledge. Many of the pressing problems in higher education are interdisciplinary in nature and require interdisciplinary solutions. The interdisciplinary thrust of Tennessee State University is in general career-oriented. The programs draw on faculty skills, student needs, and the facilities and collective activities of the following departments: communication, psychology and guidance, sociology, and government and public affairs. Specific interdisciplinary programs offered are in mass communication, mental health, and social science.

Experiential learning center. The university is also investigating the effectiveness of nontraditional learning or learning outside the traditional classroom setting. Although the traditional approach to higher education has contributed greatly to the socialization of millions of American young people, this approach functions best when the students are concerned with status quo life-styles. For the students who seek more creative and innovative academic experiences and who are concerned about helping to solve the problems of the community and society, the traditional approach to learning may become frustrating and alienating.

To provide an opportunity for these students to serve the community and to learn without attending the classroom, the university initiated a University Year for Action program in 1973. Students earn academic credits by carrying out projects and library assignments. A maximum of thirty-six credit-hours can be earned by participating in the program for twelve months. Students participating in the program work full time in nonprofit agencies. They become additional human resources with some expertise after training to assist agencies in attaining their goals and objectives. Our students work in the metropolitan public school system helping counsel high school and junior high school students on drug education and careers and occupations. They work in juvenile delinquent centers and with the outreach geriatric programs.

Programs and experiences of this sort allow our students to apply some of their academic experiences and theories to real work situations. These experiences, more than academic courses, afford socially concerned students the opportunity to participate in meaningful experiences that sharpen their sense of the real world and its relationship to academics. Our analysis and evaluation of the program indicate that the concerned, committed, and socially mature students perform quite well outside the classroom regardless of grade-point average. In fact, students with low grade-point averages had increased their grade-point average at the closing of their participation in the program. The good and excellent (in grade-point average) students either maintained or slightly increased their grade-point averages. In light of these benefits to students and the community, the university will institutionalize the program with some modification in an experiential learning center.

Every institution of higher education strives to produce students who can compete effectively with other college graduates in the job market and on the job. We strive to turn out a productive student who has a clear perception of the world, is in charge of his destiny, and understands his ability to interact with his environment. We strive to produce students who have integrity, are responsible, have taste and objectivity, and relate to the human struggles of our society.

By the above-described curriculum departures, we believe that we are beginning to develop at Tennessee State University an effective education for the underprepared student. From our experience, the task is not simple. As in all change, roles of faculty become redefined, organizational structures are modified, revised, or abolished, and new champions appear. And on each campus engrossed in breaking new ground, a certain degree of turmoil, insecurity, and frustration develops. But the price is fair if we can make the dream of every institution of higher education a reality for the underprepared students.

Outward Forms of Inward Values

MYRON J. LUNINE

PLANNING NEW DEPARTURES in curricula necessarily involves planning changes in organizational structure and institutional priorities. Moreover, if new departures in curricula are to be more than short-range exercises in faddishness, the values of the academic professions and guilds—and indeed the nature and performance of precollege schooling and of graduate and professional curricula and institutions—are also at stake.

Despite tumultuous changes during the past two decades, virtually all institutions of higher education have managed to maintain the basic compartmentalization of academic courses and programs and dichotomy between academic and nonacademic affairs. They have preserved the separate identities of the students' curricular and experiential lives.

The history and the present condition of programs that would integrate the disciplines and the various segments and services of the institution—at the same time facilitating the growth of literate, resourceful people—present a picture of piecemeal, hasty efforts at curricular changes. These attempts have neither sustained themselves nor reflected credit on the institutions that began them. Such programs as honors programs, interdisciplinary studies programs, Third World studies programs, urban studies programs, human development programs, peaceful change programs, and women's studies programs have found themselves, at best, symbols of rather than mechanisms for innovation and integration and, at worst, controversial, undersupported programs artificially attached to the main body of curriculum and of more symbolic than real value.

Educators must attempt to understand the problems, purposes, and possibilities of higher education in the context of our national and international life. Students in our colleges and universities are neither studying and learning the necessary matters nor acquiring the necessary skills and competencies for a humane and effective life. Nor are the institutions generally providing the environment that will enable us to possess and practice skills in addition to the cognitive and analytical skills—skills such as creativity, imagination, empathy, moral commitment, and ethical action.

The substance, the style, and in many cases the spirit of higher education are inappropriate to the needs of students and society. Programs that have tried to deal with the real relationship of facts to ideas to values, with the interdisciplinary interpretation of issues, and with the appropriate preparation of liberally educated humans simply cannot do the work intended even for their own participants. Colleges and universities will not have appropriate curricula and learning environments without curricular, organizational, and institutional change.

What is needed, then, is nothing less than a hard look at the appropriateness of our present institutional and curricular arrangements not only to our legacy of knowledge, values, and commitments, but also to the complexity of social reality.

A discouraging note in this scrutiny is the alacrity with which our educational institutions are returning to what many believe to be the proper job of colleges and universities. For a time, especially in the late 1960s and early 1970s, there was a necessary, fertile reformation. That reformation took place in a time of stress. Nevertheless, the yearnings and demands were legitimate: that colleges and universities practice what they teach about the dignity of the individual, the efficacy of reason, the dependency on due process and equal rights, the necessity of beauty and creativity, and the ethical and organic relationship of education to the wider arenas of human and institutional struggle and reality. These groups also demanded that our curricula enable students and teachers to understand the great problems of our age as well as the traditional academic subjects. These were appropriate demands that gave rise to errors of varying degrees of seriousness and continuity.

Has the counterreformation ended?

The counterreformation of the last six years has been bolstered by legislative and executive niggardliness and/or punitiveness, intensified and perhaps exploited by stagnation, inflation, and a tragic paucity of positions for our best educated people. The reaction has been fueled by the understandable but wrong-headed anxiety of those who would educate or train people for their first jobs only. This counterreformation is resulting in dangerous trends toward ideological conformity, pedagogical orthodoxy, and institutional homogeneity.

As educators, we must examine students' current interests and mood. We must scrutinize the institutions themselves to determine whether the pendulum has moved them back from innovation to rigor verging on rigidity and to legitimacy verging on docility. We must determine whether the post-Kent State and Jackson State impulses for liberalization and humanization have subsided and perhaps even ceased. We must continue to ask whether we can educate people capable of responding creatively to an age of profound change and proliferation of ideas and events, whether we can devise an educational style that will nurture the development of people who respect themselves and others and in whom there is a harmony of private beliefs and public actions.

Colleges and universities have talked a lot about devising such programs. Many colleges and universities enable small, dependent programs to talk about such desiderata. Sometimes they even allow some students and faculty to engage in valid and humanizing educational activities. But these programs serve too few on too shaky a basis. If they are legitimate and necessary, as they frequently are, they should be made available to everyone. At the least, what they involve should be made available to everyone. Liberal arts students should be exploring and mastering a revivified and transformed liberal arts program. Students in other programs and, indeed, institutions should be enabled to benefit from general education programs that focus serious attention on problems and issues, both current and historical.

The experience of the author in developing such programs may shed some light on the possibilities for curricular change. At a National Collegiate Honors Council meeting in 1968 I urged honors directors to transform honors programs into syntheses of what is good in conventional education and what is necessary in relevant education. I proposed that they devise programs that transcend rigid departmental and cultural boundaries and deal intellectually and experientially with the dynamic processes of ubiquitous change. Such transformed honors programs would serve well both students and instructors—especially, if they dealt with a core curriculum of four sequential, problem-oriented, interdisciplinary colloquia: The United States: Race, Poverty, and the Pursuit of Happiness; The Underdeveloped Nations: Population, Growth, and Prospects for Peace; The New Civilization: Automation, Urbanization, and the Individual; Education: Problems and Possibilities for the Age of Relevancy. In this age of the multiversity (and this condition is not necessarily a function of size), with its various and conflicting communities, its specialization of knowledge, and its disconnection of personal beliefs and public acts, the general honors program should be to the university what the university should be to the society—a chief locus and source of conscience, criticism, creativity, and constructiveness.

Making honors programs humane

Thus, I urged others to do as many were doing across the country and as we were trying to do at Fisk University: namely, to make honors programs relevant and to make them models and instruments for increasing consciousness of and consensus on the need to embrace certain values. These values would be reinforced by perpetuation of the traditional commitment to excellence; innovation in the content and focus of courses and programs; experimentation with techniques of teaching and learning and with the roles and the relationships among students, faculty, and administrators; relaxation of rules, requirements, and locksteps; creation of a learning community enhanced and enabled by communication and shared commitments.

I know from my experiences at Kent State University that honors and experimental programs in colleges within universities have provided humane environments and serious means for student and faculty—and for curricular and programmatic—development.

Kent State opened in the fall of 1970 with innovations that would make it a more humane educational institution. Foremost among these innovations was the experimental wing of what is now the Honors and Experimental College. Twelve hundred members of the faculty were invited to participate in the experimental division. The letter of invitation outlined the philosophical underpinnings of the experimental program:

> The Experimental Program is based on several notions: 1. Academic excellence and personal and societal relevance are not incompatible. 2. What many of our students and faculty want now more than ever in the University in particular and in society in general are the following values and goals—*Authenticity* of the ends and especially of the means of the educational experience, of the roles all of the participants are playing, and of the relationships of all the participants; *Personal Participation* in the dialogue and the deliberation for the sake of defining not only the game and its rules but especially one's self in relation to the game; *Involvement* of the individual with the life of the University and of that University with the life of the society so that one's education and life will be relevant intellectually, and practically, personally, and socially. 3. Experimentation and innovation are necessities in the educational process of a University in particular and of a democratic society in general.

Kent State opened that year with eighty sections involving one thousand students in five "clusters of concerns," the core curriculum of the new program. The clusters should sound familiar: war and peace; racism and poverty; natural and social ecologies; education for the seventies; individualism, dissent, and communication.

Now the time has come for such programs and colleges within universities to stop carrying the burden of truth and the redemptive role associated with and required of such piecemeal, dependent programs superimposed on the regular curriculum. If there has been any usefulness in the hundreds of programs over the past decades that have been, generally speaking, interdisciplinary, holistic, and relevant, they should have had and should now have serious support. If they are indeed legitimate, they should not be limited to the comparatively small numbers of participants in them. In other words, if some students can learn most advantageously in certain kinds of learning environments, if certain groups of people do well to understand the relationships and commonalities of subject matters and of questions of value and fact and meaning and purpose, if some students consider it essential to acquire more than a superficial understanding of the extraordinary changes in national and international life, then somehow all students should be able to experience at least some of this educational program and way of life.

In 1974, Miami University acquired the erstwhile private liberal arts college, the Western College for Women/the Western College, a liberal arts college begun in the 1850s by women from Mount Holyoke College. Miami decided to create a sixth undergraduate academic division that would be a residential college of interdisciplinary studies leading to a Miami bachelor of philosophy in interdisciplinary studies. The new institution has become a human-scale, residential college within a major public university. It has a lower-division curriculum of interdisciplinary liberal arts core courses and individualized majors within interdisciplinary boundaries, and is supported by the other academic divisions and systems of the host university.

The basic program involves freshmen and sophomores in three interdisciplinary core courses in the areas of the social and behavioral sciences, the humanities and arts, and the natural sciences and history and philosophy of science. Emphasis in the new college is on equipping the students with a working understanding of the perspectives, conceptual approaches, techniques of analysis, methodological tools, and in short, modes of inquiry appropriate to each of these clusters of subjects and activities. During the first two years students take approximately 25 percent of their work in electives in other parts of the university where their interests and needs can be served. In the junior year students involve themselves in two semester-long methodological seminars that deal especially with interdisciplinary studies in each of three programmatic areas (arts, humanities, and culture; behavior, institutions, and social change; science, technology, and the environment). The program culminates in a year-long senior project and workshop. The seminars and senior project constitute about 25 percent of the student's upper-division work. Courses in other parts of the university at the upper-division level, which constitute 75 percent of his or her work, make up the student's individualized major and related free electives.

While we at the Western College of Miami University are engaged in many of the traditional tasks of a good liberal arts college, we are also committed to the notion that a college is an evolving human institution, whose activities must do more than respond to its societal circumstances. Part of the curriculum is therefore quite honestly and openly problem-oriented, is futuristic, is focused on communities larger than the academic. We intend to provide a good kind of education with respect to both the conventional academic values and the more humane values of individual development, social awareness, and, quite possibly, institutional and social change. In our more optimistic moments we hope to serve as a model and even as a catalyst for change within Miami and quite possibly beyond Miami in higher education.

Despite the fact that we have made academic and educational progress during these first two years, we have developed a quite respectable and ever improving lower-division core curriculum and have entered the upper-division plateau with sixty juniors pursuing individualized majors. We have enjoyed a civil, creative, and quite convivial educational and educating way of life within the residential college and have had some effect—not always felicitous or popular—on the university as a whole. But we are not of course without our difficulties and complexities.

Higher education and society

Whatever the particular nature of the program, the perils and fragilities of innovative, integrative efforts raise questions about the ability of higher education to come to terms with the needs and desires of students, about the nature of sensible curricular and programmatic arrangements, and about the actual relationship of collegiate education to the world at large.

Educational validity and feasibility. Is this approach to undergraduate education educationally sound, and will it work? Are interdisciplinary liberal arts core courses with thematic and frequently problematic foci a good and proper way to provide a general educational base and orientation for human beings at this time? Moreover, are the structure and the process that have been devised for individualized programs of an interdisciplinary character sensible of the educational needs of students and are they realizable within the university as a whole?

The budgetary situation. Can an incremental growth unit be sustained and developed by a university that is moving toward a static condition if not actually retrenching?

Philosophical-cultural-behavioral tensions. There are stylistic differences in pedagogy, community life, interpersonal relations, and (in the short run at least) individual and group self-perceptions between the Western College of Miami and the rest of the university generally. The question of the levels and limits of a university's toleration of diversity might very well be tested by the growth of a college that was intended to be an alternative undergraduate division within, but obviously not identical with, the university as a whole.

If the Western College of Miami experiment is successful—and I believe its chances are about fifty-fifty—is it reasonable to propose such a model for more general implementation?

Is this a plaintive echo of the 1960s—that we have a coherence of experience in a holistic educational environment; that we have a core curriculum which provides revivified and transformed liberal arts education that is both elegant and aristocratic, problematic and inclusive; that we have an ever-improving style of teaching and learning which not only develops cognitive and analytical skills but also leads to the development of creative, active humans; that we have on our campuses and extending from our campuses a spirit of inquiry, criticism, creativity, and a sense of joy and adventure; that we graduate literate, responsible generalists with specialized skills and with especially the continuing and growing capacity to learn; and that these persons all will have learned about the realities that they will either comprehend and control or be overwhelmed and controlled by?

It is wrong for successive generations of college and university graduates to leave with degrees and without an understanding of the basic realities and problems of war, poverty, racism, pollution, and the difficulty and complexity of nonviolent change. It is wrong for students not to have developed a sense of themselves. It is wrong, it is tragic, it is dangerous—and yet it continues. We are graduating successive generations that do not understand, either intellectually or emotionally, the social, political, and ecological realities of the times in which they live. Their majors, their intended careers are irrelevant to the urgency of reforming our educational institutions to provide core curricula that fuse liberal arts values and traits with problematic and futuristic foci.

I believe that holistic, interdisciplinary education will be increasingly desired and practiced. I believe that eventually people will demand to learn what they must know—namely, information and its connections to process, and facts and their connections to issues and values. I think this way because of the increasingly threatening and demanding nature of the society we live in and because broad-gauged, lifelong learners will not only be more civilized and cultivated but also will have more "marketable skills." In short, I believe that the future lies with and depends on educated, whole human beings—educated to be human first, civil and civic second, and specialized third. I also believe that in the short run the kind of curriculum (institution) I am proposing will continue to have very tough going.

I have been arguing that the proper education of human beings is not occurring because the curricula are two-dimensional and delimited, are imbedded in vested interests, are captive within intentionally disintegrated and sometimes disorganized large institutions, and are not creating persons with the necessary and appropriate values and skills. To accomplish this we need radical curricular change. To have radical curricular change we need radical reorganization of our colleges and universities with respect to their departmental and divisional composition. To have this kind of radical reorganization, we need a transformation of definitions and values about what constitutes professionalism, professional identity, and professional mobility. To have this kind of radical transformation we need leadership and acts of faith and courage at every level of education from the elementary schools through the graduate and professional schools.

To provide the curriculum, the environment, the operative value system, and all the institutional arrangements—and not just within private liberal arts colleges but within the educational experience of every student in any kind of college or university—clearly what is required is more than new departures in the curriculum, for curriculum is merely the outward form of inward values.

Curricula to Develop
Conscience and Consciousness

COLETTE MAHONEY, R.S.H.M.

MARYMOUNT MANHATTAN COLLEGE is a small, independent, urban, liberal arts college for women. Existing as it does at the confluence of three major problem/opportunity areas of our society—namely, the future of independent education, the role of women, and the fate of the cities—the experiences of this one college may reflect more than a few common concerns.

The context in which new departures in curricula are being undertaken is a society that is struggling to make its peace with the constancy of change. The American fascination with nostalgia is wearing thin. The new romanticism of the 1960s, which idealized a simple return to the land and the methods and expectations of the past, is being replaced by a tempered optimism about the prospects of a technological society. Futurist Herman Kahn and economist Robert Heilbroner, neither of whom is a naïve proponent of blind confidence in the future, suggest a common theme in recent works. Whatever the solutions to our society's problems, they are not to be found in the past.[1]

The rapid social, political, and religious upheaval of the last two decades has shaken the traditional views on life and threatened the value system held by many. This questioning, together with the increased body of knowledge in all disciplines due to better and more rapid modes of communication, provides students today with a wealth of knowledge, opinions, ideologies, etc. To choose wisely in a way that will enable them to be more humane, free, and of service to others will be a difficult task. It certainly will be the mission of those who provide a liberal arts education to address themselves to this task.

The very term "departures" in curricula presumes that developments for the future involve some specific breaks with the past. The predictabilities of simpler times must be left behind by curriculum planners who hope to prepare leaders of today's and tomorrow's more complex societies. Teaching of the trivium and the quadrivium may have solved the curriculum problems of a highly structured society, but similar attempts to formularize education would be both false and futile for twentieth-century educators. That is not to say, of course, that the new curricula should not be structured along classical lines. The liberal arts, understood in the literal sense of intellectual skills that ensure freedom from the inability to communicate and to function in civilized society, are an indispensable component in the curriculum planning I will describe. It is wise to remember though that today's student, under the pressures of expanding education costs and a shrinking job market, cannot be expected to come to our institutions equipped with the attitude of leisure and a predisposition to recognize the value of the liberal arts. The role of educators is precisely to present the liberal arts component of the curriculum as a value. We must not fail to learn from our brothers and sisters in the business community that every product, no matter what its inherent quality, must be marketed.

1. Heilbroner, *Business Civilization in Decline* (New York: W. W. Norton, 1976); Kahn, *The Next 200 Years* (New York: William Morrow, 1976).

Developing varied skills

One way in which we at Marymount Manhattan College have tried to market the liberal arts is by deemphasizing the dichotomy between them and the programs that our work-oriented, urban students immediately recognize as practical. The liberal arts requirements run concurrently with electives throughout the entire period of study. Everything in the students' environment demonstrates that diversity is the rule of the day. They feel they must develop numerous, very specific and highly practical skills. Without denying them the opportunity to do so, the curriculum should be composed so that these practical skills have behind them a constant counterpoint of general, humanizing disciplines. Diversification is a fact of contemporary life; developing a skill for synthesis is the accomplishment. Students do not need to be taught that their culture is fragmented; they do need to be taught how to cope with the multiplicity of experience and how to understand it as a coherent whole.

New models for curricula must depart equally from solutions based on the expectation of ever-increasing financial resources. Educators who could, in more affluent times, depend on broadening offerings by hiring new faculty must learn instead to identify and develop their institution's internal potential. The more steady-state faculty of the 1970s brings with it the challenge of stimulating professional growth and the credentialing of academic competence in newer and more imaginative ways. The motivating force must come more and more from within the campus community.

Two of the ways in which Marymount Manhattan attempts to deal with the new economics of education in developing its curriculum are by using part-time faculty and by developing cooperative programs with neighboring institutions.

One of the distinct advantages of our metropolitan setting is, of course, the availability of both scholars and working professionals in every conceivable field of study. But at least a limited number of such specialists are available in nearly every sector of the country, and it seems unwise not to consider enlisting them for the academic venture. No one has ever suggested that the quality of an instructor is enhanced by exclusive affiliation with one college or university. In fact it is difficult to find documentation anywhere in the literature of higher education of the value of using exclusively full-time faculty. The use of part-time faculty and cooperative programs certainly does not diminish the importance of a strong cadre of full-time faculty and a comprehensive program of study. On the contrary, it enhances both by freeing them from the demands of excessive diversity. As educators we may have reason to be grateful for the pressures of an inflationary economy if they serve to move us beyond the competition that pits college against college at the expense of the common task of education. Economic stringency is the fact; avoiding the bankruptcy of imagination is the accomplishment.

Those who favor job training at the expense of liberal arts values would substitute for an educational product of lasting value one of planned obsolescence. It has been wisely observed that our failure to solve such problems as world hunger is accounted for more by the failure to educate for problem recognition than by a failure to educate in the uses of specific technology. The only way that technology can be made an ally in improving the quality of life is by educating beyond and around existing technology and so equipping students for its human uses.[2]

To exert a counterpressure to narrow vocationalism, we are committed at Marymount Manhattan to maintaining a full-time faculty of primarily liberal arts specialists. Another step in the same direction is the use of what we call special interest sequences within the classical program of academic concentration. While pursuing a liberal arts degree in sociology, for example, the student can build into her program a clearly job-related series of courses (an average eighteen credits) in an area such as alcoholism or gerontology. In addition, the curriculum is divided into general education requirements, concentration requirements, and open electives as a way of illustrating the college's dual commitment to liberal arts' values and preprofessional training. Student demand for sophisticated professionalism is the fact; achieving it without sacrificing broad cultural awareness is the accomplishment that identifies a successful educator.

Respect for student freedom of choice is not to be confused with abdicating responsibility for conveying structure in the academic program. The operative word here is conveying. An arbitrary structure, imposed on the course of studies for the sake of procedural convenience, is certainly undesirable. But it is equally undesirable to be so unstructured that the undergraduate is exposed to a raw and undigested mass of information. It is a common fallacy to assume that suggesting a structure for interpreting experience is identical with dictating that there can be no other effective structure. The student should be able to expect from faculty and administrators that they have dealt with fields of study in their full range of complexity, have digested what they have learned, and have become able to communicate it in some structured—that is simplified—ordered way. The structure of learning is never the absolute, but it is a framework that puts inspiration into an understandable shape so that it, and not the framework, can be internalized.

2. Martin Mayer, *Today and Tomorrow in America* (New York: Harper & Row, 1975).

In the past decade at Marymount Manhattan we have moved from a strictly structured curriculum through an open curriculum to a system of advisement that requires a student—before being permitted to enter a specific course—to consult with an advisor aware of the student's program and goals. Pressure for specialization is the fact; sensitized and expanded consciousness is the accomplishment.

In a society that moves as quickly as ours, solutions based on already recognized problems are likely to be outmoded before they can be enacted. If education is going in any sense to fulfill its traditional mission of educating society's leaders, it must move definitively beyond the survival mentality and set its sights on curricula designed to facilitate the identification of tomorrow's problems. Such an attitude shaped Marymount Manhattan's decision to exclude from its curriculum academic concentrations in strictly job-related fields. While it is clear, for example, that trained professionals are needed to undertake the education of the adult retardate, it has seemed to us more academically sound and more sensitive to equip students with the basic vocabulary of traditional disciplines. They can then be acquainted with the specific practical applications of their fields of concentration, by special course sequences, for example, that underscore the fact that within a single field of study one can be equipped to identify and respond to a potentially unlimited number of social and procedural problems.

The problems of the contemporary environment are the obvious and often inherited facts of the students' lives. The accomplishment of education is to equip those students to choose their own future.

Goals of departure

The expression "departures in curricula" suggests that breaks from the past are made for the sake of certain definite future goals.

The increasing involvement of the government in education through federal government titles, affirmative action programs, and the like must be recognized for what it is: an effort to increase the accessibility of higher education, leaving quite untouched the issue of the quality of education.

Conscience, and conscience alone, is the only proper stimulus and goal of the educational process. Legislation can never substitute for it, and educators must guard against being lulled by the slow grinding of legalistic procedures into the illusion that they are somehow excused from maintaining the inspiration that fires the educational mission.

The goal in curriculum development is to move far beyond law abiding into the area of enlightened responsibility. In the early 1960s, before many of the currently available sources for funding minority students could be tapped, Marymount Manhattan felt a responsibility to make its educational resources available to students who might not have access to the college without some additional, creative planning. A community leadership program was evolved to recruit and provide continuing moral and academic support for students who might not otherwise have qualified for entrance to institutions of higher education. Developmental skills were offered in addition to continuing tutorial and advisement services so that the student, once admitted, was not abandoned, and that the college, once its academic standards were set, would not be asked arbitrarily to waive them. As it happened, this impulse of conscience proved historically sound, and the community leadership program students presaged and prepared the college for broad changes in the student population, in the direction of nontraditional candidates. Courses in developmental skills such as reading, written communication, science, and mathematics are now a regular part of the curriculum. Conscience should, in short, lead the way in education, looking to legislation only to confirm what educators have recognized to be just and fitting. As the range of nontraditional students broadens, stimulated sensitivity in communication will become an increasingly important principle in curriculum planning.

Another objective of departures from traditional curricula is the increasing recognition that the only invariable in the liberal arts tradition is the student-teacher dialogue. Treating time, space, location, size, and the like as true variables will automatically increase the quality and the variety of courses. One of the ways this has been attempted in practice is through cooperative programs with institutions such as Mannes College of Music, the Kennedy Child Study Center, and the New York School of Interior Design, which permits students to pursue courses at these cooperating institutions. This sort of cooperation may seem an obvious direction for contemporary institutions, but its real difficulties test the motivation of those who undertake it. Complex legal issues and subtle psychological questions of identity must be solved.

Under the direction of the division of continuing education, Marymount Manhattan courses are being offered on the premises of some major New York-based corporations and in extensions in various boroughs and neighborhoods. Courses are scheduled when students are able to attend, with the result that the college operates from early morning until late at night throughout the calendar year.

While these measures make good economic sense, we firmly believe that such efforts to go more than half way to meet the potential student are equally a demand of conscience and responsibility. A dramatic example of this principle is the Malcolm-King: Harlem College Extension.

This fully accredited extension initiated by Marymount Manhattan and cosponsored by Fordham University and the College of Mount Saint Vincent operates from several centers in the Harlem community and is designed to serve the educational needs of older black men and women largely forgotten by contemporary legislation. Now long past the experimental stage, Malcolm-King has shown that by going into the neighborhood a college can have a far more important leavening effect on a community than it ever could if college attendance became identified in the minds of the people with escaping from the neighborhood.

Education must demonstrate as well as give lip service to the movement from information to choice. This is shown in the curriculum by courses built around creative syntheses of scientific-ethical subject matters. Provision must be made for opening the classroom to the discussion of such issues as the conflict between technology and humanism highlighted by recently publicized debates on the so-called right to die.

In addition to broadening the content of curricula, an attitude toward instruction should also be encouraged that could be called the content-plus-conviction approach. By this I mean the readiness the instructor demonstrates to speak of the personal synthesis he or she has made of scientific facts and freely chosen principles of conduct or operation. Indoctrination need hardly be cautioned against, because it is as out of fashion as it is undesirable. But perhaps some caution should be expressed against teachers forcing themselves within the artificial limits of an impersonal teaching machine. The student is not being asked unquestioningly to adopt the instructor's syntheses, but merely to observe that the progression in humanistic education is from fact to judgment to action. In short the desired effect is to convey that there are consequences to learning. In an era of antiheroes, a revival of the Mr. (and indeed Ms.) Chips figure could surely be refreshing. If the content of education does not include inspiration as well as information, then much has been lost.

Problem-approach courses are of considerably more importance than giving a relevant look to the curriculum. They represent an effort to simulate the complexity of the culture in the classroom. At Marymount Manhattan, that effort stretches from the design of individual courses to the entire parallel structure by which the liberal arts and preprofessional studies are combined at every point of the degree program. One well-justified critic of memory-test examinations objected to them because they suggested that the postgraduation life of the student was to be spent without books.[3] A similar criticism could equally be leveled against teaching that suggests that the formation of attitudes is somehow unrelated to

3. Ross Wetzsteon, "The Education Hustle: If U Cn Rd Th Artcl, U Cn Gt a Gd Jb," *Village Voice*, Special Supplement, August 23, 1976, p. 56.

the learning process. The education of attitudes and the development of an interdisciplinary view of issues are intrinsic parts of the Marymount Manhattan curriculum, as demonstrated by the fact that the current curriculum is structured around sixty-five programs of study within five divisions, whereas the curriculum was formerly built around seventeen rather narrowly defined academic majors.

Although much is being made in the media about the arrogance of power, educators might better be on the alert to combat the arrogance of powerlessness in all segments of the academic community. To the degree that the admissions policy and the curriculum open a college to an increasingly diversified student body, they become the tools of increasing the individual student's sensitivity to his or her cultural context. To the degree that the administration opens the way to faculty involvement in the shaping of the curriculum, it becomes the tool of increasing the individual faculty member's sense of involvement in the future and the fate of the college. The current curriculum at Marymount Manhattan is the product of an intensive four- to five-year creative effort on the part of the faculty under the direction of the academic dean, and were it not, it would be hard to imagine how it could be effectively implemented.

It is often those who lack power who most lack responsibility. Without the opportunity to exercise responsibility, faculty, students, and, yes, even administrators can lose sight of the fact that power has both a positive and a negative side—power to create morale or to destroy it; to promote change or to resist it; to develop enthusiasm or to kill it. The shared power of the college must be put at the service of creating a climate for learning. Nothing can more effectively short-circuit that venture than the arbitrary or negative use of power.

In the scheme of the new curricula, a college is no longer definable by an analysis of its student population statistics and a sentence in its charter. The true principles for defining the college and its curriculum are the thrust and the intention that supply its dynamic motivating force. In practice that means that a women's college can be of equal service to its male students without losing its identity as a women's college. It means too that a liberal arts college can offer a program such as Marymount Manhattan's preprofessional training for women in management without removing the student from the liberal arts context. Management, like all human skills, is demonstrated to be a partially specialized function of the effective human being. Courses are designed to illustrate that all the components for successful functioning as a business executive are contained within the liberal arts tradition. The talent for intuitive thinking developed in a study of Romantic poetry, for example, is experienced as equally important in the forming of an effective executive as the accounting skills necessary to measure cost-effectiveness.

In summary it is important to note that it is not enough for curricula to look different, still less to look merely stylishly relevant. Unless a curriculum develops from a living and dynamic core of convictions—a heart—it runs the risk of being a more than slightly embarrassing monstrosity, like some examples of modern architecture that stand witness to their builder's lack of a point of view.

Rigidly traditional and strictly analytical education and the curricula that perpetuate them deserve to be supplanted. But what comes after them must stand the test of being founded on a sense of values. The new curricula—what is taught and how and to whom it is taught—must demonstrate the colleges' dedication to synthesis, to choice, to conscience, and to consciousness.

New Quality Ratings:
A Force for Reform

DAVID W. BRENEMAN

DURING THE 1960s, the American Council on Education sponsored two assessments, or ratings, of graduate program quality, the Cartter and Roose-Andersen reports, which are both well known.[1] In the preface to the second report the authors wrote:

> In light of the serious problems facing higher education today and the necessity to reexamine priorities, it seems unwise for the Council to make a commitment to use its resources for regular updatings of the ratings. If there is an ongoing purpose to be served by such ratings, the Council urges discipline areas or perhaps the Council of Graduate Schools in the United States to repeat the survey as necessary. The American Council on Education stands ready, if requested, to provide counsel and guidance in such studies.[2]

The American Council accepted this suggestion and does not plan to sponsor another round of ratings. The Council of Graduate Schools (CGS) devoted a plenary session of its 1971 annual meeting to discussion of whether the Council should publish a third in the series of ratings; it rejected the idea. Instead the CGS, in conjunction with the Graduate Record Examinations Board (GREB), initiated a project titled "Dimensions of Quality in Doctoral Programs," an investigation of some thirty program characteristics that had been judged important to quality. A grant from the Fund for the Improvement of Postsecondary Education will allow CGS to present the results of the study at several regional conferences.

In spite of this activity, interest remains strong in several quarters in having the ratings redone (with whatever methodological improve-

1. Allan M. Cartter, *An Assessment of Quality in Graduate Education* (Washington: American Council on Education, 1966); and Kenneth D. Roose and Charles J. Andersen, *A Rating of Graduate Programs* (Washington: American Council on Education, 1970).

2. Roose and Andersen, *A Rating of Graduate Programs,* p. xi.

ments seem warranted) and the results published. The Conference Board of Associated Research Councils (composed of American Council of Learned Societies, American Council on Education, National Academy of Sciences, and Social Science Research Council) agreed to sponsor a planning conference to investigate the issues involved in redoing the ratings. The conference was held September 1976 at Woods Hole, Massachusetts.

Why redo the ratings?

There are several reasons to prepare a new assessment of graduate program quality. First, the most recent ratings, by Roose and Andersen, are based on a survey conducted in the spring of 1969 and thus are out of date. Second, the universe of graduate programs eligible for inclusion in such a study has grown considerably since 1969, and these unrated departments should be evaluated and added to the information base available to potential graduate students and other users. Third, in addition to the informational uses of the ratings for various decisionmakers (including students), the ratings, if current, have considerable value to researchers and policy analysts concerned with graduate education.

These considerations are commonly advanced to support an update of the 1969 survey, but I wish to focus on a fourth rationale—the effect (for good or evil) that a new round of ratings could have on the subsequent development of graduate education in the United States. It need hardly be stressed that the economic circumstances of graduate education have deteriorated dramatically since the last quality survey, and forecasts for the 1980s and early 1990s point toward a further deterioration of conditions.[3] Although an average of 27,000 junior faculty members were hired per year between 1962 and 1972, such hiring is projected to fall to an average of not more than 16,000 annually between 1972 and 1982 and to not more than 10,000 annually between 1982 and 1992.[4] In recent years, our graduate schools have awarded approximately 33,000 Ph.D.'s annually, and some projections are that the figure will increase to more than 40,000 annually in the late 1970s and early 1980s. Although only half of the people with new doctorates in the 1960s took teaching jobs after graduation, the percentage able to secure such employment in the next ten to fifteen years will be sharply reduced, and in fields such as the humanities that have traditionally placed 85–90 percent of new graduates in college teaching, the prospect is particularly grim.

3. National Board on Graduate Education, *Outlook and Opportunities for Graduate Education* (Washington: National Academy of Sciences, 1975); and Allan M. Cartter, *PhD's and the Academic Labor Market* (New York: McGraw-Hill, 1976).

4. Allan M. Cartter and Lewis C. Solmon, "Implications for Faculty," *Change,* September 1976, p. 38.

Faced with this pronounced and extended decline in the academic market, policy recommendations have tended in one of two directions. Some have argued that substantial excess capacity exists in graduate schools, that the leading twenty-five to fifty universities could easily produce all the new Ph.D.'s needed, and that lesser programs should be closed down. This line of argument is often accompanied by a recommendation that the federal government take the lead in identifying "National Universities" and then concentrate all federal support for research and graduate education in these institutions. Note that this approach implicitly accepts a single standard or model for doctoral education, with the Ph.D. viewed exclusively as education in and for research. Both the Cartter and Roose-Andersen surveys were based on this view of doctoral education.

The alternative approach has been to urge much greater diversification among graduate programs in their purposes and the clienteles they served.[5] Advocates of this approach do not disparage the value and continued importance of traditional Ph.D. programs, particularly in departments of established research excellence; but they argue that such programs do not meet other equally important and legitimate needs, such as the training of practitioners for nonacademic careers or the education of teachers for the unique needs of community colleges. The research effort sponsored by the Council of Graduate Schools and the Graduate Record Examinations Board grew out of a perceived need for multiple indicators of quality to correspond to diverse program purposes. It is not surprising, therefore, to read in the CGS-GREB report:

> We were not prepared for the consistently strong and pervasive influence of the research and scholarship model at the doctoral level, and the correspondingly light emphasis given to preparing teachers and practitioners. Though the idea of fitting assessment indicators to the purposes of doctoral programs sounds reasonable in theory, in practice its impact is muted by the simple fact that the overwhelming majority of doctoral programs in the country appear to identify the preparation of researchers and/or scholars as their primary goal. This was certainly true for the graduate departments in our study, even though we intentionally included a number of programs in our sample which were not among the elite in their respective fields.[6]

5. The Panel on Alternate Approaches to Graduate Education endorsed this approach with sweeping rhetorical flourish in its report, *Scholarship for Society* (Princeton, N.J.: Educational Testing Service, 1973), as did the National Board on Graduate Education in *Outlook and Opportunities for Graduate Education*.

6. Mary Jo Clark, Rodney T. Hartnett, and Leonard L. Baird, *Assessing Dimensions of Quality in Doctoral Education* (Princeton, N.J.: Educational Testing Service, 1976), pp. 11.7–11.8.

The CGS-GREB findings confirm the experience of other observers that new models for doctoral programs have not yet jelled. The new quality assessment provides an opportunity, however, to identify and help establish new approaches to graduate education.

Assessing new doctoral models

An essential issue to consider is what stance a new assessment of graduate program quality should take on these alternative directions for development of graduate education. I say this because the assessment, if done, will exert a considerable influence on the direction taken. If the new survey is conducted as the last two have been (even if the methodology is modified by introducing objective correlates of research quality such as publications, citations, and research grants), the message driven home will be that doctoral education serves the singular purpose of educating people in the tools and techniques of scholarship and research, and that all doctoral programs should be rigorously evaluated in those terms. As soon as the word goes out that a new quality rating will be done along lines similar to Cartter and Roose-Andersen, those who are attempting to modify or alter graduate programs to serve new purposes will be undermined, and pressures to emulate the Harvard-Berkeley model will be reinforced. The perfectly understandable fear is that a new set of ratings, published in 1978 or 1979, will be used by administrators and state agencies to eliminate low-rated programs[7] and will produce powerful incentives against experimentation.

Alternatively, if the new assessment were structured to recognize and support diversification among graduate programs, it could be a powerful force for change. The process of evaluation would become considerably more complex, for, within each discipline, several departmental clusterings might be developed, reflecting different program purposes. Departments might be classified by national as opposed to regional designations or be grouped by differences in research orientation or the employment market served. Criteria would likely differ by discipline, another reason for supporting the suggestion that five or six fields be evaluated each year as part of a continuing cycle of five to ten years. As the various categories and subdivisions within each field were developed, each department could specify the group in which it wished to be included and would be rated accordingly.

7. This observation causes one to wonder whether faculty evaluators (if that technique were used) would rate programs honestly. Just as grade inflation can be traced, in part, to the Vietnam era and the unwillingness to fail students while the draft prevailed, so might departmental evaluations be biased upward in a similarly threatening environment.

This approach to quality assessment holds the promise of eliciting a much more creative response from the graduate community than would another ranking of departments on a single dimension. A repetition of the Cartter and Roose-Andersen reports will do little more than prove that the University of Eastern West Virginia's English department has once again failed to match Yale's. Rather than doom Eastern West Virginia to a futile, frustrating, and wasteful attempt to increase its rating by goading its faculty to an ever larger volume of publication that nobody wants or values, the new procedure opens the prospect that E.W.V.'s English department might become one of the finest regional departments specializing in doctoral programs for current and prospective community college teachers—and be publicly recognized as such.

The key distinction between these two approaches lies in the incentives that are produced. Simple repetition of the previous surveys would, I believe, send out all the wrong signals to the majority of new and developing doctoral programs, encouraging them to strive for a type of excellence that they are not likely to attain and that the country does not need from them. (The twenty-five to seventy-five departments in each field that wish to be classified and evaluated as national research departments would, of course, be unaffected by the additional categories developed under the second procedure.) The second approach to quality assessment would be more complicated and not as neat and circumscribed methodologically, but it would have the great merit of helping to set new directions for large numbers of programs that were brought into existence by the excesses of the 1960s, and that are now stranded in an educational no-man's-land. The attempt to develop alternative models for doctoral education may be an abject failure, but the time is surely right to explore the potential for a redirection of effort. A new quality assessment, if done wisely and creatively, offers that opportunity.

Reassessing Graduate Education

LAURINE E. FITZGERALD

LEADERS in higher education should be more concerned with the challenges and the opportunities for graduate education, the necessity for collegiate institutions to reassess the nature of graduate programming and the process of curriculum development, and with the administration of graduate education. About a thousand years ago, when the Judgment Day was thought to be imminent, estates were ordered turned over to the ecclesiastical authorities *appropinquante mundi termino:* "the end of the world being now at hand." The end of the graduate world is not at hand, but there are clear indications that significant opportunity exists for innovation, reassessment, and reorganization.

The role of the graduate dean is one of the principal concerns of graduate education. College and university presidents and chancellors should assess the "charismatic" aspect of the role in terms of *authority* in the academic scheme versus the *responsibility* and increased significance of the role as anticipated in this and the coming decade of steady-state economic support, growth of graduate enrollments and programming, and the involvement of the graduate dean in academic administration.[1] If the dean has limited budget or limited authority in direct involvement with the curriculum and faculty, to what extent should (or can) he or she be held responsible for projecting graduate enrollments, increasing graduate enrollments, developing curricular programs to meet public needs and interests, innovating in program style or delivery of educational offerings? Each institution should consider a review of the roles for the graduate dean or director.

There is increasing concern about the nature and scope of graduate degree programs as they now exist within postsecondary collegiate institutions. We will not attempt here to analyze the issues of external degrees, "poolside" or "weekend" graduate seminars, the use of adjunct faculty located all across the country, or nontraditional thesis/dissertations. But the changing nature of the master's or first graduate degree is certainly a major problem for administrators of graduate programs, for accrediting agencies, and for graduate students. More than 330 special names of master's degrees are used by collegiate institutions within the United States. This number of nontraditional degrees does not include the broadly applied M.A., M.S., and the fairly wide range of generally accepted professional degrees, such as M.B.A., M.F.A., M.A.T., which may also be considered terminal degrees in some fields.

Renewed emphasis on the master's degree

The master's degree has a history that can be traced for nearly a thousand years. In medieval Europe, masters, or teachers, and their disciples often lived and studied together in scholarly communities. A bachelor's degree holder wanting to become a master was required to pass an appropriate examination to qualify as an *artium magister.* In early America, the degree of master was highly respected. It gradually fell in prestige

1. Oliver C. Carmichael, *Graduate Education: A Critique and a Program* (New York: Harper & Brothers, 1961).

until the latter half of the nineteenth century, when the degree *in cursu* was replaced by the degree *pro meritus.*[2] Earlier in this century, the degree lost much of its significance as a research and scholarly achievement for students. However, current societal factors and institutional responsiveness in the provision of innovative and specifically targeted programs strongly point to a resurgence of popularity of the master's degree and to the expansion of graduate study at the master's level.

In addition to degree proliferation, the expansion of scholarly and professional fields for graduate study has produced subspecialties requiring trained scholars to exploit their potential. So significant is this expansion that it has been estimated that an expansion rate of 2–3 percent per year would be needed merely to keep abreast of the expansion of knowledge while maintaining zero growth in graduate work.[3] Licensing and/or certification of many occupations and professions will require additional postbaccalaureate education. Persons seeking to sharpen skills and broaden knowledge will view the master's degree as the natural documentation for closing out their college or university student career, much as the undergraduate degree is perceived now.

Economic factors will enhance institutional support for master's programs since they are relatively inexpensive and frequently lend themselves to innovation. Interdisciplinary and flexible areas of emphasis, as a supplement to the basic graduate discipline, enable students to obtain degrees that reflect and meet needs for individuality.

Reforms in calendar and cooperative ventures

Innovation within the university framework may include reforms of the institutional calendar to provide restructuring of course timeframes. Innovation may also generate renewed interest in instructional methods. Both of these reforms would better meet the needs of "new" populations of graduate students. Flexible and modular core components, graduate instruction based on competency, and course formats that are specifically geared to each individual student are regenerating interest in graduate-level education. A few graduate degree programs allow credit for experimental life involvement/experience. Many degree programs no longer require "residency," and opportunities have been developed for full-time homemakers, the unemployed and/or underemployed, and full- and part-time employed adults to return to their education as part-time

2. W. S. Eells and H. A. Haswell, *Academic Degrees* (Washington: Government Printing Office, 1961), p. 25.

3. "Scholarship for Society: Report on Graduate Education," Commission of the Council of Graduate Schools of the United States (Princeton, N.J.: Educational Testing Service, 1974).

students. In these cases, the institutions retain their traditional concerns for quality educational involvement and cohesive curriculum, albeit in the nontraditional setting.

An interesting dimension of innovative programming for graduate education is the formation of consortial clusters of universities on a cooperative and/or regional basis, providing a program of graduate curricula from several institutions. Examples include the Committee on Interinstitutional Cooperation (CIC), which consists of the "Big Ten" institutions and the University of Chicago; statewide programs endorsed by several midwestern states; and the regional concept of graduate education, based on geographical clusterings of institutions *within* a state. Wisconsin endorsed the regional concept in 1972; two graduate regions have been identified and are now in the developmental stages. (Thus far, a new, jointly administered curriculum and degree are available, and two students have received regional M.A. degrees.) The goal of graduate education in this regional program is to foster cooperative instructional efforts among the institutions within identified geographical areas for greater numbers of graduate students in a broader area than could be served by a single participating institution. The graduate programs are perceived as a single expanded program of graduate education, with the duplication of curricular offerings and degrees eliminated or materially reduced. Further, the range of educational opportunities is expanded throughout the geographic area beyond that possible by a single participating university.

Focus on graduate curriculum in planning

Collegiate institutions of postsecondary education are increasingly involved in planning. All plans tend to include graduate programs and course offerings at the academic departmental or division level, and they frequently project new and advanced degrees or proliferation of "tracks" or emphasis areas. But coordination of the curricular projections tends to occur only at the college level. As a result, parallel, duplicative, and competing programs frequently coexist on the campus, housed in separate colleges of the university. (Examples may be competing programs within psychology, educational psychology or counselor education, and social work; prelaw emphases in history and political science.) In addition to overlaps in the degree program, duplication of courses and their content may develop in many more areas.

Thus, a review of the roles for graduate education by any concerned institution must include a centralized analysis of graduate curriculum, separate from but concurrent with any undergraduate planning process. An ambitious undertaking, to be sure, but it is a necessity if graduate education is to be responsive to emerging populations and the institution is to maintain its fiscal well-being. The focus of planning should be on the quality of available offerings, the evidence of sound curricular management by academic units, and the responsiveness to emerging trends in professional, general, and liberal educational practices.

Fitting graduate education to society's priorities will require that the institution focus, perhaps for the first time in many years, on the administration, planning for, and delivery of this important dimension of its educational program.

Graduate Education as Liberal Education

PATRICIA ALBJERG GRAHAM

WE IN THE ACADEMIC COMMUNITY view graduate education, in part, as liberal education. This suggestion has a heretical quality. I am not arguing that graduate education should be only liberal education; nor am I arguing that liberal education be only at the graduate level. Rather, I am arguing that a legitimate function of graduate education is liberal education, and that universities would do well to be explicit about that purpose. Further, I believe that such a conception would benefit the students, the faculty, the universities, and the society.

Heretofore, graduate education has been explicitly vocational. The assumption has been that the requisite liberal education has occurred previously, either at college or high school. The graduate schools constitute the only segment of the educational system that has prepared people strictly for jobs, the whitest of white collar jobs. This success has been most notable in the case of the professional schools, but even the rather amorphous Ph.D. programs have functioned efficiently until the recent job shortage.

Until relatively recently, the rhetoric of educators below the graduate level has not been job-oriented. The principal exception has been the rhetoric of proponents of vocational education, chiefly at the secondary level, for children of working-class families with low academic ability for whom a blue collar job seems appropriate.

Within the last few years, however, the educational establishment, in an effort to respond to the increased demand for salable skills among college graduates, has begun to speak of "career education," a concept which, we are told, is more than vocational education insofar as it prepares one not simply for a specific job but rather for a total career.

Career education occurs primarily at the undergraduate level (not at the high school level) and is directed toward white collar jobs, which are now much more numerous than they once were.

One impetus for the interest in career education is professional educators who recognize that a new college population is no longer growing but leveling off. Many of the students who make up this new college population come from families in which higher education has not been a tradition. For them, the educators believer, higher education must be defended in economic terms, since cultural ones seem inadequate to justify the expense of higher education today. The familiar rationale for a liberal arts education ("to be a gentleman") is both unacceptable and unattainable.

Broadening the base

Traditionally the notion of a liberal education has been linked to an elite, typically a social elite, although it is sometimes defined as an intellectual one. Often there was considerable similarity of membership between the social and intellectual elites. The student body that participated in higher education in this country until the 1920s (less than 10 percent of the age group) had a relatively homogeneous social and economic character and did not seek job-related skills as part of the bachelor's programs. Predictably, those higher educational institutions that were most accessible by their fee structure to a diverse social and economic student body—the state and municipally supported institutions—were the ones to move most rapidly away from an exclusively liberal arts program. They led in adopting a curriculum that included a variety of subjects, many of which were related to specific problems, which, if one mastered them, could lead to a job. I refer specifically to the state universities, which, in addition to their liberal arts departments (sometimes referred to as "service departments"), pioneered in offering courses and later majors in such technical subjects as agriculture, engineering, home economics, and, along with the normal schools and teachers colleges, elementary and secondary education. Subsequently even more specific majors—occupational therapy, radio-television communications, or special education—emerged from these institutions that catered to the children of noncollege parents.

The bastion of the liberal arts remained the expensive and often very selective private institutions, those epitomized by the Ivies and the Seven Sisters. Here the ideal of the liberal arts remained untarnished, but the proportion of undergraduates enrolled in such institutions dropped sharply as the overall percentage of the population aged eighteen to twenty-one attending college jumped from 12 percent in 1930 to 46 percent in 1970. Although many of these institutions significantly broadened the socioeconomic representation of their student bodies, they retained a higher proportion of sons and daughters of the wealthy (often their alumni) than did their publicly supported sister institutions.

To attract the "new" college student, frequently from a nonprofessional family, higher education today justifies itself by citing the economic return that will be realized in later life by the college graduate. This is particularly a device of the many institutions that are concerned about shrinking enrollments. The curriculum of the institution must therefore be tailored to provide the skills that will honor the claim. This accounts for the relative decline in majors in the pure liberal arts and the increase in the applied subjects, such as health professions, public affairs and services, and business and management. The forecasters estimate that these fields will continue to grow and the liberal arts to decline. At the same time requirements in what was once called general education have been significantly reduced.

Certainly these undergraduate curricular trends coincide with the claims of the career education enthusiasts. The recent popular criticism of the economic value of a college education has vigorously argued that unless one could demonstrate that college would lead to a better (meaning better paying) job than would be likely without college, then one should eschew the expensive undergraduate experience.

Such an argument was not the rationalization for college education in an earlier era. However much parents wanted their children to be associated with others of similar background during the turbulent years of late adolescence, they and the educators at least gave lip service to the notion that the content of a liberal education was inherently desirable.

An intriguing and interesting education

No one today would seriously maintain that a liberal education provided to the populace would prove a panacea to the nation's ills. A liberal education is not useful in that mechanistic sense. But, to use Benjamin Franklin's typology, it is more than ornamental. Most of all a liberal education is interesting.

The ideas that intrigue people now and have intrigued them for centuries make up the essential content of a liberal education. Whether these be humanistic or scientific, contemporary or historical, verbal or visual, these ideas challenge us to look beyond the routine of our days, of our jobs, and to learn about a world that transcends our own narrow experience and may even help us to understand that experience a little bit better.

The college graduate of a generation or two ago at a minimum received as an undergraduate the tools necessary to carry on these investigations in later life. Today the college graduate is much less likely to have those tools or to be exposed to those issues in a substantial way in college. An undergraduate program in chemical engineering or accounting or physical therapy leaves little room for study of unrelated matters. College administrators find it hard to argue that a chemical engineer will get a better job with DuPont or Dow if he has studied philosophy rather than an extra semester of thermodynamics, and they are probably right.

The chances are that a person with a degree in accounting is much more likely to find employment upon graduation than a person with a degree in history. Perhaps it is even the case that the study of these larger issues is wasted upon the young. As John Dewey told us so many years ago, we must learn from our experience and must build on our experiences in order to learn. For most young people the necessity of finding a job and deciding on a career is a much greater personal imperative than to understand more fully the ideas that have shaped their culture. Only when those immediate needs of their own lives (job and careers) have been resolved —and when they have exhausted the creative opportunities of their jobs, which happens increasingly rapidly—will many of them be seriously interested in exploring subjects in the liberal arts. Since many of them will already have a bachelor's degree, this exploration will need to occur on the graduate level.

The students, then, who would enroll at the graduate level for a liberal education would be likely to be older than the traditional undergraduate and considerably more experienced than the proverbial sophomore in introduction to philosophy. Their motivations would undoubtedly vary considerably: curiosity about subjects missed in a previous technical education; investigation of a new field with a possibility of exploring it further; study as an alternative or supplement to a dull job; and the perennial explanation for college or university attendance—an opportunity to meet new people respectably.

Probably the most important characteristic of these students would be that they would all be studying on their own initiative. Unlike many adults who are employed full time and who study part time, these individuals would not be enrolled in order to maintain a teaching credential required for their employment or to fulfill the requirements for a continuing education unit for their job in the health field. Rather, these students would be enrolling in courses that would be for them essentially elective. There would be less pressure for them to remain in the course if they found it not to their liking and more incentive to take full advantage of a course that they had chosen of their own free will. Classes with such students might well be a marked contrast to those filled with individuals enrolled to meet a requirement.

For the faculty, too, these students, with their varied backgrounds, could conceivably add interest to a class of potential professionals in a field. For most of us professors the shock of offering courses at the graduate level to persons who have not already committed themselves to following our profession will be severe. For those of us in the humanities, particularly, we at the graduate level have been nearly exclusively engaged in vocational education, or replicating ourselves professionally. In the social sciences and particularly in the sciences the replication has not been so direct, since opportunities for Ph.D.'s in those fields do exist outside academe. We might even discover some of the joys of yore, teaching our subject to nonspecialists, to persons not narrowly committed to our profession. Further, we would be spared the agony of trying to find them jobs or at least the pain of alerting them to the likelihood of the difficulty of finding jobs in this field. Two or three intelligent nonspecialists in a master's-level colloquium might well leaven the lump of professionalism, particularly in the humanities and social sciences.

The humanities and the social sciences

Clearly such nonspecialists cannot enroll in courses that have specific prerequisites, as do many mathematics, science, and language courses. Probably the best courses for such graduate liberal education are those in the humanities (the fields that are suffering most in the present dearth of graduate students) and the social sciences that either study a broad base of material or deal intensively with one subject that touches on a number of related issues. Both kinds of courses, one, for example, on American social history from 1865 to 1918, or another on irony in Elizabethan drama, would be amenable to and enhanced by this mixed student body. Ethical issues in contemporary medicine could easily attract potential professional philosophers as well as others with little formal training in philosophy.

Most students seeking such a liberal education would ordinarily be doing so at what we euphemistically call the master's level. Traditionally at the immediate postbaccalaureate level we have provided the professional training for the liberal arts graduate that would make him or her employable. I think specifically of the L.L.B. for lawyers; the M.B.A. for business people; the M.L.S. for librarians; the M.S.W. for social workers; the S.T.B. for ministers; or the M.P.H. for public health specialists. While rigorous, the content of those academic programs is not dependent upon having previously acquired a specific body of knowledge. Most courses in the humanities and the social sciences, often upper division ones cross-listed for juniors and seniors as well as beginning graduate students, are similarly rigorous, but nonspecific in requirements. Such courses would certainly be suitable for persons interested in obtaining a liberal education at the graduate level.

Institutions considering such students would need to reexamine their assumptions and policies for part-time students. In many places such students are either discouraged or prevented from taking part in the regular departmental offerings, being consigned instead to the nether reaches of the university, extension or continuing education for women. While these offerings are sometimes excellent, there seems little reason to assume that these students cannot compete successfully with regularly enrolled graduate students. Various institutional safeguards could be established initially to prevent what some might fear—a lowering of standards in the regular graduate program. Given the current shortage of graduate students in many of the humanities and social science departments, faculty members may be more enthusiastic about these new students than they would have been in the halcyon days of the late 1950s and 1960s.

Fee structures for such part-time students would also need investigation. What Stephen Dresch has called the "net incremental cost" of such students would need to be established.[1] Whether that cost should determine the charge to the student is another matter that would require evaluation of the value of such students to the total university and to the society generally. Assuming that such students were either employed or otherwise economically self-sufficient, the institution would have less need to subsidize them either directly or indirectly than it would conventional graduate students heading for the Ph.D. as a professional degree.

Most of us would agree that a student body unified by ability but diverse in experience and age is desirable. Most of us, I suspect, remember the callowness of our own days as graduate students with a shudder and complain over our coffee or cocktails to our colleagues about the immaturity and inadequacy of our present graduate students. The only group of students I ever remember faculty members being uniformly enthusiastic about, not only in retrospect (when we are often more charitable) but also at the time they were enrolled, were the veterans studying in the late 1940s on the GI bill. Customarily grumpy and cynical professors spoke enthusiastically about the academic energy and eagerness to learn that characterized that group. I am suggesting that graduate students seeking a delayed or renewed liberal education might have some of that same academic enterprise.

Finally, I would argue that not just the students, faculty, and the

1. *An Economic Perspective on the Evolution of Graduate Education* (Washington: National Board on Graduate Education, 1974), pp. 31–32.

universities would benefit from more opportunities being made available for liberal education at the graduate level. The society at large has much to gain and little to lose by its members pursuing such activities. Within this century there have been phenomenal shifts in adult priorities away from religion, community, and family. Much of the personal investment that formerly was diversified among church, town, and home has become concentrated upon job. While a job and the income it provides are both necessary and important—as the women's movement has shown us— they are not psychically fulfilling. As we look ahead at the kinds of jobs most people will have in the future, they are even less fulfilling than those many of us have now and consequently they are even less worthy of their full psychic energies. Education or training that increasingly prepares people for a job and that does not broaden their horizons beyond it is an inadequate preparation for the ennui of adulthood. Some other preparation is necessary, and I believe that more opportunities for liberal education at the graduate level may be one type.

9. REVISING AND CUTTING
ACADEMIC PROGRAMS

Doing Well with Less

RANDOLPH W. BROMERY

IT IS INCREASINGLY necessary today for educational programs and policies to undergo continual reassessment. The ever-expanding market for higher education has begun to sense its own outer edges, and the educational "Bulls" in and out of our institutions of higher learning have begun to make place for the "Bears." The philosophy of almost limitless growth that characterized the 1950s and 1960s has been replaced by the concepts of limited resources and the need to prove higher education's worth to a somewhat less receptive society. The academic community is under new pressures, new public scrutiny, and new constraints.

It is deceptively simple to generalize, but it seems to me that most of these constraints are the stepchildren of the recent national recession and have to do with inflation, overextension, and tight money in general. Their other parent appears to be a concurrent questioning of our institutional aims, structure, and policies—a questioning even of the ultimate worth of our product.

Most of us in the academic community have gotten out of practice in dealing with a shrinking universe. We have, to varying degrees, grown fat and complacent until rather recently, when a marked change began to be felt in the national attitude toward higher education in general, and, I may add, toward public higher education in particular. Now we are in the lean years and are being forced to rediscover what our indispensable elements really are. The forces behind our efforts at adaptation wear many faces and have many names—the taxpayers' revolt, overeducation, cultural parity, dwindling endowments, changing times—but their ultimate impact is similar. They lead us toward a personalized view of how to do well with less.

In the public sector, the cutting edge between increasing costs and diminishing resources is applied to higher education by the state legislature in the form of a curtailed budget and restrictive legislation. The shifting national attitude toward higher education is sharply focused when seen in the state legislative microcosm. In the main, legislators have come to share public perceptions that a degree may not help get a job, that the educational process can be wasteful and highly inefficient, that the ivory tower is full of fat cats, and that many educational programs have no bearing on the real world.

Such ideas, coupled with increased demand for expanded social services statewide, have produced relatively harsher attitudes toward public higher education on the part of many legislators. These attitudes, in turn, produce not only budget cuts but devices such as mandated teaching loads, salary freezes, and the like.

One factor that has strengthened the general feeling that it is time to do something about the mushrooming growth of educational empires is the steady advance of public employee unionization, particularly that of faculty in higher education. The unionization process has shifted the public perception of professors from an elite class of scholars to that of yet another labor group trying to apply pressure for a bigger slice of the pie. In the view of many, the faculty has suffered the effect of a process of "your friendly next door neighbor," which has stripped it of prestige and lowered its common denominator. The effect is paradoxical, because the faculty aim was simply self-betterment, an expanded role in institutions of higher education, and popular understanding of its problems.

Both public and private higher education share an institutional time-frame that extends well beyond the seasonal or the annual fluctuations in their fiscal climate. They share common obligations of tenure and contract to their faculties and other employees; they share moral obligations over a five- to seven-year span to incoming and current students in the high school to graduate school pipeline. Neither can expand or contract in general or in part by the month or by the semester and continue to meet basic public expectations. For both public and private colleges and universities, there is a difficult balance that must be maintained between the institution's absolute responsibilities and its need for financial flexibility.

Speaking only from the viewpoint of a public institution, it appears to me that the time-frame of the budget process is more complex for public institutions than for private institutions, partly because public institutions must operate on annual budgets set up one or two years at a time and partly because the academic year and the state budget year do not generally coincide. There can be no five-year plans for programmatic or fiscal matters if the state legislature may change not only the expected revenue but also the regulations governing how it is spent at any time. Witness such devices as Massachusetts' freeze on hiring regardless of the pattern of employee and faculty attrition. Our university is now beginning to recover from a year-long, state-imposed, blanket hiring freeze. On the Amherst campus alone, the number of vacancies rose from 233 at the close of fiscal year 1975 to 560 at the close of fiscal year 1976, an increase of 140 percent. These figures translate to ending an academic year without 15 percent of our needed faculty and staff.

How, then, are we to maintain this balance between responsibility and financial flexibility? How do we cut back deeply on a living thing such as a university without inflicting a crippling wound? The answer lies beyond the process and the options, although these are of great importance. The answer lies in the reasoned care of our approach, which can only be achieved by consultation with all groups involved, well in advance of the need for action, so that an agreed-upon framework and system for responsible change may exist before, rather than after, the fiscal events they are supposed to control.

If our overall budget is cut back sharply, what are the alternatives? Basically, there are two: to cut back everything across the board, or to cut selectively by individual program and function. A third approach, which I personally favor, is a judicious combination of the two. The first alternative—to squeeze everything down, possibly by a percentage factor—is the most simplistic and the easiest. However, it has two major drawbacks: It works only on a small scale and as a temporary measure, when combined with a cut in enrollments; and it is inherently dangerous to the very life of a college or university. It is dangerous in that it implies to the public that an institution of higher learning is a simple system like a department of motor vehicles, in which you can just knock a little off the top. Maybe close the doors two afternoons a week, and come up with a 15 percent saving. It is easy for the public to ask, if you achieve a 15 percent cutback, why you did not go further, since money is so tight, and chop off 20 percent. It is also dangerous because ground lost in such a general blindfolded cutback is seldom, if ever, regained. The second basic alternative is to cut programmatically. This is more complex, in that it absolutely requires foresight and planning of a specific nature. It involves a long-range approach in which institutional problems and public needs—quite aside from financial emergencies—must be seen coming down the road.

It is only fair to admit that, at the time our budget crunch struck, the University of Massachusetts at Amherst was not adequately prepared to make an immediate response by the programmatic reduction route. Decisions on the best potential program cuts must be made approximately a year or more in advance of their effective date, and our mechanisms and procedures for dealing with massive potential budget cuts were not forged until the fiscal fires swept across the state in 1974. The magnitude of the statewide problem was not clear until early 1975; as a result of state actions in fiscal 1976, we sustained what may have been the most severe budget cut of any state university in the nation, and yet we feel confident of our ability to adapt intelligently to the realities of fiscal year 1977, now already upon us.

Coping with recession

What are some of the steps that can be taken by a college or university before the slope of institutional decline becomes precipitous?

1. Flexibility must be built into the planning and budgeting system so that major budgetary units—MBUs, as we call them—can affect dollar budgeting with dwindling resources at their own levels and with their own internal expertise. The individual MBU may then assess its own predicted program needs and divide the available funds on the basis of its own allocation. No longer can an institution afford to plan that each of its subordinate units will require a fixed percentage of the whole for any operational category. No longer can every line in any budget afford to end with three zeros.

2. We need very much to effect an attitudinal change in regard to long-range planning at the department level. It is no longer healthy for a university to flesh out a long-range plan every five or ten years for legislative and media consumption, with input limited to a blue-ribbon committee of administrators. The muscles necessary to forge a long-range plan that will stick must be exercised with regularity, and they must extend from top to bottom within the body of the institution. Everyone involved, from those seeking funds to those spending them, must begin to think in terms of steady-state systems, plus or minus specific increments. Year-by-year processing and planning is not sufficient today to deal with faculty matters involving contracts, tenure, bargaining, policies, guidelines, and practices. Yet, in general, faculty members view their institution and their role within it on an annual basis. Systematic longer-range planning does not come easily to many faculty members, not because of any inherent lack of facility, but because of the spottiness and variability of the data with which they must work. Administrators would do well to bear this in mind and sharpen their awareness of the faculty viewpoint.

3. An expansion of roles must be encouraged at all levels. To function effectively in the long-range budget revision process, individual faculty members must assume a greater level of departmental concern, and department heads need to become administrators. This is not an easy task. In order to accomplish it, a role reversal as well as role expansion is needed. The administration must become faculty to teach its revised budgetary ethos to the faculty, and the faculty in turn must become students of the new discipline. Indeed, the entire educational process is

somewhat reversed for the occasion. Whereas formerly academic input slowly affected the body politic, today the political realities become the corpus for the academics.

4. Upon successful accomplishment of the previous three steps, the institution can then match its dollar resources to its specific plans. Here the public higher education budget system has certain advantages, not the least of which is the fact that its budget officers are accustomed to the multiplicity of line and item detail that realistic budgeting requires. "Guesstimates" are no longer in style.

5. The college or university must set out clearly its targets for the coming year and for several years, and it must assign the stringent kind of priorities that will allow for attrition or expansion with some degree of calm if not comfort. The difficulty here, of course, is that some areas will decline or disappear, while others remain level or even receive increased support. The prime need, once such decisions are made, is to explain them satisfactorily to all involved, including the professional college-watchers. Without such explanation, some may tend toward the view that if a single high-visibility program does not suffer, things in general really cannot be all that bad. If a distorted view of the cutback procedure becomes back-fence gossip around the state, another legislator or two may go sour on educational appropriations.

6. Students and faculty must be given a real participatory role in governance and decisionmaking in general, and in program and fiscal matters most specifically. At the University of Massachusetts at Amherst, such roles are played, along with administrators and the professional staff, by such groups as the program and budget council, the kingpin in any plans for revisions and cuts, and the academic program review task force and graduate review committee. All educators are aware of the scope and duration of the process for initiating a new academic program, but sometimes we do not share the same awareness when it comes to program elimination. Such matters ought to be deliberated by a group such as the program and budget council well in advance of immediate need. This must be done from a standpoint of educational value to the institution as well as any potential budgeting utility. Both students and faculty should realize that just as dropping a program can save money, creating a new program requires additional money. Such funds must be identified within a total fixed dollar amount and can only be made available for the new purpose at a measurable cost to another program or programs.

7. The administration must retain its sense of final authority and responsibility throughout this cooperative governance procedure. The bottom line is clear: no group of faculty, staff, and/or students can properly close down or create a program. This the administration itself

must do, within the contexts outlined above. The buck, even if diminished, still stops there.

In many ways, dealing with these types of programmatic budgetary concerns at the highest to the lowest levels is a new experience for colleges and universities. Industry has dealt with this very process for many years, but we in higher education have worn our charter with a difference. We have not seen ourselves as dealing with simple supply and demand in the marketplace. Perhaps it is time for a new concept, based on our assessment of supply and benefit. Are we as institutions to supply what our publics demand—that which they see as necessary and proper for themselves—or are we to proffer those things that our publics need—those things that will bring about the greatest public good? And who among us is to decide that question? There can be no stronger argument for collective decisionmaking.

These adjuncts are necessary to institutional success: fiscal flexibility, acceptance of the need for long-range planning, diversification of roles, dollar budgeting, fixed priorities, broad participation in governance, and a sense of administrative responsibility.

Of course, some of the fringe detriments of hard budget times are still noticeable among us: the pressure for more teaching per hour and more hours per contract, coupled with an apparent trend away from teaching, a withdrawal into research where brighter laurels may be won for the individual. Other spinoffs from the problem include a strong faculty expectation of guaranteed tenure, leading to unionization, and a tendency to indulge in interdisciplinary effort for the purpose of establishing a broader base of support, rather than for pure educational benefit.

Although we entered this particular arena of program revision and justification for reasons of current crisis, we are convinced that the results of our efforts will be highly beneficial to our institutional future. I sincerely recommend a similar internal reassessment and rethinking process to all college and university administrations everywhere, regardless of the fiscal pressures upon them.

Although we have not yet broken the grip of decades of "growth psychology," we feel that Massachusetts and the nation have turned a corner. Massachusetts has lifted the hiring freeze, the university's economic climate has stabilized, and its operating budget is $1.6 million greater than a year ago. Nationally, we see signs of improving economy and a curtailment of economic decline, at least for a time. We see students becoming more and more serious about their educational opportunities, and we see evidence of a renewed dedication to learning. We are moving ahead with optimistic caution. But no matter how hopeful the view, a little sunshine should never persuade us that we need not learn how to put up an umbrella.

Retrenchment: The Case at CUNY

EDMOND L. VOLPE

MY EXPERTISE in cutting academic budgets derives, as the bard might put it, from a foul configuration of the stars. I was not born a college president. My own trajectory placed me in a placid orbit around the sun of literary criticism. Then, some powerful magnetic force, undoubtedly that same sin that felled the angels, thrust me in July 1974 into this wild, careening orbit, which sensible people sample occasionally at the fair grounds with a short trip on the roller coaster.

By July 1976 I had handled two annual budgets. The first required a reduction of 10 percent. The second, scaled, I assume, to take advantage of my expertise, required a reduction of 17.5 percent. If I had known higher education was entering the lean years, I would probably still be in my study working with figures of speech (and mixing my metaphors) rather than with budget figures. I sometimes envy my more experienced colleagues their years of plenty. My sole comfort is that it is probably easier to adjust to austerity if that is the sum of your experience.

Euphemisms are as endemic to academia as faculty orators; and colleges merely contemplating the possibility of lean years tend to think in such terms as "revising and cutting academic programs." When the fiscal crisis hit CUNY, up-beat terminology had little currency. During 1976 the operative term was "retrenchment," which, appropriately, has the unpleasant connotation not only of a military exercise but also a military strategy designed to accommodate defeat.

The dreadful fact is that "retrenchment" is an accurate term. What I discovered is that revising and cutting academic programs is not what budget cutting is all about. On paper, an academic program consists of a number of requirements and a series of courses. In actuality, the program is inextricable from the staff teaching it. In a budget-cutting process, you deal with faculty positions and teachers rather than programs. If you dismiss one staff member, you have revised the program. Dismiss a few key people, and the program is eliminated.

Theoretically, because we are dealing with educational institutions whose primary obligation is to the students, any cuts in the budget should be carefully and intelligently planned to maintain the quality of those programs essential to the mission of the college. In actuality, all kinds of regulations, state education laws, academic traditions and taboos, such as tenure, college politics, and even the personalities involved in the budget reduction process govern which faculty members will be dismissed.

Given these taboos and regulations, a reduction of the instructional budget begins and ends with the roster of faculty that can be dismissed and the order in which they can be dismissed. Guidelines, based on the law and accepted academic practice, are absolutely essential, as I shall try to illustrate, for any kind of orderly and fair budget reduction. But, in a period of retrenchment, no intelligent or rational plan to revise or cut academic programs can be devised unless the academic community, specifically the faculty, is ready and willing to confront the issue of tenure by separating its current interpretation (as a guarantee of job security) from its original and only justifiable intent (as a guarantee of academic freedom).

I should like to demonstrate the reasons underlying this conclusion by describing the retrenchment process at the College of Staten Island in July 1976. Long-range planning to reduce the instructional budget cannot be neatly isolated from the actual process of retrenchment, and it will, I think, be helpful to those who are beginning to plan to be aware of the complexities that lie ahead.

Retrenchment under pressure

As a direct result of the budget crisis at CUNY, Richmond College, an upper division institution on Staten Island offering junior-, senior-, and master's-level study, was federated with Staten Island Community College. On September 1, 1976, they were reincarnated as the College of Staten Island. The term "federation" requires some clarification, because it may well be a newcomer to the jargon of academia, and because it is relevant to the budgeting procedures under discussion. The federation had its roots in the fiscal crisis. Because of the difference in the funding formula for community and senior colleges, it was less expensive to maintain the community college funding for the first two years and the senior college funding for the last two years than to finance the merged institution as a four-year senior college. Federation consolidated the administration and instructional support services but retained separate faculties in two divisions on separate instructional budgets. Most large colleges and universities are, in fact, federations of the liberal arts college and the professional schools. The College of Staten Island is thus a horizontal rather than a vertical federation.

Though economics may have dictated the structure, the concept of federation is advantageous on academic grounds. It provides the kind of flexibility and diversity in academic programs that the heterogeneous student body in an urban institution requires. The community division can maintain its mission by offering two-year career programs as well as associate degree transfer programs. The senior division can continue to offer special programs for community college graduates. Together, both divisions can offer traditional as well as coordinated and new four-year programs.

The federation process at the College of Staten Island began June 1976 and continued during the first year as a single college, with top priority being given to curricular planning and development, which meant reduction in some programs, expansion of others, development of new ones. Such alterations will, of course, require a reallocation of resources; many colleges with shrinking budgets will have to undertake this process. We at the College of Staten Island have the advantage—or perhaps the better term is traumatic disadvantage—of having already endured a brutal retrenchment process under great time pressure, and, it is to be hoped, learned something from that experience.

Initiating the budget reduction process

Our budget year begins on July 1. Because of the protracted battle over the free tuition policy, the state legislature did not act on the university's budget until the middle of June. I did not receive from the chancellor the budget for the federated college until June 30. The new budget called for a reduction of $4.3 million. The preceding July, the two independent colleges had been required to cut a total of $1.8 million. The new budget represented an additional 17.5 percent reduction, which meant that in one year the combined budgets had been reduced by $6 million, considerably more than 20 percent.

The fiscal crisis in New York City had made crystal clear that higher education was low on the list of priorities; the two colleges had prepared, during the year, for a reduced budget. The combined budgets had, through nonreappointments, retirements, resignations, and attrition, been reduced by approximately $2.3 million. The nonpersonnel portion of the budget had been gleaned the preceding year for all possible savings. All that remained to be done, therefore, was to remove from the payroll, as quickly as possible, sufficient personnel to reduce expenditures by an additional $2 million. On July 23, after three weeks of brutal work, the task was completed. On July 26, dismissal letters were mailed.

Because livelihoods and careers are at stake, a broad-based, elaborate consultative process is a sine qua non. Our committee had representatives of the faculty, students, the professional administrative staff, the secretarial force, and the nonprofessional staff. Nonteaching personnel tend to be realistic about budget reductions, perhaps because their role in the college is supportive rather than central and perhaps because their skills are more readily adapted to other institutions and jobs. The faculty, obviously, is the most difficult to deal with, not only because its members cannot readily use their talents and training in other types of work but also because they are intensely committed to their careers, their disciplines, their departments, and the institution as a whole. Professors balk, and rightly so, at the thought of dismissing a colleague to reduce the budget. The intrusion of mundane money considerations on normal academic concerns and procedures is abhorrent to people who chose their career to avoid such concerns. At the same time, professors balk even more, and rightly so, if they do not participate in a process that impinges on their proper concern, the academic program.

Dealing with committees on such a sensitive and volatile issue is time-consuming, emotionally exhausting, and physically demanding. It would be much easier and more pleasant for a president to sit down with his deans to allocate the budget and draw up a retrenchment plan. Such a plan might be more rational than that produced through consultation, but its implementation would probably create a furor that the administration could not survive.

My problem was unusually complicated because I was dealing with two colleges that retained their status as legal entities until September 1. I had therefore to deal with three sets of committees: joint committees and separate committees from each college. The two most essential committees were concerned with budget and retrenchment. On July 6, I distributed to the college community a description of how the consultative process would work, listing the committees, their specific charges, and deadlines that had to be met.

Perhaps one of the most important decisions was to separate consultation on budget allocations from the process of developing plans for dismissing personnel. The budget committee was to advise on gross allocations and amounts to be cut from nonpersonnel expenditures and from the administrative, instructional support, and instructional budgets. The retrenchment committee and its subcommittees was to develop specific recommendations by identifying positions which, if cut, would meet the cuts established by the budget committee. If these two processes are not separated, and the retrenchment committee not given specific instructions that have come through another faculty committee, it will insist on reallocating the entire budget to avoid having to develop plans that require the dismissal of colleagues.

No matter how pressing his other obligations, it is advisable for the president to take command of the entire operation and to work with the committees. His is the ultimate responsibility for every decision, and he alone has the authority that must be constantly exercised throughout the process. His presence at committee meetings will help to create the feeling of a responsibility that administration, faculty, and staff must share to do a job, unpleasant as it is, that must be done and done together.

Involvement with the committee in its deliberations requires tact and diplomacy. Presidential participation will be eagerly interpreted as an opportunity to make decisions by majority vote; it must be made clear that the committee's power is restricted to recommendations to the president. Presidential participation can also evoke charges of interference. Nevertheless, those dangers are worth risking, because every other administrative officer, except perhaps the provost, is inevitably an advocate for his area of responsibility. Only the president has both the full responsibility for all college functions and total overall perspective. Faculty members, for example, are primarily concerned with instruction, and the academic deans tend to share that concern. All other functions are considered peripheral to instruction and will be readily offered up for sacrifice.

In most colleges, the political strength of the faculty resides in the liberal arts departments. If the chief executive officer is not wary and ready to use his authority, all innovative programs, interdisciplinary programs, professional programs, community and adult education programs will be proffered by the liberal arts faculty as nonessential. With faculty jobs at stake, the academic needs of the students tend to be overlooked, and the president must constantly remind the faculty that though jobs are certainly important, the faculty is there to provide the students an education.

The importance of candor

No president is without his own priorities, and ultimately these will influence the decisions that are made. Candor about these priorities and the decisions that will flow from them will not muffle objections, but it will, at least, not undermine trust. Candor about the entire budget, in a period of fiscal crisis, is also wise, despite the immediate problems that might ensue. Though the average faculty member usually cares little about budgeting and tends to be confused by the process, when jobs are in question, everyone discovers within himself a latent accountant.

Any action that aggravates the usual faculty suspicion that the administration is withholding budget information raises to an uncontrollable level the paranoia that is normal in academic life. If the faculty is to participate intelligently and responsibly in the decisionmaking process, it requires full budget information and all the available data. Besides, unless the faculty committee is absolutely convinced that there are no secret funds stashed away and that all options for cutting nonpersonnel funds are exhausted, the process of reducing personnel expenditures can never get under way.

A fiscal crisis provides for the staffs in the business and budget offices their moment in the sun. Their concerns, which academics tend to consider peripheral, suddenly become pivotal, and they are ready and eager to provide all kinds of data concerning class size, work loads, cost per full-time enrolled student, costs per student by discipline, program, class, height, weight, heredity, anything. They are also prepared to provide formulas for improving the cost effectiveness of every college function but the business office. I do not want to denigrate, in any way, the importance of data and formulas; but a president, faced with serious budget problems, could very easily succumb to those who seem to have pat financial solutions and end up with a college that offered no philosophy, foreign languages, even science. These days, cost effectiveness analyses, if followed, would turn our institutions into colleges of social science.

Over the long Fourth of July weekend, the administrative and budget staff analyzed the implications of the budget reductions and prepared information for the faculty budget committee. Everyone on campus was, of course, tense and fearful, and it was necessary to prepare carefully the information and data and present them in a manner that would make comprehensible our budget situation. Unrefined budget data are useless and misleading. To the uninitiated, a budget that deals in millions of dollars seems capable of handling every possible contingency. It was, therefore, necessary to identify clearly controllable from uncontrollable funds and expenditures, provide comparative figures, and establish parameters for possible reductions. By July 7, the staff had prepared a document containing ten exhibits; I was then ready to meet with the budget committee.

After rehearsing the committee's charge and emphasizing that its role was advisory to the president, I explained the various exhibits and then discussed the options available to us. At this stage of the process, executive authority must come forcibly into play. As representatives of various constituencies, committee members are under great political pressure to save jobs. It becomes necessary for the president to declare that books will be purchased for the library, oil and electricity bills must be paid, supplies purchased.

Only when it was finally clear to the committee—or at least most of its members—that other options were exhausted, could we turn to the personnel budget. I suggested that the budget committee send along to the retrenchment committee requests for several levels of reductions in the three areas of personnel expenditures: administration, instructional support, and instruction. For example, a request was passed along that plans be developed for budget cuts in the student service area for three levels of cuts: $200,000, $300,000, $400,000.

These preliminary plans were designed to serve three functions. Of most importance, they provided me and the budget committee specific information on the effect of the possible reductions in each area of our operations, and they greatly assisted the committee in establishing overall perspective. In the area of administrative services, I suggested that the committee request plans for sizable reductions. The suggestion was seized by faculty members who tend to forget the administration serves the faculty and who always see the administration as an expensive frill. When the preliminary plans came back, it became clear to the faculty members that without a payroll office they could not get paid; without registrars, we would have no students in the classes; without secretaries, departments would have trouble functioning.

Requesting plans for various levels of cuts also provided valuable information about problem areas. The lowest suggested cuts produced patchwork plans that did not attack any problems. The more severe cuts produced plans that established priorities and dealt realistically with such problems as overstaffing. Finally, planning for various levels of cuts produced good psychological side effects. When we finally decided that a $200,000 reduction would suffice for student services, the subcommittee felt relieved to the point of triumph.

The work of the budget committee was suspended until the preliminary reports of the retrenchment committee were submitted. The committee was informed it would be called back into session for consultation on final allocation decisions when the reports were analyzed.

Working with the retrenchment committee

Our retrenchment committee consisted of six faculty members, a student, a representative of the secretarial staff, a representative of the professional staff, a representative of civil service workers. The six faculty members constituted the academic subcommittee. The administrative and instructional support subcommittees were enlarged to include the deans of those areas and other representatives. The first meeting of the committee was spent attempting to do again what the budget committee had already done, arguing against the justice of the allocations, insisting there were other sources of funds, backing away, in other words, from the reality of their responsibility. It then broke into subcommittees and began its proper function. I worked with each of these committees as much as possible, attempting to maintain overall perspective and point out why various functions could not be eliminated.

After receiving from the retrenchment committee its preliminary plans for the various levels of cuts, I consulted once more with the budget committee and then sent to the retrenchment committee final decisions on cuts for each of the three areas. The retrenchment committee and its subcommittees went back to work to develop final recommendations. I worked closely with the committee, indicating whenever possible what recommendations were within the realm of the possible, which I could not accept and why. The final recommendations were not all acceptable to me. But when the president's official retrenchment plan was published, it did not contain any surprises for those who had been involved in the work of these committees.

The final recommendations of the retrenchment committee differed markedly from those in its preliminary reports, because the legal restrictions that governed the dismissal of personnel had now to be taken seriously. Essential to the retrenchment process is a set of guidelines. At CUNY, the chancellor's legal staff, after consultation with various groups, produced a document entitled "Retrenchment Guidelines." Primarily, the guidelines were based on the education law, the university's bylaws, and, whenever applicable, the university's contract with the faculty and professional staff union. The education law stipulated that dismissals necessitated by fiscal exigency were governed by seniority. Seniority was divided into two categories, tenured and nontenured.

The guidelines required the establishment of discrete units for retrenchment of staff. In the instructional area, these were mandated as the academic departments. In accordance with the university's bylaws, faculty members were appointed to a department and their appointments with tenure were restricted to their department. In the administrative and instructional support areas, the guidelines permitted greater discretion in establishing retrenchment units. The business office, for example, could be considered as one whole unit or broken up into smaller units. Decisions on these retrenchment units, once published, could not be altered, and they could prove crucial. At our university, most of the nonacademic administrative staff is civil service. Seniority had to be strictly observed for such employees, and had we not planned our retrenchment units carefully, the application of the seniority rule might have eliminated an entire essential function, such as accounting.

In the academic retrenchment units, no tenured person could be dismissed until all untenured personnel within that particular unit were terminated. The seniority rule, in the tenured category and in the untenured category, could be broken only by invoking a special educational reason. If, for instance, in a language department, an untenured German instructor and an untenured French instructor had more service than an untenured Spanish instructor, they could be dismissed despite their seniority if the president declared that Spanish was essential to the academic program. If all three had been tenured, and the department had no untenured personnel, the junior Spanish instructor could have been retained and the others dismissed for the same reason. But educational reason could not be invoked to retain an untenured instructor and dismiss tenured personnel.

Though such guidelines proved restrictive and made reducing the budget an elaborate process not unlike a chess game, they are essential. When livelihoods and careers are at stake, a set of rules, based on the law or on accepted practice or principle, such as seniority, must be established and known to all involved. Human beings are willing to accept impartial rules; they will not tolerate actions and decisions that are based on no known rules and that are therefore seen as the arbitrary and capricious decisions of another human being in whom final authority happens to rest.

Litigation follows dismissals in academic life as inevitably as night follows day, and unless the ground rules are clear-cut, impartial, and based on law or accepted principle, everyone dismissed would be back on the payroll within a year, with back pay and litigation costs draining the budget into bankruptcy. One of the ironies, among many, that evolve from the budget reduction process is the necessity of putting money that could be used to retain staff into reserve for litigation costs.

Planning for reduction of the instructional budget

As necessary as are guidelines, the restrictions they impose cripple the possibility of intelligent planning. The status of personnel takes precedence over programmatic needs and tends to determine which academic programs can be revised or cut. Though private institutions may not be under such rigid regulations as public colleges, their freedom, too, will be restricted by past hiring practices, seniority, and the academic taboo against dismissing tenured faculty.

Given the rules and regulations with which we had to work at the College of Staten Island, I am not at all certain that the retrenchment plan we developed under intense time pressure would have differed much if we had had many months for preparation and planning. I am also not certain that serious planning, which has as its goal the elimination of personnel from the payroll, can ever get underway unless the moment has come when the dollars are just not there. Intelligent planning for reducing the instructional budget must, of course, give priority to the mission of the college and the academic needs of the student. But such planning is not possible if precedence must be given to the status of personnel.

The options available to any committee facing the difficult problem of reducing the instructional budget are very limited: (1) dismissal of untenured staff, wherever available; (2) across-the-board reductions, department by department; (3) selective elimination of academic programs; (4) selective cutting of overstaffed departments.

Dismissing untenured staff is the easiest method, because it avoids the volatile tenure issue, but the consequences can be serious. New programs, usually staffed by untenured faculty, will be the first to go. Such programs undoubtedly include the new ethnic studies programs, and our campuses could generally be denuded of recently recruited minority faculty members. Dismissal of younger faculty also saps the vitality of an academic department and undermines the future of the college.

Across-the-board reductions, if they were applied without touching tenured personnel, would leave untouched the overstaffed departments, which are overstaffed only because the faculty is fully tenured. This option would hit hardest the departments that are shouldering the major burden of the curriculum and that have the greatest need for staff.

The only truly sensible way of cutting the academic budget is to reduce overstaffed areas and carefully select entire programs for elimination. Any other method jeopardizes the quality of the total academic program.

I think I share with most of my colleagues in academia a firm commitment to the principle of tenure as a guarantee of academic freedom. I also share a sense of responsibility to the students we educate. In a period of real budgetary contraction, neither college presidents nor the faculty will be able to fulfill that responsibility if the tenure problem is not confronted.

As instruments of their boards of trustees or of their state legislatures and as chief executive officers, college presidents cannot recommend dismissal of tenured faculty on the grounds of fiscal exigency without raising the issue of academic freedom. Only the faculty can shoulder that responsibility. My prediction, which may surprise you, is that when faculty committees actually face the options available for reducing the instructional budget and the impact of those options, they will not sidestep the issue. I base that prediction on a startling experience. One of the academic retrenchment subcommittees with which I worked recommended in its preliminary report the dismissal of four tenured faculty members in two overstaffed departments. If that committee action is symptomatic, and it may well be, then the tenure issue will be faced, and intelligent planning for a period of contraction will be possible.

Urging consideration of the dismissal of tenured personnel sounds, I know, callous. But dismissing any staff member is painful, and if one must be involved in the process, it might just as well be in accord with a plan that does not irreparably damage the academic program.

The inescapable choice between maintaining a balanced academic program or dismissing tenured faculty creates a paralyzing moral dilemma. I have tried to be realistic about our obligation, as educators, to the students and their program needs and the options available to fulfill that obligation in a period of fiscal contraction. I am, at the same time, painfully aware of our obligation to senior members of the faculty who have devoted their lives to their institutions. Neither obligation can be morally avoided.

In planning for revising or cutting the academic program, we must also consider devising means for mitigating the impact on the faculty. One obvious option, of course, is early mandatory retirements. Even earlier retirements for faculty in their fifties might be made attractive if the institution made up the difference between retirement income and full pay by providing the retiree the opportunity to teach as an adjunct. Such a system would allow for the retention of younger faculty members, preserve the services of experienced professors, and still save a great deal of money.

Another possibility might be to split tenure lines, allowing two faculty members to retain all rights and privileges by teaching one semester each or a half program each, both semesters. Many faculty members, particularly writers and artists, or those whose specialties are in demand for consultation, might welcome the combined security and freedom such an opportunity offers.

Local, state, or even regional cooperation among colleges could develop an information center that would allow the interchange of faculty that might be in excess in one college but needed in another. Colleges in a region might jointly support one quality department of, say, classical languages, rather than ten minimally staffed and underused separate departments.

The retraining of faculty, at the expense of the institution, is an alternative to the dismissal of tenured faculty that makes both economic and humane sense.

There must be other possibilities. I am not advocating an attack on tenure. I am advocating an honest confrontation of the dilemma shrinking budgets create for us. As administrators, we can expose the problem, but we cannot resolve it. Solving the problem must be done by a faculty deeply concerned with the fate of the institution, which means a faculty that is intimately involved in the budgeting process and that knows the resources of the college and the problems it faces.

It is a painful dilemma to confront, but by wrestling with it together, faculty and administration may well make a reality of the concept of shared responsibility that dominates the rhetoric, if not the practice, of academia.

Managing under Depressed Funding

E. T. YORK, JR.

WE AMERICANS are by nature builders. From our beginning as a nation of immigrant builders, we have been enamored of growth. Indeed, for most of our first two hundred years, we have equated our progress as a nation with the amount and rate of our growth in most areas of human endeavor. "More" and "bigger" have been virtually synonymous with "better"—and the "American way of life."

The economic recession of the 1970s has, therefore, hit this generation particularly hard. We were not prepared for it psychologically, and we are finding adjustment to it perplexing. This has been especially true of those of us in education. During the past two years, higher education in Florida—as in other states—has experienced major financial constraints, so major that some now contend the "3 R's" in education refer to "Reassessment, Reduction, and Retrenchment." We realize that the old order has changed in American higher education, that we are, indeed, in a different era, and that we must adjust accordingly. I would add, however, that the new order is not all bad—some positive things can be said about what is happening, assuming, of course, that we can survive the process.

A period of reassessment and adjustment such as we are now experiencing has been inevitable and, I believe, can produce some very desirable results. It was inevitable because American higher education experienced a period of growth and expansion during the quarter-century following the Second World War unequaled in American history. Such rates of expansion in both student numbers and levels of funding were not likely to be sustained indefinitely and there had to be, sooner or later, the period of leveling-off and adjustment we are now experiencing. Other factors, such as the competing needs of other segments of society that have been given higher priority in use of available resources, have contributed to this period of adjustment.

Furthermore, much could be said for such a period of reassessment and adjustment. No society can afford the luxury of wasting its public resources. I am not suggesting that there has been gross waste or mismanagement in higher education. (I would recognize that there are two types of potential waste: doing a given job poorly or inefficiently and doing the wrong job. The second may be more significant than the first.) In recent years, however, an attitude developed among legislative bodies and among many segments of the public that universities were not good managers and that we were "fat cats" with more money to spend than was really needed to get the job done. Such attitudes have contributed significantly to the financial stresses the academic community is now experiencing. Finally, we would be less than candid if we did not recognize that with the sort of growth and expansion that has occurred in higher education in recent decades, there have not always been the pressures to manage and use our resources in the most efficient and effective manner. We have, in effect, "lived" on growth and have gotten along reasonably well. However, our well-being has in many cases been somewhat of an illusion.

The Florida experience

During the past fifteen years, enrollments in Florida's state university system have increased more than fourfold, growing at the rate of approximately 6,000 new students annually, the equivalent of adding one average-sized university to the system annually during that period. While appropriations increased significantly during that period, the level of support failed to keep pace with growth and inflation. For example, full-time enrollment increased almost 80 percent during the seven-year period 1968–75, but appropriations (in constant or noninflated dollars) increased only 40 percent, or less than half as much. In the last four years, the level of support per student (in real dollars) actually declined by approximately 20 percent.

Despite this steady erosion of support over a period of several years, we did not feel the serious financial crunch until about two years ago, when there was a simultaneous leveling-off, at least temporarily, in enrollment and a sharp economic recession in our state, both of which contributed to a marked reduction in the rate of appropriation growth. The limited growth that did occur was insufficient to cope with the rapid inflation or with the sharp rise in enrollment that occurred during the second year of the recession (1975–76).

While higher education in other parts of the country has faced similar problems, the difficulties in Florida have been particularly acute because of very rapid growth in the educational system and a narrow tax base, which made it difficult to support a greatly expanded system, particularly during a period of depressed economic conditions. Until the mid-1950s, Florida had only three state universities and five public community colleges. In the last twenty years, it has added six new universities and twenty-three community colleges. Many of these institutions are still in the early developmental stages and have heavy demands for start-up resources. In 1975, Robert Graham, chairman of the Senate Education Committee aptly characterized the problem by saying: "The State has written a lot of checks for postsecondary education which are now beginning to come in to be cashed." The problem of redeeming these checks was made very difficult during the recession by the narrow tax base (no personal income tax and only 4 percent sales tax, with many items exempted), which produced limited revenue growth.

As we attempt to adjust and respond to these circumstances, we are doing little more than trying to be accountable for the stewardship of the public resources entrusted to us, which is our basic responsibility. But we are doing this in a setting different from that in which most of us have worked. I would suggest, however, that this is the type of educational leadership that may well be demanded of us all in the future. And in many respects it can be more challenging and possibly more rewarding than the leadership demands of the more affluent times in our immediate past.

In addressing our financial difficulties, we did not limit our efforts to cutting and adjusting academic programs. Indeed, attention was first directed toward cutting back administrative and management costs and considering other means of conserving resources, such as significantly reducing utilities consumption. Our primary objective was to do those things that might ultimately strengthen and improve the quality of academic programs while at the same time meeting the total higher education needs of the state. For example, the primary goal in attempting to reduce administrative costs or to eliminate unnecessary bureaucracy was to free resources that could be redirected to improving academic programs. In all these efforts, our primary goal was to avoid weakening and, whenever possible, to strengthen academic programs as we adjusted to limited levels of funding.

Improving efficiency and effectiveness

Let me examine some reforms we have undertaken to improve management and efficiency, eliminate waste and unproductive effort, and provide improved accountability for the stewardship of available resources. Some of these efforts were already underway before we were caught in the serious financial crunch that began two years ago. We have, however, greatly intensified our efforts to improve the management of our resources as funds became more limited.

Major efforts have been carried out statewide to identify and eliminate wasteful or unproductive administrative procedures. A systemwide task force, involving each university and the central office, has made a comprehensive study of the problems and has identified many ways to reduce administrative costs.

The task force found, for example, that a significant portion of the increased campus administrative workload was externally imposed, much of it by the legislature and agencies of state and federal governments. We have worked with our state legislature and with executive agencies of state government to change laws or administrative procedures to secure greater management flexibility and reduce the red tape in purchasing, data processing, handling of surplus property, reporting faculty assignments, accounting and budgeting reporting requirements, and a host of additional bureaucratic processes.

We have also tried to set our internal house in order. At all administrative levels, we have examined and adjusted policies and procedures in efforts to reduce unnecessary bureaucracy. Organizational changes have been made to lower administrative costs. Departments and colleges have been consolidated, thereby reducing the number of administrators. Full-time administrators have been encouraged to devote a portion of their time to classroom teaching. In one university, for example, every administrator with academic credentials, from the president on down, is teaching at least one course.

For several years, the legislature has encouraged the university system to increase its level of summer enrollment, thereby lowering the peak demands for facilities and support personnel. During the past two years, major efforts have been made to achieve such a goal. Various incentives, such as preferred admission, lower tuition, and reduced dormitory rates for summer attendance are being used to induce students to attend voluntarily. The board of regents has recently made attendance at one summer term mandatory for all students admitted with two or more years remaining in the undergraduate degree program. As a result of these efforts, Florida already has one of the highest, if not the highest, levels of summer enrollment of any university system in the nation. Policies now in effect should result in even higher levels in the years immediately ahead.

Various approaches have been used to accelerate educational processes for many students and reduce the time and effort within the university, thereby lowering the cost of educating these students. These efforts, including early admissions, dual enrollment arrangements, College-Level Examination Program, and other credit-by-examination mechanisms, saved the state $8 million in instructional costs and the students $3 million in tuition charges in 1974–75 alone.

Florida's nine universities are now part of a library network tied into a computerized bibliographic data base of more than 2 million items. This effort provides access to a huge bibliographic center that enables libraries to catalog books on a shared basis more rapidly and at a substantially lower cost than with a manual system. Interlibrary loans have been stimulated, thus obviating in many instances the duplicate purchasing of materials.

During the past two years, we have been involved in a comprehensive cost study aimed at developing detailed data on the cost per credit-hour by level and discipline and the cost per major by level and discipline for the several hundred academic programs within this system. We have moved to a charge per credit-hour, based on a percentage of instructional costs, as a means of maintaining a reasonable and readily identifiable division between student tuition and state funding.

We are also developing systemwide management information systems, with uniformly defined data bases on personnel, academic programs and activities, students, and facilities. These systems will improve the quality and availability of data for both institutional and systemwide management.

We believe that these and other efforts are contributing significantly to better management and more effective use of available resources. Furthermore, we hope that these efforts can increase our credibility with both the legislature and public in demonstrating that the universities are indeed carrying out sound management practices.

Academic program management

Since a major share of available resources in a university goes into academic programs, these programs will obviously be affected when resources are deficient.

The terms "management" and "efficiency" are not popular among many academicians. We are not, however, discussing "managing" the content or the style of courses. Neither are we talking about trying to make individual faculty members intrinsically more efficient, although I am sure there are opportunities for improvement with most of us. We are discussing managing resources that are used to support academic programs so that the greatest good can be derived from them in meeting basic higher education needs.

Faced with the prospects of no increase and possibly a decrease in funding for 1976–77 and the need for additional resources to meet inflationary costs and provide salary increases, we initiated a contingency planning process in the fall of 1975 to prepare to accommodate depressed funding levels, should they occur. As a means of saving resources to accommodate recognized needs without additional funding, we asked the universities to continue to do everything possible to reduce administrative costs and to examine carefully opportunities to eliminate programs or activities that could not be clearly justified, especially where such termination could result in freeing resources that could be better used for other purposes. We also asked that careful consideration be given to institutional goals and priorities in considering what programs might be reduced in scale or scope to accommodate these objectives. In cases where personnel reductions might be needed to meet these goals, careful consideration was given to the timing of notice requirements, particularly nonrenewal notices for nontenured faculty. These contingency plans had to be developed with the assumption that enrollment would be limited to 90 percent of the current year's level. Admissions were then controlled by each university to achieve that level until the legislature met in late spring and passed an appropriation bill.

In the legislative process, appropriations for 1976–77 (as in the previous year) were actually increased, although not enough to meet inflationary needs or to compensate for earlier losses. As a result of legislative action, it was not necessary to limit enrollment, and funds were provided for modest salary and inflationary adjustments.

The adjustments that were made as a part of the contingency planning process have resulted in savings which, with our lump-sum appropriation and budgeting authority, could be applied to higher priority needs. I am sure we can say that many of the adjustments made in this process needed to be made irrespective of the current financial difficulty.

We were committed to conducting a comprehensive role and scope study for the system before we were confronted with our recent economic difficulties. Serious problems of inadequate funding, however, prompted us to move forward as rapidly as possible in addressing many critical issues through the role and scope study that have significant financial implications.

The philosophy of a system of state universities under a single governing board embraces the concept of looking at the total higher education needs of the state and the way in which these needs can best be met by the *total system,* without each university having to address every need. Such a concept obviously calls, first, for defining the total statewide needs; and second, for allocating responsibilities to the various universities so that the total needs can be met with a minimum of duplication or overlapping of effort. Achieving these two objectives is essentially the goal of the role and scope study.

The process obviously begins with what is rather than what should be. Most American universities and many of their major programs were created by legislative action. Over time, the legislative attitudes and circumstances that may have contributed to such attitudes frequently change. At any rate, the board of regents has responsibility for making recommendations concerning the ways in which the total higher education needs of the state can best be met.

We are now in that process, of asking and attempting to find the answers to many of the hard questions affecting the future direction of Florida's system of higher education. Some of these questions are:

- Does Florida need nine state universities? (Many contend it does not.)
- Would there be economic or other advantages resulting from merging some of the present institutions, making one of the partners involved in the merger a branch campus of the other?
- How many comprehensive research and graduate institutions does Florida need and is it willing to support? (Many would contend that not even one is currently being adequately funded.)
- What should be the primary mission and orientation of each of the nine universities? What segment of the total state need should each university address?
- Is there a need for nine colleges of education, four colleges of engineering, nine colleges of business, two colleges of agriculture, and so on? If not, how many are needed, and where should they be located?
- Is there adequate justification for maintaining more than one high-cost, low-demand program within the state in certain fields? Can the maintenance of even one such program be justified when the program could be secured out of state, if necessary with a state subsidy, at less cost than maintaining the in-state program?
- To what extent can we utilize the capabilities of private colleges and universities in the state to meet some of the public system's needs? (A recent state law authorizes the state university system to contract with private institutions for the conduct of academic programs or the use of facilities when it is found to be advantageous to the state to do so.)

These are a few obvious issues being addressed in the role and scope study. The effort offers a potential for making significant improvements in the management, effectiveness, and efficiency of our total program.

A process of evaluating and controlling academic programs, which was initiated five years ago, was greatly intensified during the past year both at the system level and by the individual universities. This review process has led to the elimination or consolidation of sixty academic programs (eight doctoral, nine master's, and forty-three undergraduate). Furthermore, authorization to plan many new programs has been denied in the absence of adequate justification. Because of changing circumstances, universities have not proceeded with the implementation of many new programs, even though they were included in original university master plans. A moratorium on new doctoral programs has been in effect since 1971.

In October 1975, the board of regents endorsed a comprehensive review process for all academic programs in the system. The objective of this process is to provide a review of each authorized degree program within a five- to six-year cycle. In this process degree programs, grouped into major disciplines or subject categories roughly paralleling the Higher Education General Information Survey classifications, are being examined throughout the system to determine the need for and effectiveness of each program in meeting institutional as well as statewide higher educational goals.

Major considerations in the review process include program quality, institutional and system priorities, career implications, program administration and management, and the relationship to other programs within the university. Input concerning programs under review is being obtained from the widest possible range of sources including faculty, students, administrators, lay persons, state and federal agencies, other educational institutions, and business and industry. One key to the credibility of this process is the use of outside evaluators who are educators of unimpeachable reputation.

Following each program review, the chancellor will make recommendations to the regents that may call for the initiation, expansion, consolidation, transfer, or termination of academic programs.

The first three program reviews have been completed and recommendations will be made to the board of regents this fall. As a result of these reviews, it becomes apparent that serious consideration will be given to merging, transferring, and eliminating certain programs.

Greatly concerned over the potential impact of program cuts on personnel, particularly on tenured faculty, we are currently developing clearly defined procedures for terminating personnel when it becomes necessary to reduce or eliminate programs, especially during periods of financial emergency. At the same time, however, we are attempting to soften the impact of such actions by providing special grants for retraining, as well as making special efforts to relocate affected personnel either within the university or within the Florida state university system. Significant relocation has been achieved in the past when programs have been terminated.

Numerous approaches have been used to achieve better systemwide cooperation and to avoid unnecessary duplicating and overlapping.

For example, a cooperative program allows state universities without doctoral degree programs to offer joint programs with other system universities that have approved programs in order to meet such needs with less resources.

We are also making effective use of systemwide institutes in such expensive programs as oceanography and solar energy, thereby permitting all universities to participate without duplication of effort.

After reading the comments of my fellow panelists, I think it is obvious that we have not been subjected in Florida to the extreme financial difficulties, requiring the traumatic adjustments in academic programs that a system such as the City University of New York has undergone. I fervently hope we never have to face such circumstances. We have, however, been experiencing serious financial problems in Florida for the past two years when funds have not been adequate to permit us to maintain quality programs.

In assessing the impact of depressed funding levels, I should point out that this situation coincided, although it was coincidental, with legislative authorization for state employees to bargain collectively. The vote by faculty to unionize came after the state had failed to provide annual salary increases and when operating funds were very limited. Many attribute the faculty decision to unionize to the unfavorable economic climate prevailing at the time of the vote. At this time we cannot fully assess the impact of the collective bargaining process upon the system.

Florida's economy is now improving, and we would hope that this improvement would lead to more normal circumstances, including better funding for higher education. In retrospect, however, it is obvious that "normal" funding levels of the past have been inadequate to build the quality programs we aspire to achieve. Consequently, we intend to continue and, hopefully, improve the efforts we initiated during a period of financial stress. Our continuing objectives will be to reduce the bureaucracy and administrative overhead associated with our efforts, to eliminate unnecessary duplication and overlapping of programs, and to do whatever else we can to manage our resources so that they may be maximized to meet the higher education needs of the state.

In improving our efforts, we will obviously save some resources that can be put to more effective use. But perhaps more important, we may regain some of the credibility and public confidence that higher education has apparently lost in recent years. This must be done if the academy is to be given the sort of priority consideration it once enjoyed with the public and legislative bodies. The realization of this goal could enable us to avoid future financial difficulties that may otherwise beset us.

Implementing the Regulations

BEVERLY E. LEDBETTER

THOSE who have been associated with education for some time must long for the days when the federal government's presence in the field appeared to be limited to school lunch programs in secondary education and loan funds in higher education. They may even have dreams of a constitutional amendment that recognizes the separation of school and state in much the same manner as church and state.

How, indeed, does one respond to federal regulations? The response preferred by agency officials is one of unquestioning compliance with the regulations as articulated by the agency. Institutions of higher education often prefer to respond by presenting objections and questioning the efficacy of the regulations. The effectiveness of the regulations may well depend on both types of responses at different times.

Many agencies establish a time period for receiving public comment on proposed regulations before they become final. Institutions can and do use this period to make known their objections. Although the objections include the burdensome nature of the provisions relating to implementation and the high costs of compliance, the most often expressed objection relates to interference with the traditional educational process and the apparent lack of a rational relationship between the proposed regulation and the aims and objectives of the institution.

Daniel Aldrich of the University of California has warned that unwarranted federal intrusions will neither strengthen democratic participation nor lead to equity. Chancellor Aldrich could have been speaking of the Title IX guidelines, IRS regulations, the Rehabilitation Act of 1973, or a host of other federally imposed regulations. He was, in fact, testifying before a Senate subcommittee on education and referring to one of the latest concerns of the Congress, the Cranston Amendment.

Dr. Aldrich does not stand alone in questioning the government's benevolent concern. The proliferation of regulations in the past few years has provoked spirited comment, if not outright rebellion, by many institutions. The much publicized comments of the president of Brigham

Young University, the declaration of independence by several District of Columbia universities, and the court challenge of Bob Jones University are evidence of the concern by many that federal intrusion may be never-ending.

At the present time, the federal government's presence on campuses is reflected in everything we do from the keeping of student records to the operation of day-care centers, from the construction of parking lots to the provision of toilet seats. We are required not only to keep access records, but to fill out numerous EEO-6 reports—and now to file environmental impact statements. Nevertheless, before dismissing the regulations as impossible, burdensome, unduly restrictive, and so on, the university should make one last attempt to examine the causative factors leading to the adoption of the regulations.

Responding to special interest groups

The rules and regulations enacted by the agencies are, in and of themselves, responses to mounting pressure from the general public to curb both real and imagined abuses by corporate powers over which they have no control. Special interest groups have found that by banding together with groups with common interests they can make their needs and desires known to the government and, relying on the government's well-established right to regulate government contracts, can get results. If intervention is forever to be tied to the receipt of federal funds, then no governmental contractor can be exempt from the regulations. Educational institutions, in particular, have found that they cannot hope to maintain their current level of operations without the aid of federal funds. There is little or no hope that we can be free of regulation if our resources do not allow us to function independent of federal financing.

Once the regulations become final, the institution must make a move. If the institution has failed in its quest to delimit the regulations and has dismissed "financial independence" as an impractical way of escaping increasing regulation, then it is left with defiance or compliance as alternative responses. Pure defiance should be dismissed as counterproductive. It is unlikely that universities and colleges will ever choose to cooperate gleefully with laws that they feel are so remote to their purposes, but it is inevitable that they will comply, unless the agency has promulgated regulations or guidelines so complex and contradictory that neither the institution nor the agency can determine what is required for compliance. At the present time, the situation is further complicated by the fact that the government is churning out regulations faster than any institution can respond, either by objecting or by complying. The institutions do, however, keep trying.

The institutions may need a full-time staff with no other obligations than to keep up with the multitude of regulations currently being issued by the Department of Labor and the Department of Health, Education, and Welfare—not to mention the Environmental Protection Agency, the Equal Employment Opportunity Commission, and the Internal Revenue Service.

In lieu of the full-time staff, the institution must develop an internal process for complying with the law. Institutions are, of course, hampered in the development of such processes by the fact that they operate under a system similar to that of the federal government—one that is characterized by red tape and red ink.

Our task in colleges and universities, until such time as the great tide of regulatory controls subsides, is to implement the provisions of the regulations with a minimum degree of disruption to our own process. The confusion begins with the method by which most of us are informed of the regulations. As the regulations are proposed or adopted, they are first transmitted to the institution by one of three means: (1) *Chronicle of Higher Education;* (2) the newsletter of a professional association; (3) notice to a division of the institution that it must furnish data for or a statement of compliance with a regulation the division has never before heard of. Although the above serve to make members of the institution aware of the regulations, they do not relieve the institution of its responsibility to its various components.

The university may take several steps to comply with federal regulations and not be overwhelmed by them. The most important and seldom realized action that can be taken by the institution is internal communication. Federal rules are never tailored to fit the university's distinctive manner of operating, so we must take primary responsibility for interpreting the laws and translating them into meaningful internal policy and procedure.

To be effective, communications must be timely. By the time most institutions disseminate internal policy guidelines for operating within the scope of the new regulations, the staff, faculty, and student body have long since developed distinct opinions about what the regulations call for and how they will implement or demand implementation of them. Although institutions claim to be devoted to independent thinking and creativity, they will hardly benefit from creative thinking in regard to government regulations.

Before issuing written statements on implementation, the university should review its objectives for doing so. I suggest that the following are applicable: compliance for the purpose of maintaining status as a federal contractor; avoidance of confusion, unnecessary delay, costs associated with improper responses, and defiance; and a belief in the purpose sought to be accomplished by the regulation. The last is the most important. If there is not a genuine belief in the purpose sought to be accomplished, "good faith" compliance is difficult, at best. This belief cannot be relegated to written statements, it must be translated into action.

For example, I believe that most institutions had demonstrated a genuine concern for the privacy rights of students before the publication of the Buckley Amendment. Internal rules and restrictions were already in effect at most institutions. Generally, the discussion was about internal access to records and confidential letters of recommendation. It appeared that on many campuses, the problem with privacy was that it was so highly regarded that even the student did not have access to the record. For all of the fuss, institutions have responded admirably to the Family Educational Rights and Privacy Act.

Having examined your objectives in compliance, you must now decide what you are going to communicate. The communication should consist of legal guidelines, apparent policy changes necessary for implementation, personnel requirements, if any, and rationale for cooperating.

How to communicate

The method of communication is almost as important as the content of the communication. Most major policy changes are communicated from the chancellor or president to the deans. Seldom is there significant communication on regulations from the deans to the departmental heads, and there is never any from the departmental heads to the instructional staff (the same is true for middle management and general staff).

In addition to communication to staff and faculty, the university must play a major role in communicating its intent with regard to regulations to others, specifically the student body and the public. We should take the initial steps to inform them firsthand of any new requirements. Not only does this serve to relieve tensions associated with external imposition of regulations, but it also demonstrates the administrative commitment to compliance.

The form of the communication is also critical. Attorneys, of course, prefer *most* actions to be committed to paper. We generally get what we ask for by having the most arbitrary and utterly unsupportable decisions memorialized on paper, listing the arbitrary and utterly unsupportable reasons for those decisions in much detail.

The second requirement in establishing a mechanism for response is an organizational structure that acts as a catalyst for change rather than an inhibitor, one that promotes rather than retards. Delegation of responsibility for implementation to a vice president or dean who is a nonbeliever or a nondoer defeats implementation early. The man or woman at the top does not always have to be given the assignment.

The last obligation with regard to effecting internal response to regulations is the monitoring of compliance. I have been and still am opposed to the lengthy, burdensome, and totally ineffective guidelines that are so frequently issued by federal agencies. In many instances, they ensure noncompliance by making it so difficult to comply. I have no doubt in my mind that Health, Education, and Welfare Secretary Caspar Weinberger was speaking of implementing regulations and their attendant guidelines and requirements, and not the laws themselves, when in a written statement prepared for inclusion in the record on hearings on Implementation of Executive Order 11246 as it applies to higher education, he said that he had concluded that many of the Department of Labor requirements are "simply unworkable and counterproductive in the area of academic employment."

Establishing a mechanism for response is important because we can almost certainly expect more government regulations.

In addition, the regulations may, in many instances, be supported by concurrent court rulings. Since regulations primarily adapted for industry are applicable to higher education, many see no reason why current case law enforcing government regulations in industry should not also be applicable. Thus, rules articulated in *Duke Power, Albermarle Paper,* and *Gardner-Denver* are frequently cited in cases against the university.

Although we are not to see an end to the proliferation of federal regulations, we should perhaps be encouraged by the introduction of a new element of awareness in the drafting of the implementing regulations. Former Secretary of Labor W. J. Usery, Jr., in discussing the affirmative action obligations of contractors in the hiring of the handicapped, said that the regulations would illustrate the department's efforts to "let common sense play a proper role." The university would also be wise to heed these words.

If there is one lesson in life that both the federal government and the university should learn from, it may well be Samuel Butler's warning:

> There are two great rules of life, the one general and the other particular. The first is that everyone can, in the end, get what he [or she] wants if he [or she] only tries. This is the general rule. The particular rule is that every individual is, more or less, an exception to the rule.

Educational Leadership or Institutional Reflex?

CECIL MACKEY *and* STEVEN WENZEL

RESPONDING to federal regulations and regulators is not unlike wrestling with an alligator—if it doesn't get you first, and, if you can keep its mouth shut, there is some hope, provided, however, that the tail does not get you.

On a more serious note, the problem and challenge of responding to federal regulations governing the conduct of institutions of higher education have become, and will continue to be, one of the most interesting and frustrating functions of institutional management.

Federal regulations govern, in some instances to the extent of nearly determining, decisions regarding the admission of students, awarding of financial aid, the facilities in which students are housed and taught, the recruitment and selection of faculty and staff, and the manner in which they are paid, promoted, and discharged. Displacing regents, trustees, legislators, and governors from educational management leaves Uncle Sam with a loud voice, but perhaps little direct responsibility for getting the job done.

But it is a mistake to expect a fair fight, for the federal agencies have not allowed for continued federal funding during the resolution of disputes. The Corporation for Public Broadcasting, for example, the agency upon which most educational television and radio stations are dependent, has a standard contract provision which dictates that further funding will be immediately withheld if any federal agency determines the grantee to be in a state of noncompliance with federal equal opportunity requirements. Federal agencies, like the people in them, make mistakes. Jeopardizing an ongoing program while a mistake is being corrected is inexcusable.

Despite these and other significant obstacles to successful relationships with federal agencies, some techniques have been developed and tested that seem to alleviate some of the difficulty.

A major obstacle to institutional compliance with federal directives is the practical problem for the institutional decisionmakers of gaining access to those directives. One person, perhaps institutional counsel, can review the *Federal Register* daily and route both proposed and final rules of federal agencies to the appropriate decisionmaker for review and implementation.

Reviewing the *Federal Register* facilitates the implementation of another technique for a healthy relationship with federal agencies. The Federal Administrative Procedure Act requires that federal agencies afford an opportunity for public comment on proposed rules. If proposed rules are reviewed on a timely basis by the administrator who will be responsible for living under them, there is a meaningful opportunity for comment to the agency on problems related to compliance with the rules. As demonstrated by Secretary David Mathews' retraction of the Department of Health, Education, and Welfare's proposed rules on review of equal opportunity complaints, federal agencies have, at least on occasion, been responsive to public comment.

If the institution elects to comment on rules, I would suggest that the responsible first-line administrator study the rules and draft proposed comments. Proposed comments should be reviewed by the highest-level university administrator responsible for the area to which the rules relate and also by institutional counsel. In some instances, the university president's review of rules and proposed comments is time well invested, if for nothing more than as a personal reminder of the realities of management at the firing line. The same holds true for chancellors and central staff, regents, or trustees. Proposed comments, when properly reviewed, should be presented to the agency by counsel or some other administrator charged with continuing liaison responsibility.

Coordinating institutional and agency activities

Another technique for meaningful institutional response to federal regulation is directly related to the last suggestion—it is the careful coordination of institutional contacts with any given agency. Two approaches are available to implement this technique. First, contacts between institutional managers and agency personnel can be coordinated through a single university official, such as the vice president for university relations or the equivalent. This officer is charged with responsibility for monitoring the relationship, maintaining contact on good terms so that agency personnel hear a friendly voice as well as an objective one, and making decisions on approach, timing, and follow-up. A second approach is to charge a single institutional officer with responsibility for all contacts with a given agency. While this approach requires that the officer be briefed by each of the institutional managers responsible for the areas affected by the federal agency's rules, its values should not be minimized. The private sector has used an ombudsman approach very successfully in improving consumer relationships, and the application of this technique has met with success in the higher education field also. For example, at the University of South Florida, the general counsel was the contact with the Equal Employment Opportunity Commission and the Department of Labor as well as with the Office for Civil Rights of the Department of Health, Education, and Welfare. The responsibility included both positive contacts as well as negative ones when problems arose. While the approach requires the institutional contact person to be and to remain a generalist, it is a mechanism well worth trying.

A major theme for successful management of relationships with federal agencies is awareness of institutional rights as well as responsibilities. The Federal Administrative Procedure Act, Freedom of Information Act, and privacy legislation are all sources of institutional rights as is the Constitution, particularly the due process clause of the Fifth Amendment. While counsel for federal agencies are aware of the requirements of such legislation, frequently agency personnel, as well as institutional managers, are unaware of the attendant rights.

While an institution's own counsel is clearly best suited to give both an overview of institutional rights and advice concerning a solution to specific problems, several publications on federal agency procedures are available and useful to nonlawyers. Both the Bureau of National Affairs and the Commerce Clearing House offer subject-matter-oriented publications, which contain, for example, the procedural rules of all federal agencies having authority over personnel practices. A not infrequent problem in dealing with federal agencies is that they fail to follow their own rules on notices of charges, data collection, and disclosure of data to the institution. Institutions have a federal constitutional right to be treated by federal agencies in accordance with the agency's rules and not the whims of agency personnel. Reminding agency personnel of the rules is frequently a sufficient solution to relationship difficulties. Sometimes more is required.

A related theme underlying successful relationships is the need for being rational but firm in dealing with agencies. Being firm does not mean being consistent to the point of sacrificing flexibility and adaptability. Rather, at the heart of this theme is the philosophy that there is a rational response to virtually every problem and that in the context of solving a problem with a federal agency, institutional management should develop, through some rational process, a position that it will advocate and stick to. When federal agencies push beyond this rationally derived position, there must be an institutional commitment to fight. In short, it is the iron fist in the velvet glove.

On August 31, 1976, the University of South Florida finished another chapter, perhaps the final one, in four and one half years of litigation with a faculty member who resigned rather than face formal charges incident to his termination on the ground of moral turpitude.

Four days after his resignation was signed and accepted, the faculty member, who had filed racial discrimination charges with the Equal Employment Opportunity Commission and the Department of Health, Education, and Welfare sought to withdraw that resignation. The Department of Health, Education, and Welfare investigated the complaint and entered a finding that the university had not discriminated. The faculty member initiated litigation in the federal district court on numerous grounds, including racial discrimination. After lengthy pretrial proceedings, a trial was commenced and the defendant university was granted a directed verdict at the close of the plaintiff's case in chief. No appeal was taken. Two other lawsuits, essentially variations on a theme, were commenced and successfully concluded.

Taking firm and rational action

Meanwhile, the Equal Employment Opportunity Commission had done nothing in response to the faculty member's initial complaint. He filed a suit seeking that the court order the Commission to do its job. In turn, the Commission advised the university that it would open an investigation. The university maintained that a federal agency investigation and a full federal court action was a complete remedy for the faculty member, and the university need not therefore submit itself to further investigation. When the threat of investigation became imminent, I, as the university president, intervened in the federal court action between the faculty member and the commission. When the court allowed the motion for intervention but denied the motion to enjoin the Commission from investigating the university, an appeal was taken. In addition, to protect the legal question, I filed suit against the faculty member and the Commission. When the first case was remanded from the court of appeals, it was consolidated with this action. On August 31, 1976, the district court granted a motion for summary judgment filed by the university's general counsel on my behalf. In his order, the district judge said:

> Mackey's motion [for summary judgment] asserts that the claim of racial discrimination has been or could have been adjudicated in *McDonald* v. *Mackey*, Case No. 72-563-Civ-T-H, and is therefore barred from relitigation here by the doctrine of *res judicata*.
>
> The complaint in 72-563-Civ-T-H alleged a coerced resignation in deprivation of Plaintiff's due process rights. Count II alleges that the motivation for the coercion was Plaintiff's complaining of the University's "discriminatory practices based upon race." A non-jury trial was commenced but adjourned prior to completion, and was not resumed for five months. In the interim, Plaintiff filed a motion to compel discovery which was in part based on the fact that documents sought

"tend to support the Plaintiff's claim(s) of racial discrimination, duress, and denial of due process."

After review of the record in Case No. 72-563-Civ-T-H, it appears that Mackey's position is well taken. Whatever claim of racial discrimination in employment McDonald may have had, it has been conclusively determined as a result of the earlier litigation.

The Court recognizes, of course, that a prior adjudication is not binding upon those not parties to the proceeding, and the EEOC, defendant in both of these cases, was not involved in Case No. 72-563-Civ-T-H. However, the relief sought by McDonald is to force the EEOC to investigate a claim which has been resolved adversely to McDonald in this Court, thereby eliminating any justiciable controversy.

I believe that this is the first case in which a form of administrative res judicata has been applied. I offer it not so much because it may be a partial solution to the problem of multiplicity of remedies under equal opportunity regulations, but rather as an example of the "be rational and firm" principle—one that shows that the principle works.

Another apparently successful technique is an adaptation of "the squeaky wheel gets the grease" principle. When the personnel or regional offices of a federal agency are unresponsive and are given a formal opportunity to correct an error but refuse to do so, contacting supervisors in the agency is appropriate. In some instances, it may be helpful to enlist the aid and assistance of other university supporters in this effort. Governors and senators and representatives are often successful in cases in which a university seems to have reached a dead end. A second technique for solving the stalemate is an appeal to the senators or representatives who sit on the congressional committee charged with supervising the agency. While there is occasionally the danger of overzealous committee staff members who may have their own ax to grind, careful application of this technique seems to net some success. I stress the importance of having given agency personnel an opportunity to respond to the problem. First, the higher authority will inevitably require that you do so anyway. Second, for the sake of tolerable relations after such an appeal, it is important that the agency officials have been in part responsible for the problems that fall on them after such an appeal.

While I have certainly not detailed all of the approaches and techniques for institutional leadership response to federal regulation, I have provided some guidance to promote something more worthy than mere reflex. The problem is not solved and will not be solved easily. It demands our attention; simple creatures act reflexively; institutions with the complex capabilities of colleges and universities deserve to do better—that is our challenge as the leaders of those institutions.

Making the Case
for Higher Education

LATTIE F. COOR

FEW ASPECTS of higher education are undergoing such substantial changes as are the relationships between the state and the campus. These changes have occurred in part because state financial support for higher education has declined somewhat—from 16 percent of state revenues in the late 1960s to 14.6 percent in 1974–75.[1] Another, more important reason for the decline is that the nature of state-supported higher education is undergoing review. Inasmuch as colleges and universities have a substantial stake in the results of the review, it would be prudent for them to play an active role in shaping the outcome.

A significant part of the debate is, to some extent, already over, as state after state has adopted new mechanisms for consolidating or coordinating its colleges and universities. Lewis B. Mayhew recently concluded that "the days of individual, autonomous institutions in the public sector are gone," and he added that "for at least several years there will be questing for new mechanisms and new patterns of relationships."[2] Thus, state higher education policymaking is timely for discussion. For the public university, no other policy area has such far-reaching implications.

State policy, much more than federal policy, has a special bearing on public institutions. It is the state that provides the bulk of support for public institutions—more than three times as much as the federal

1. Lyman A. Glenny and James R. Kidder, *Trends in State Funding in Higher Education: A Preliminary Report* (Denver: Education Commission of the States, January 1973), p. 10. Carnegie Foundation for the Advancement of Teaching, *The States and Higher Education: A Proud Past and a Vital Future* (San Francisco: Jossey-Bass, 1976), p. 76.

2. *The Carnegie Commission on Higher Education* (San Francisco: Jossey-Bass, 1973), p. 58.

government in recent years.[3] It is the state that determines a public institution's charter and its governing board. It is the state that reaps the broadest benefits from its colleges and universities: educational opportunities for its citizens, young and old; a trained labor force for its businesses, industries, and professions; cultural enrichment for its communities; and support for its economic well-being. It is to the state that the public college and university must look for continuous, broad-gauged support.

Several developments in recent years have altered the partnership between the capitol and the campus. These include the rising costs of higher education to the state and to parents, questions about the utility of the college degree, evidence of overbuilding on some campuses, conflicting and competing claims among the various institutions of higher education in the state, a perceived overemphasis on research as compared to teaching, and concern about the life-style and value system of the campus.

While differences of opinion have always existed between policymakers on the campus and in the state, some characteristics of the current relationship warrant special attention:

1. The state's stake in higher education is now large enough, in absolute dollars and as a percentage of the state's total expenditure, that the state pays closer attention to the campus than it has in the past. As Leon D. Epstein has said: "There appears to be an inevitability about the exercise of substantial state power, in one way or another, whenever higher education becomes a larger and expensive government service."[4]

2. Management information systems have developed to a point that persons in many areas of state government—the governor, the executive office of management and budget, the appropriations committees of the legislature, the state coordinating board—can have a free rein in assessing the performance of a college or university and making decisions on the basis of that independent assessment. "With larger and increasingly sophisticated administrative staffs, governors and legislators tend more confidently to use their budgetary power to affect substantive policies."[5]

3. New persons and new groups have entered the arena of policymaking for higher education, most significantly in state coordinating and governing boards. By their nature, these bodies have had an impact on the focus and nature of policymaking for higher education. Thus, policy-

3. Department of Health, Education, and Welfare, National Center for Education Statistics, *Digest of Education Statistics,* 1975 ed. (Washington: Government Printing Office, 1975), p. 122. See also comparable data in digests of previous years.

4. Epstein, *Governing the University* (San Francisco: Jossey-Bass, 1974), pp. 63–64.

5. Ibid., p. 55.

making for higher education at the state level is undergoing some significant changes in both form and substance.

The political context for policymaking

The political context for the formulation of state higher education policy deserves some attention before we consider steps to influence that policy. In their 1968 survey of legislative attitudes, Heinz Eulau and Harold Quinley found that "higher education has low political salience for state legislators because articulated demands from a broad section of the population are missing."[6] Citizen concern is lacking, apparently because public approval for higher education has declined in recent years. Legislators thus feel much freer to exercise their own judgment about matters concerning higher education than they do about other issues of greater political salience, such as support for elementary and secondary schools and for welfare. Further, in the absence of an active political constituency for higher education, legislators and executives have felt a freedom to trim university budgets without encountering untoward political consequences. Equally important,

> Higher education funds are tempting targets for economy; in most states they constitute one of the few substantial budgetary segments financed on a discretionary basis from general funds, in contrast to the many segregated, dedicated, or earmarked funds.[7]

Rapid expansion, the proliferation of campuses, and—often combined with these—conflicting and competing institutional demands for support have lead to a "suspicion ... among state office holders ... that the state is being asked to provide funds for institutions whose programs and expenditures have been established by internal drives rather than public needs."[8] This situation has led to a "continued quest for effective mechanisms of overall educational planning and allocation of budgetary resources."[9] As a result, higher education, with a limited political base, is faced with state officeholders who are concerned about the cost of higher education, can deal with those costs with relative impunity, and are suspicious of the goals espoused by the institutions themselves. This, to put it mildly, is an unenviable state of affairs.

A new base must be built for the formation of higher education policy within the state, both with respect to the substance of that policy

6. *State Officials and Higher Education: A Survey of the Opinions and Expectations of Poilcy Makers in Nine States* (New York: McGraw-Hill, 1970), p. 50.

7. Epstein, *Governing the University*, p. 45.

8. Ibid., p. 46.

9. Ibid., p. 61.

and to its political salience, so that higher education may in the future have a solid footing. In building that base, two characteristics of the current political context must be recognized.

First, the campuses themselves and their presidents are no longer the prime force in setting the agenda for the issues to be discussed with respect to higher education. The initiative for shaping the issues to be considered in formulating state higher education policy has moved away from the campus, often to state boards and commissions that were established to coordinate and review the various institutions of higher education.

Second, attention to management concerns, such as mechanisms for cost determination, criteria for resource allocation, and the organization of multicampus systems, has influenced the debate on higher education to an extent that such concerns often become the whole debate rather than simply a part of it. As a result, the broader dimension of higher education and its role in the state and in the society are lost to consideration when state higher education policy is being formulated.

In view of these developments, the new base for formulating higher education policy should incorporate two features: the development and articulation of the case for higher education, broadly defined in the larger context and not limited to management information; and the systematic development of a statewide network of citizens concerned about higher education. In both instances, it is imperative that college and university presidents take the initiative.

The broader case for higher education. American higher education has had great educational leaders in the past. Charles W. Eliot at Harvard University, James B. Angell at the University of Michigan (and before that, president of the University of Vermont), and other academic statesmen shaped a nation's values as they led their own institutions. Their counterparts today, caught in a quagmire of cost-per-credit-hour computations and multiagency interdigitation, all too rarely speak on the broader issues of higher education, its strengths and weaknesses, and its role in building and nurturing the larger society. As institutional leaders have become bureau chiefs, responding to requests for information on agenda that are determined elsewhere, the broader discussion of the importance of higher education has been shunted aside.

This point must not be misunderstood. Recent developments in management information systems and management techniques have greatly enhanced the capacity for colleges and universities to manage themselves. The same developments also enhance the capability for state and national groups to develop comparative data to evaluate what is happening statewide and nationwide. I believe these instruments and techniques should be used. They should not, however, become substitutes for a full description and discussion of the college and university. These management processes do not tackle such basic questions as the nature of the liberal arts in contemporary society, the relationship of the liberal arts to professional education, the role and capacity of the institution in responding to the problems of society. All too often these broader questions are not raised. For the health of higher education and its relationship to society, they *must* be, and the college and university president bears the responsibility for seeing that these issues are raised.

A broader constituent base for higher education. A well-developed and well-articulated case for higher education will have only modest impact in the arena of state policy unless it is accompanied by the development of a cadre of supporters throughout the state who can give it high political salience. A network of many spokesmen for higher education must be developed throughout the state. The single institutional voice will no longer suffice. Recent experience suggests that developing knowledgeable and articulate supporters for higher education will not be an easy task. Political realities suggest that it is an essential task.

Here again, the college and university president must take the initiative in identifying key leaders throughout the state—college and university trustees or regents, alumni, parents, students, business and professional leaders, and interested citizens—and bring them into active dialogue on the significance and importance of higher education to the state. This cadre of leaders, knowledgeable and concerned about higher education, is essential if higher education is to have a fundamental impact on state policy formation.

A strategy for forming higher education policy

Translating the broader base of citizen support and the more fully articulated case into policy for higher education requires each institution to develop a long-term and a short-term strategy. Five basic principles should obtain in the development of long-term strategy.

Each college and university must get its own house in order. The broader discussion of the nature and role of contemporary higher education has been as lacking on the campus as it has been in the larger society. Colleges and universities must take the initiative for developing a clearer definition and understanding of what they are doing and how what they are doing fits the needs of society. An essential first step is campus discussion that explains institutional purpose and mission and that gives clarity to each program, especially in the often poorly understood world of the liberal arts. Because colleges and universities have been derelict in their responsibility for sharpening the issues as seen from the campus, they have been constantly in the position of having to react to definitions of their enterprise which have been developed elsewhere. In my experience, nowhere has this shortcoming been more evident than in the failure by complex research universities to define themselves in their own terms. I sat for two years on a committee of the Association of American Universities which sought to develop a project to define accurately the special characteristics of the complex research university so that such institutions would not forever be responding to inadequate definitions developed by NCHEMS and other management information systems. Surprisingly, given the large research budgets of many of these universities, not one of them had done that job, and, sadly, the AAU project never got funded. If institutions cannot understand and describe themselves in the broader dimension, they forever will be forced into describing themselves in terms set by others.

Getting the institutional house in order calls for a tough-minded, critical review of mission and goals to be conducted and for each program in the institution to be subjected to systematic review. A well-defined, well-articulated case for what the institution is and its place in the larger scheme of things is a first essential in a long-range strategy. Experience suggests its difficulty.

Institutions must make a commitment to develop a strategy for influencing state higher education policies. The need to do so is self-evident. My conversations with other presidents suggest, however, that such a commitment is not always present—not self-consciously at any rate.

Institutions must regularly analyze state policy trends as they relate to higher education and formulate reasoned positions on the trends. Epstein describes four principal instruments of control the state has over higher education: creating the institutions' budgets; creating the structure of higher education; providing for the selection of board members; and imposing administrative controls.[10] Institutions should regularly analyze the policy trends in relation to each of these controls and formulate their positions with respect to them.

Institutions must regularly assess the breadth and quality of commitment to higher education by the statewide network of leaders. The nature and effectiveness of the network of leaders who serve as spokesmen for higher education must be reviewed periodically and its composition updated as leadership in the state changes and as the issues shift.

Institutions must establish an internal mechanism—person or committee—to be responsible for both the long-term and the short-term strategies. The mechanism must ensure that the long-term strategy is

10. Ibid., pp. 54–55.

carefully thought out and regularly updated and that the short-term strategy is consistent with the long-term goals.

The discrete items, or short-term strategies, that higher education confronts each year in its dealings with the state are numerous and ever-changing. Each issue must be treated as it arises. The key is to respond to the immediate items with an unshakable commitment to the long-term strategy and to formulate the university's presentation each year on such prime items as budget and resource allocation in such a way that they fit the institution's long-term goals.

Concern about influencing state higher education policies must be at the top of the agenda for colleges and universities, especially those in the public sector. Low political salience for the colleges and universities coupled with mounting concern by state policymakers over the nature and cost of higher education may well lead to policy changes that ignore the importance of higher education and the contributions it can make to the state and the nation.

The campuses themselves, led by their presidents, must take the initiative for building a new agenda for higher education, ensuring that the case for higher education is well reasoned and articulated. They must ensure further that spokesmen of significance throughout the state are brought actively into the process of influencing state policies of higher education.

How to Work with State Legislatures

WILLIAM E. DAVIS

ELEVEN YEARS AGO, newly appointed to the presidency of Idaho State University, I was embarking on my first trip to the state legislature to appear before a budget and appropriations committee, when I encountered a salty old judge. A grizzled and battle-scarred veteran of many a political war, he warned me: "Young fella, when you tangle with those wily legislators, just remember—the only time you can be sure of an even split is when you walk off the airplane and into the path of a whirling propeller. So clean the wax out of your ears, keep your back to the wall, and sleep with one eye open."

It was good advice, somewhat cynical, but practical. I now have eleven campaign ribbons testifying to eleven years of riding off to the wars in the legislative halls. I have never doubted the worthiness of the mission, never begrudged setting as a high priority the attempt to influence higher education policies as they emanated from legislative and executive branches of state government. One of the most important roles for a university president is to provide the leadership necessary to obtain funding, resources, and policies to move the university ahead.

From a very personal standpoint, this posture seems to make good sense. In terms of the president's mental and physical health, adequate financing makes the campus a happier place. It tends to keep the faculty and students sullen but not mutinous. Poverty, on the other hand, makes people mean; extreme poverty makes them extremely mean.

Aside from the urgency and importance of these pilgrimages to the state capitol, I simply enjoy these involvements with the legislature. Politics is one of the ultimate arenas for competition. It attracts a special breed, and I enjoy having a ringside seat—even being a part of the action.

Winning and losing

In these encounters with the legislature, I have learned to win and lose. As the old judge says, it is better to be an arrogant winner than a whining loser.

In winning, I suggest:

1. Be humble, whatever the temptations of arrogance. Victory is never permanent, and defeat is always close at hand. You can be sure you will be tested again—and soon.

2. Give credit where credit is due. I am reminded of the old Michigan State University football coach, Duffy Daugherty, who at the end of a great season culminating in a Rose Bowl victory stated: "I would like to give all the credit to my fine staff of assistants. After all, had we suffered through a miserable year, I fully expected to give them the blame."

3. Don't carry grudges; be forgiving.

4. Never take anything for granted. If something can possibly go wrong, it probably will.

If you lose:

1. Know that you can't win them all. The perennial battle cry of football coaches and presidents is: "Wait 'til next year." That has led more than one critic to remark: "When are we going to have *next* year *this* year?"

2. Fight ferociously, especially if you're getting beaten. I remember the sign on the ceiling of the wrestling room at the University of Northern Colorado: "If you can read this, you're in trouble. Fight like hell!"

3. Arise and fight again. Defeat and shortcomings are a part of any competition. Learn by mistakes and be better prepared for the next encounter.

4. Find the bright spot and philosophize. When I was head coach

of the University of Colorado football team, Oklahoma beat us 62 to 0. The president called me into his office and said, "The alumni are getting restless. What do you have to say about last Saturday's score?" I replied, "Thank God we were up for the game."

Actually, in sixteen years of working with legislators and governors in four different states and four state universities, I have found no pat answers or formulas for influencing state higher education policies. The states in which I have had experience are Colorado, Wyoming, Idaho, and New Mexico. They are all characterized by vast distances, sparse populations with few large cities, and heavy rural influence on all legislation. So the guidelines I set for myself apply and are adapted to personal experience and my own prejudices about what I think might work. These guidelines are geared to legislative relations pertaining to funding, but I try to apply the same principles to other state policy decisions affecting higher education. Likewise, I try to apply the same philosophy to governors and other elected or appointed state officials and agencies.

The president must lead the legislative effort

A university president's principal responsibility is to assume leadership in coordinating the legislative program. This task is too important to be delegated. Legislators want to deal with the top man, the one who can speak for the total institution. I think legislators expect that when the university comes to the capitol with a package, the institution has already examined its needs and established internal priorities. The president must let them know that these have been set and what they are.

Self-appointed, uncoordinated lobbyists, in the form of well-meaning deans, directors, sometimes students, can often be counterproductive in roaming the legislative halls and hearings and buttonholing legislators to promote their own disciplines or programs. This kind of lobbying should be done within the halls and councils of the institution, not in the capitol. If the president needs to call on special expertise for more detailed reports on specific areas, as is sometimes the case, he has those human resources at hand and must use them startegically and wisely. This is the *"Don't call me, I'll call you"* principle.

The president should avoid the tag of "lobbyist." I have always refused to register as a lobbyist. I am a state official, and high on my list of duties and obligations is that of assessing the needs and projecting and interpreting the perfomance of the university. All of my contacts with government officials are in the line of duty, not lobbying or pressuring or cajoling for a vested interest. In many of our states, the total budgets for public schools and higher education exceed half the total state tax expenditures. Education is every legislator's business.

Know the state

The president must know the state and get around the state. The president must be knowledgeable about its history, its literature, its art and culture. Most important, he must be knowledgeable about the nature of its people, where they work, their level of income, the patterns and characteristics of their aspirations for education, their willingness and ability to support it. When I arrived in New Mexico this past year, I embarked on a reading list of 200 books on the history and background of the state. I also made it a point to visit every one of the major communities in New Mexico during the year. (This is not too difficult in places like Idaho and New Mexico, where there are fewer than twenty communities with more than 5,000 people.) It is important to me in my work to know the kinds of schools, communities, and homes our students come from.

Another task the president must set for himself is to identify the power structure, both formal and informal. Know who the decision-makers are. I was told that most of the decisions in New Mexico are made by fewer than 200 people. I believe it is important not only to know who they are, but also to know them personally.

Know the power structure within the legislature itself: the leaders of the key committees. Often, this leadership boils down to a few powerful persons who hold the cards when it comes to critical issues and votes. In the pressure of a session, when time is short and events are moving fast, know whom you can talk to in order to influence the most votes. As my old friend the judge told me: "Politics is fought in the desert. If you want to win, grab the water bottle."

Know the legislators personally

Know the legislators personally in the context of their own communities as well as the state scene. I try to visit as many of them as possible in their home towns well ahead of the legislative session. I do this in the late spring, summer, and early fall when they have time to sit down and discuss the total higher education arena. The visits provide an opportunity to hear their concerns and criticisms as well as the chance to familiarize them with what we are doing and what we want to do. These talks prove far more fruitful than those in the harried atmosphere of a hearing or in a few stolen minutes in the heat of the session. Informal meetings also provide clues about which other legislators and officials they respect and whose opinions they listen to in their own communities. The visits also let me learn which students or graduates come from, or contribute to, their communities.

I do not hold to the adage that familiarity breeds contempt. Quite the contrary. I find it much more difficult to become angry with or dislike people I know on a personal basis. When disagreements or misunderstandings arise, personal contact and mutual respect make it so much easier for either party to pick up the phone and ask, "Mr. President (or Mr. Legislator), what the hell is this all about?"

With legislators, I think it is helpful to know who your friends are, where you can find support when the going gets tough. It is also important to identify your adversaries and then to strive to win them over or to neutralize them.

The president must be knowledgeable about local politics, who is standing for reelection, who wins, who loses. I always try to maintain contact with the losers as well as the winners. Like Lazurus or General MacArthur, many do return.

Perhaps it is obvious that a president should stay out of partisan squabbles and elections. He must work with the winners in both parties. In our Western states, legislation pertaining to education seldom follows partisan party lines. More often it involves some coalition among factions of both parties. Every vote counts.

When legislators call about a problem, I think the president should be responsive. Legislators are usually representing a specific concern or need that has been passed on to them by one of their constituents. They feel an obligation to represent their people, and their role of serving as advocates of persons or groups in their district is a time-honored political principle. A university or its officials should always have time to address individual problems as they arise.

In responding to legislators, I believe in giving them a straight answer. Sometimes your reply is not what you think they want to hear. Most often, however, requests can be met without infringing upon or compromising the integrity of the institution or any individual concerned. And in the political atmosphere, where quid pro quo is part of the game, legislators respect and appreciate attention to personal concerns on behalf of their constituents.

The president must recognize that legislators also have a tough job. There are many demands on their time and the state's resources. They have as many problems in allocating funds and setting priorities for the state as university officials do in allocating funds and setting priorities within the institution itself. But the president should let them know that these difficult decisions have been made internally, and that requests do reflect an honest and realistic assessment of needs rather than a blue-sky "wish" budget. The president must know the financial situation in his state. What are its capabilities and its limitations? To avoid complete frustration on the part of the state officials as well as within the institution itself, requests must be within the bounds of the possible.

If you don't get what you want or feel you need, don't whine. Avoid criticism of legislators as persons or as a body. Give them credit for what they do do. Lick your wounds and gear up for next year's session. As in football, each week or each year is a new ball game, and preparation begins the minute the current contest is over.

Keep presentations simple

In presentations, I like to rely on the old K-I-S-S principle: Keep It Simple, Stupid. Concentrate on a few, highly visible objectives and interpret them in a fashion that doesn't require a Sears-Roebuck catalog of material as a backup. By the time the legislature convenes, any member has a stack of background material on every conceivable subject of importance to the state, often reaching head-high, in reams of paper that would take a speed-reader months to assimilate. Give them what they need for decisions, or specifically request, but don't try to dazzle them with paper work. Personally, I like to stay away from elaborate presentations. If I can't explain it to them in straight language, I am not communicating. I also like to leave enough time to allow them to ask questions, to find out what their criticisms are, where their interests lie.

As for statistical data, I have found legislators much more concerned with the quality of programs and performance, concerned with what these programs mean to the enrichment of individual lives and the welfare of the people of the state.

Don't threaten or bluff. Someone may take you up on what you say. The institution is not going to close its doors if the legislature does not appropriate the requested funding. It is going to do what other state agencies do when their appropriation levels are not met: It will retool, reorganize, and live within the budget. But a drastic differentiation between needs and levels of funding may result in a deterioration of quality. That is a point that can be made with fervor and emotion.

On a more positive note, the president should make the distinction between what it takes to get by at a survival level and what truly is needed to provide a margin of excellence or progress. Legislators need to be asked, How good do you want us to be? Just as our institutions affiliate themselves with different athletic leagues for competitive purposes, so we belong to different leagues in terms of standards of excellence in our halls of learning. What league do they want your institution in? Can your state be dedicated to less than the full opportunities afforded by the best of your kind of university or college in neighboring states, or in all states?

After the legislature has determined what kind of an academic league it wants you in, what is required to get there or stay there? If the legislature meets your request for progress or that margin of excellence, specifically what are you going to do with the new money? How will it change the university for the better? And, if the funds you request are granted, then ensues the follow-up. What did you do with the new money the legislature gave you last year? The cycle is continuous.

When the legislature is in session, the president must keep tabs on what is on the agenda. Bills must be analyzed for their potential effect on higher education as soon as they are introduced. Louis Pasteur noted that chance favors the prepared mind. Be alert, be prepared, and don't be surprised.

Know how decisions are made

Know how decisions are made. In many states, highly sophisticated formulas—computerized and data driven—project the needs of institutions, and the basic decision is relegated to a bottom-line figure generated by the governor or the fiscal committee. In the states with which I am most familiar, however, this practice is only a fragment of the legislative process. The actual judgments are often made late in the session, sometimes in the early hours of the morning of adjournment, when decisions take on a highly personal tone and negotiations are scratched on the backs of envelopes. What is available in funds and how much they really think you need become highly subjective questions. In such situations, the credibility of the top official of the institution can be a key ingredient. It may boil down to an issue of personal trust and may reflect more faith than science.

It is my opinion that most positive legislative decisions are based on an overall confidence in the institution and its administration. All the quantitative data and statistics compiled will not build a confidence that has been destroyed by poor example and service. For example, the most glorified and publicized research projects will not offset a reputation for mediocre or indifferent instruction. Quantitative evaluators, while perhaps more precise and scientific, simply do not measure the quality of a program.

In a state university, each student receives the equivalent of a scholarship, which even in the most conservative terms would exceed a thousand dollars a year. It is not enough for the institution to say, "We are the experts. Just give us the money, then let us alone." The state expects a return for its investment, usually in the form of educated and productive young men and women who graduate from its halls of learning. At the highest level, the goals of the university and society are the same: the preparation of a trained intelligence which, with integrity and compassion, will do the work of the world.

People support those things they believe in. If they lose confidence and stop believing, they often stop paying the bill. The public is not looking for gimmickry or gadgetry in education. Quite the opposite. Philosophically, the public is quite pragmatic: Will it work? The chief test of "will it work" in education is how successful we are in educating the people of the state and their sons and daughters. The products speak for themselves when they come home from the university or college campus, whether they bring with them a sense of failure or high achievement. I have found that students, parents, townspeople, legislators all prefer to talk in terms of human accomplishment rather than cold statistics. Our greatest accountability is what we do with those resources we have at hand: human lives.

Leadership and lemonade

In conclusion, let me note: Don't expect that among the joys of leadership you will find gratitude. If the college president purports to know the answers and shows confidence in his decisions, there are those who will call him arrogant. If he "runs a tight ship" (regardless of how hard he tries to govern by democratic processes), there are those who will call him dictatorial. If the university goes to seed under his leadership, many will call him inept.

A president I knew well once called a subordinate (me) into the office and instructed him to find out just what the faculty thought of their president. The unlucky messenger returned and with considerable embarrassment stated, "Mr. President, I am so sorry to report this, but the faculty regards you as arrogant, dictatorial, and inept." The president considered this and, with a wry smile, replied: "Arrogant, perhaps. Dictatorial, maybe." Then with gravel in his voice, he concluded: "Inept—*never!*"

All of this brings me back to another saying of my friend the wise old judge: "If, in the end, your outraged critics howl you down and throw lemons at you—make lemonade."

The Higher Education Climate: Separating Facts from Myths

STEPHEN HORN

EDUCATORS are all concerned with finding new ways to shape public policy in regard to higher education. That the job has never been tougher reflects, I believe, our enormous past success. But, it is no longer 1955. We are no longer loved for simply saying that whatever we do is for the creation of a better tomorrow. To use political analyst Samuel Lubell's phrase, "Much of the future has already happened."[1]

In recent months we have discovered that what we are doing, and not doing, is grist for the muckracker's mill. Questions that would have been unthinkable a decade or two ago are coming in at us from all directions. As Adam Yarmolinsky put it:

> America's mammoth educational system is simply among the last of a long line of now battered institutions whose usefulness as agencies of constructive social change has come increasingly into question.... Every substantive question is up for grabs....[2]

His article's title, complete with the academically essential colon in the middle, was: "Challenges to Legitimacy: Dilemmas and Directions." A recent issue of *Playboy* magazine, I am told included an article on student consumerism. The title was "Sue the Bastards." So much for questions of legitimacy.

Yes, we are being lambasted for many things: grade inflation, inadequate placement, high salaries, indiscriminate granting of credentials, and many other alleged sins. No institution seems to be sacrosanct or immune. Who can forget that long lead article in *Harper's* entitled "Harvard on the Way Down"?

Our traditional inclination is to ignore this kind of criticism, dismissing it as the handiwork of primitive know-nothings. I think we cannot do that any more. In the first place, much of the criticism, though not precisely accurate, is symptomatic of actual problems. We *do* have grade inflation. We *do* have high budgets. We *do* find it takes more and more effort to get our graduates placed in the jobs for which they were educated.

The danger in these articles is not in their specific charges; rather, it is in their tone, a tone that can do us immeasurable harm. After all, these articles are in mass-circulation publications. They are read by vast numbers of people. Last winter's cover story in *Newsweek* was this fall's *Reader's Digest* feature. The title: "Who Needs College?" These ideas are picked up and replicated ad infinitum by television and radio commentators. The result is a change in the climate in which we operate. What is worse, this publicity can alarm students and their parents, alienate faculties, and rob us of all credibility before the general public, our trustees, and our state legislators.

1. *The Future While It Happened* (New York: W. W. Norton, 1973).
2. *Change,* April 1976, pp. 18–26.

The myths

The problem in dealing with all this is that no two of our critics talk about precisely the same aspect of what we are doing. They manage to apply their brushes to all students, in all programs, in all institutions, with one big, indiscriminate stroke. At the same time, they reinforce the inaccurate notion that today's colleges and universities are doing the same sorts of things they did in the 1920s, for the same sorts of people, in the same traditional ways. The implication is that at one and the same time we are responsible for all of society's problems, while we remain aloof from the political and economic life of the general populace.

That is simply not so. We must hope that it is not too late to start separating facts from myths. Unfortunately, many of our problems stem from the myths that have arisen from our past successes.

Take the myth of "the kids." I suspect that most institutional administrators have the same experience I do when they talk to political leaders and members of the community. They frequently refer to our students as "the kids." Kids, indeed. Nearly 40 percent of them are what we now call "nontraditional" students. Many of them are older than I am. They are not kids; they are mature men and women. They have mortgages and families. They have jobs. They come to us because they see our offerings as steps toward better or new careers. How any journalist can relate these students to whatever the trends are in high school reading scores is beyond me. If they have deficiencies—and many of them do—it is because of something that happened in the schools five, ten, or twenty years ago, not necessarily because of what is happening now.

Take the myth of "academic standards and grade inflation." This myth presumes that everything was perfect in the good old days, that the "gentleman's *C*" of the past represented genuine *C* work, not *D* efforts through a friendly prism. It also presumes that there was no fraternity or sorority house files of past examinations that gave some students the edge, and that there was no cribbing. That is simply not true. Standards have always been subjective, with variations among institutions, departments, and individual instructors.

And then there is the myth that "the truth can be divined by comparing the results of standard examinations given over the years." Those who do this sort of thing usually spot the slippage of recent years. They then go out to interview the experts: college presidents and English professors, social scientists, and high school principals. It is curious that the people concerned with these questions rarely, if ever, interview the parents and the students themselves. One could argue that those percentiles which dropped in the recent past represent a decline in student anxiety and fear and do not really represent a drop in intellect or learning. How long has it been since you have heard a high school student worrying about getting into college? We should face the reality that most students know they will be able to get in somewhere.

We must also deal with the myth that "college professors are residents of ivory towers and are not affected by the rough and tumble of the marketplace." How often have we met total strangers who accusingly report to us that "Professor so-and-so of *your* faculty says such and such...."? Usually, it is a statement that the students these days are not up to the dear fellow's high standards. Chances are the professor is not a full professor. He or she may have been passed over for tenure or promotion; or the professor or the subject he or she teaches is no longer popular, and his enrollment is almost nonexistent. In other words, beneath all the talk of standards is usually a simple fact: the professor is threatened, professionally, emotionally, and, most important, economically. He is not an objective observer.

I could go on and on with this list of myths. There is one, however, of particularly recent vintage that strikes me as extraordinarily cynical and dangerous. It is usually uttered by someone who has already obtained a degree, but not necessarily an education. It goes like this: "Well, not everyone, you know, belongs in college." The premise is that for some people—not your children or mine, of course—less education is somehow better than the opportunity for more.

These myths, however, do have a way of working against the cause of higher education. The experience of the City University of New York (CUNY) seems to show the extent of what may happen when all of the myths come home to roost. When New York City itself faced default, it did not take long for elected officials throughout the city and the state to decide that CUNY would have a low priority on the list of New York's essential services. Its rapid expansion and its open admissions policy endowed all the myths with the weight of the gospel truth in the perceptions of a city racked by racial antagonisms and social unrest. The result was a tragedy: a university with hundreds of thousands of beneficiaries found itself without a constituency.

Behind the myths

The problems of race relations and integration have been commingling with problems of the economy and inflation. The competition for jobs and opportunity and the anxiety of most citizens to hold on to what they have are significant factors behind the current assault on the educational establishment. The difficulties are apparent in the competition between private and public institutions for taxpayers' dollars. While private institutions are indeed feeling the twin pinches of inflation and declining enrollments, a more subtle and more dangerous argument is being advanced. What is being said, and, regrettably, believed by many members of the public, is that the ability to pay should again be made a criterion for access to higher education. If it were, then the sons and daughters of the rich and moderately well-off would once more have a head start toward the education that they will need to corner the jobs of the future. All others—minorities, the poor, the immigrant, the young in general—will have to "shape up" or else remain forever with their faces pressed against the glass of the American candy store.

I, for one, think we should not sit back and wait to see what will befall us next. I think we in the academic community have a positive story to tell the public and those who will make the decisions that will affect our institutions and our students. I am not talking about cosmetic public relations. If there is one thing that must be done, it is to involve our communities in the activities of our campuses. I have found that when citizens have actual contact with students, most of the images created in the 1960s are dispelled. Most people are impressed with the sincerity and diligence of our students. Whether these contacts take place in the classroom, on the gym's bleachers, or in the art gallery or concert hall makes little difference. It is also important that the university actively work to place its students in working internship experiences off campus, where the product can be tested and judged on the merits.

We must attempt to keep the curriculum in balance and to make it sensitive to regional economic and social needs. If this means adding a new curriculum or institute, we must try to find the way. At Long Beach our purpose is not to add programs like so many charms on a bracelet. Each new addition must meet a real need and have an educational purpose. Such an endeavor is our new center for public policy and administration, a graduate program that was designed to serve the needs of the tremendous number of local governmental jurisdictions in southern California. It has been highly successful. In less than three years, it has attracted 1,000 students to the Master's of Public Administration program.

At Long Beach we have attempted to trim away as much of our bureaucratic red tape as possible. Our aim has been to eliminate the kinds of institutional frustration that make students go away angry. For that reason, we have stepped up our efforts to make computer-assisted registration work. We have designed our student services/administration building in such a way that no student need make a detour to find it. It is literally on the path from the parking lot to most classrooms, and it is designed with the path running through it. And, while serving the trend toward early specialization in various career fields, California State University, Long Beach is attempting to strengthen its efforts to provide every student, regardless of school or major, with a meaningful general education. Our aim is to produce graduates who understand the workings of the economy, legal and political systems, and the cultural achievements of civilization. We may perceive our clientele as a student generation, but the fact remains that they are enfranchised citizens and, in the main, taxpayers. It is to everybody's interest to prepare them to exercise their rights with clear thinking and maturity.

Influencing state policy

Yet the job of influencing state policy toward higher education is a never-ending task. It is a continuous process and not a science or an art. Elected officials come and go, just as students, faculty, and even college presidents. I have no package of sure-fire and select gimmicks and techniques to keep state policies firmly influenced in our favor; we must use them all. What I do have, however, is the conviction born from experience that we must devote as much energy and talent as possible to the task.

Most of our problems start right under our own noses: faculty members who complain in public about students and administrative policies; students who gripe about their professors, their courses, their frustration in fulfilling their expectations; staff members who talk idly about administrations. The campus gossip of one day is a tattling letter to an editor or a legislator the next.

There is no university president alive who can exercise much power over this phenomenon. I, for one, do not think very much of the notion that the First Amendment should be curtailed. Rather, to the best of our abilities we must find and alleviate the major sources of campus concern.

At the same time, we must utilize every tool we have to keep the public informed about the many good things that occur on our campuses. It is said that good news is not newsworthy in the eyes of some editors. If that is so, then let the good news be carried by word of mouth—by students, alumni, visiting committees, parent groups, volunteers, or any member of the community who has any relationship at all with the university. To do this, of course, we have learned that we need a lot more than splendid facts and mind-boggling statistics. We need the involvement of our internal constituencies. In short, all the data in the world do not tell the story as clearly and persuasively as our own articulate, likable—yes admirable—students, faculties, and staffs. While Mies van der Rohe's statement that "less is more" makes no sense when applied to higher education, his other architectural maxim that "God is in the details" should become our motto as we seek to influence public opinion and the legislative process with solid facts rather than empty rhetoric.

Within our academic settings we have many resources that have gone untapped. Until recently, planning, if there was any, was often limited to an opinion in the president's head or unfulfilled hopes on the part of isolated faculty. Now we need to broaden the base of the planning process to involve as many elements of campus life as possible at the grass roots program level and thus attempt to secure a reconciliation of faculty aspiration, student interest, and societal need. At our institution, through the use of regular surveys, we have also included the alumni in the planning process. Our aim is to make planning continuous. By being sensitive to the views of our various constituencies, we can demonstrate our capacity and willingness to keep our own house in order without outside interference.

Yet we are witnessing in California and throughout the country a new kind of legislative interest in university affairs. Hundreds of bills affecting higher education are introduced in Sacramento each year. These measures frequently deal with substantive issues: codification of layoff procedures, record keeping in regard to faculty promotions, and grievance mechanisms. These measures, when enacted, usually usurp the powers of trustees and university presidents and frequently work against the general public interest. What this amounts to is piecemeal policymaking, all too often for the benefit of special interests, rather than the formation of broad public educational policy based on an open discussion of all possible options.

How do these measures come into being? Why do legislators take it upon themselves to make campus policy? The fact of the matter is, most of the ideas for legislation emanate from various constituent groups within the universities. Today, when someone shouts "There ought to be a law," he may well get one.

The time has come for those of us concerned with higher education to work together to reverse this trend. On the issue of legislative intrusion, all educators, in the public sector and the private sector, need to work together in our states, just as we have cooperated in academic relationships. We can share information about legislative issues. We can formulate common responses. And we can mobilize those public-minded citizens—the business executives, philanthropists, labor leaders, and patrons of the arts who are concerned about higher education—to speak out in our behalf within each state. What I am calling for is a permanent blue ribbon panel to articulate the very important notion that if universities and colleges are to function properly, the powers of their boards of trustees and their presidents must be preserved.

While all of us in the academic community should, of course, continue our efforts to keep legislators informed and welcome their visits to the campuses to meet students, faculty, and staff, we must also let them know of our deep concern with respect to the dangers in the long run for both higher education and society if legislative intrusion continues.

The work of a citizens' panel in each state would assure greater credibility than our isolated individual voices. Such panels could do what none of us can do alone. They could, for instance, monitor public attitudes by commissioning ongoing longitudinal studies that would relate higher education to the other important concerns of the taxpaying electorate. A citizens' panel made up of persons of the highest integrity could be a force for restraint and reason as state governments ponder the increasingly serious problems of fiscal affairs and higher education.

Baudelaire once described life as a hospital in which each patient feels his chances for survival would improve if only someone would shift him to another bed. Although there is ample evidence that there are many in higher education who share that opinion, I do not. I think what we are doing is so important that we must all survive. What we must do, however, is make sure that no one destroys the hospital.

AMERICAN COUNCIL ON EDUCATION

Jack W. Peltason, *President*

The American Council on Education, founded in 1918 and composed of institutions of higher education and national and regional associations, is the nation's major coordinating body for postsecondary education. Through voluntary and cooperative action, the Council provides comprehensive leadership for improving educational standards, policies, and procedures.